PRIESTHOOD TODAY

PRIESTHOOD TODAY

Ministry in a Changing Church

Edited by

EAMONN CONWAY

VERITAS

Published 2013 by Veritas Publications
7–8 Lower Abbey Street
Dublin 1, Ireland
publications@veritas.ie
www.veritas.ie

ISBN 978-1-84730-518-3

Line from *Familiar Strangers* by Brendan Kennelly, courtesy of Bloodaxe
Books Ltd. 'Anthem' lyrics by Leonard Cohen; copyright 1992 Sony/ATV
Music Publishing LLC. All rights administrated by Sony/ATV Music
Publishing LLC. All rights reserved. Used with permission. Line from 'The
Great Hunger' by Patrick Kavanagh is reprinted by kind permission of
the Trustees of the Estate of the late Katherine B. Kavanagh, through the
Jonathan Williams Literary Agency.

10 9 8 7 6 5 4 3 2 1

Cover designed by Dara O'Connor, Veritas Publications
Printed in Ireland by SPRINT-print Ltd, Dublin

*Veritas books are printed on paper made from the wood pulp of managed
forests. For every tree felled, at least one tree is planted, thereby renewing
natural resources.*

Contents

SECTION TWO: Spiritual and Theological Foundations

SECTION THREE: Person and Role

SECTION FOUR: Sign and Sacrament

Foreword

There is a season for everything under heaven, and every so often there comes a time to pause and reflect. For priests in Ireland that time is now. Ireland needs a conversation about priesthood. Like the disciples on the road to Emmaus, many of us priests have been talking together about all that has been happening. Sometimes we've done so with faces downcast – our hope had been that ...

Enter Pope Francis at the end of the Year of Faith, teasing us, telling us that an evangeliser should never look like someone who has just come back from a funeral (*Evangelii Gaudium*, 10)! Quoting his predecessor Paul VI, he continues by challenging us to 'recover and deepen our enthusiasm, that delightful and comforting joy of evangelising, even when it is in tears that we must sow ...'

Since my ordination twenty-seven years ago, the landscape in which we have been living out our priestly ministry has shifted enormously. Turn the clock back a further twenty-five years, to the time just before the start of the Second Vatican Council, and the context is scarcely recognisable.

Hence we need that conversation about priesthood, and this collection of essays provides a useful catalyst for debate. The discussion might not be easy at times, complicated by the reality that the priests of Ireland are likely to begin from a variety of theological and pastoral starting points. All the more reason to open up the conversation, and, as the apostle says, to 'bear with one another charitably' as we drill down together for the bedrock of our vocation and discover there the profound dignity of the priesthood.

The Council's Decree on the Ministry and Life of Priests, *Presbyterorum Ordinis*, reaffirmed that, at ordination, priests are 'sealed with a special mark by the anointing of the Holy Spirit and thus are configured to the priesthood of Christ' (PO, 2). Sometimes it is difficult for us to appreciate that by ordination we act 'in the person of Christ the head of the body'. Talk of 'ontological change' or the permanent 'stamp' and 'character' of the priesthood is not much in vogue nowadays. As far back as my ordination reception in the late 1980s, I remember smiles around the room when my elderly missionary cousin read, with tears in his eyes, 'The Beautiful Hands of the Priest'.

And yet the reality is that we are not in any ordinary 'job' or profession. Each of us has responded to God's call and given ourselves to Father, Son and Spirit. We do this in an ongoing act of surrender and life-long commitment that consumes our whole lives. A generous self-emptying can transform our person, intellect, emotions, desires and sexuality in a faithful, fruitful, joyful relationship in the Church with Christ the High Priest. The challenge before us of course is to lead lives worthy of our vocation. In facing this challenge, the grace of the sacramental moment of the laying on of hands can help us 'fan into a flame' the gift that God has given us in the priesthood.

The Dogmatic Constitution *Lumen Gentium* rightly and richly reminded us of the common priesthood of all the baptised and opened up the implications of this for the critical mission of laypeople in the Church. It also drew attention to the distinctiveness of the ministerial priesthood, pointing out that it was a distinctiveness 'in essence and not only in degree' (LG, 10). Above all, the Council emphasised that the ministerial priesthood serves the common priesthood of the faithful and that, in reality, there is only one priesthood – the priesthood of Christ.

In the years following the Council, much was written about a 'crisis of identity' amongst priests. More recently, priests have spoken about a 'crisis of compass'. As so much shifts and changes in our familiar role and surroundings, we have to some extent 'lost our bearings' as priests. The shocking child abuse scandals have sapped our morale. The decline in vocations has increased our workload. Change continues at a rapid pace. We must ensure that new developments and initiatives are introduced carefully and sensitively so that priests are not disoriented further. I am thinking, for example, of the development of pastoral areas and so-called 'clustering'; the introduction of the permanent diaconate; increased co-responsibility with dedicated laypeople for the life and mission of our parishes; wider involvement of parish and diocesan pastoral councils; the contribution of parish and diocesan Faith Development coordinators to the implementation of *Share the Good News*; enhanced expectations of governance and accountability associated with charity legislation; the integration of 'new' ecclesial movements into the life and work of the diocese; a harnessing of the potential of new media in bringing the Gospel to the 'digital continent'. All of these important initiatives can be perceived as either opportunities or threats to our identity as priests. It is essential that, as priests, we engage in regular 'reflective practice' so that change can be embraced and the fruits of these exciting developments can be realised.

I am convinced that an open and creative conversation about priesthood in Ireland today will help all of us respond to what the Spirit is asking of the Church at this time. It will also help to restore our confidence in encouraging more young men to consider a vocation to the priesthood. The involvement of supportive lay faithful and religious in these conversations would act as an antidote to the clericalism and 'self-absorption' that Pope Francis keeps cautioning us against. A conversation about priesthood would provide a valuable backdrop to our efforts to realise Pope Francis' dream for a 'missionary option'. He calls for 'a missionary impulse capable of transforming everything, so that the Church's customs, ways of doing things, times and schedules, language and structures can be suitably channelled for the evangelisation of today's world rather than for her self-preservation' (EG, 27).

At my episcopal ordination in April 2013, I remarked that we live in a time of change, challenge and opportunity and that we need to find fresh ways of presenting the message of Christ in all its richness. My episcopal motto: *Cantate Domino Canticum Novum*

– Sing a New Song to the Lord – suggests for me 'renewal' and new life. But how can we sing the song of the Lord in these strange times? The answer is: by showing others that our believing in Christ makes a real difference in our lives as laypeople, religious, priests and bishops. Saint Augustine said, 'The one who has learned to love a new life has learned to sing a new song' (*Sermo* 34.1-3, 5-6)!

God continues to call all priests to new life in Christ. That new life is nourished through prayer, meditation and study of the scriptures, celebration and adoration of the Eucharist and closeness to Mary, the Mother of God. It grows through fraternity with our brother priests, honest and meaningful friendships, and through pastoral and spiritual accompaniment of our people, especially the sick, the poor and suffering. It flourishes when we are prepared to take time to evaluate, review and renew our ministry.

I commend this volume to your study and reflection. I thank the editor and all those who have contributed these essays. With this book in one hand, and *Evangelii Gaudium* in the other, priests might usefully hold a series of fraternal meetings in every diocese in the country to contemplate the dignity, joy and challenge of priesthood today. Let the conversation begin!

O Mary, Queen of the Clergy, pray for us. Obtain for us many holy priests. Help our students who are preparing for the priesthood.

+EAMON MARTIN
COADJUTOR ARCHBISHOP OF ARMAGH
December 2013

Introduction

There are times when 'the self knows that self is not enough,/the deepest well becomes exhausted' (Brendan Kennelly, *Familiar Strangers*). At such moments of weakness and vulnerability, we find it somewhat easier to give God a leading role in our lives. But it takes courage and confidence to take the precarious path of self-surrender joyfully and willingly, and diligence and discipline to do so as a matter of life-habit. This can be especially true of those 'professionally' involved in Christian faith as ministers. Our busyness with the business of faith can at times become a means of avoiding undertaking our own faith journey.

It has been a focus of the ministries of Pope Benedict XVI and Pope Francis to call all Christians to recognise that our relationship with Christ is the key to genuine personal fulfilment as well as to the renewal of the Church. Writing in *Deus Caritas Est*, Pope Benedict said:

> Being Christian is not the result of an ethical choice or a lofty idea, but the encounter with an event, a person, which gives life a new horizon and a decisive direction. (DCE, 1)

Pope Francis began the post-synodal exhortation *Evangelii Gaudium* by inviting Christians everywhere to a renewed personal encounter with Jesus Christ, 'or at least an openness to letting him encounter them' (EG, 3). A personal encounter with the saving love of Jesus is also the first and primary reason he gives for evangelisation and for a renewed missionary impulse (EG, 262ff.).

Putting it negatively, *nemo dat quod non habet*: we cannot give what we haven't got. Putting it positively, we lead others to Christ most authentically and effectively when we ourselves can draw upon firsthand experience of the profound joy, healing, forgiveness and forbearance, balance and maturity that a relationship with Jesus Christ brings.

It is the hope and the intention of the contributors to this volume that first and foremost this book will help priests to deepen their own faith and hope in and love of Christ.

What is it like being a priest nowadays? Just over a decade ago, Paul Zulehner, then Professor of Pastoral Theology at the University of Vienna, conducted one of the largest ever empirical research studies on the priesthood. He surveyed bishops, priests and deacons in a number of mainland European countries: Austria, Germany, Switzerland, Croatia and Poland. Over 2,500 clergy responded (ca. 40 per cent of those surveyed; apparently a good result). Of these, two-thirds indicated that they were generally content in their priesthood; that the rewards outweighed the burdens; that they did not regret their decision to become priests; and that if they were beginning their lives again they would make the same decision to become priests.[1] The results were surprisingly positive, so much so that he took the title for the resulting publication from Isaiah 40:31: 'They shall walk and not faint.'[2]

Many priests in Ireland today would concur with these results. Despite the many challenges, some of which are explored in this book, they get on with their ministry and feel supported and encouraged by people at local level. In addition, many have put supports in place such as ministerial reflection groups, prayer groups and pastoral supervision, which enable them to keep a balance in their lives and hold challenges and problems in perspective.

At the same time, we don't have to delve too deeply into pastoral journals or attend too many priests' gatherings to know that there are also many priests who are experiencing a deep sense of hurt, isolation, loss and even bitterness (as, of course, are many of the faithful, but the focus here is on priests).

It is our hope that this book is realistic in regard both to the positives and the negatives of priesthood as it is experienced today. Beyond this, it is our wish that this book has manifested a genuinely hopeful stance. Gerald Arbuckle sees the time we are going through in the Church as one of grief, but he says that by acknowledging it as such, we can move on from it:

> The truly hopeful in the Church name the pain of the chaos and of their myriad losses. When the pain has been named it can be let go in order to give space for the impossibly new to enter.[3]

It is the hope of the contributors that this collection will play a part in helping us to hold steadfast and faithfully to what is essential, and to let go of what we need to let go of, so that the renewal that might now seem impossible to us can be realised through God's grace.

The essays in this volume have their origins in an invitation from Veritas to the editor to 'pull together' many of the resources being made available to priests in the context of in-service programmes that take place annually in dioceses and religious orders. In structuring the volume it was decided to follow loosely the elements of priestly formation identified in the post-synodal exhortation, *Pastores Dabo Vobis* (1992).

It has been said that those who best survive and even thrive in contemporary culture are those who can live with uncertainty and most readily embrace change. As people who live by faith, this should come easy to us, but it doesn't always. The first section of the book looks at aspects of the changing landscape of ministry, the kind of issues mentioned by Archbishop Martin in his foreword: the emerging role of the laity, the demands of collaborative ministry, implementing new parish structures, attempting to read contemporary culture and engage with the new social media.

John Henry Newman reminded us that change can be a virtue: 'To live is to change, and to be perfect is to have changed often.' To change or not to change is seldom an option; usually, the only choice is to choose change calmly and wisely instead of having to change in a reactive way and under pressure. In order to choose change wisely we need to be guided by our spiritual and theological foundations, and the second section of the book explores some of these: Christ, Mary, the role of scripture, Ignatian and Franciscan spirituality (incidentally, chapters commissioned before Francis became pope), the ministerial priesthood and the priesthood of all the faithful, and the importance of ecumenism and the Church's moral teaching.

The third section of the book deals with the human formation of the priest and issues in relation to his role in the Church. Early in his ministry, Pope John Paul II set the bar very high for effective ministers:

> There is a need for heralds of the Gospel who are experts in humanity, who have a profound knowledge of the heart of present-day man, participating in his joys and hopes, anguish and sadness, and who are at the same time contemplatives in love with God.[4]

Becoming an 'expert in humanity', beginning with one's own humanity, is no easy task, and it is also a life-long task. Yet it is an essential one because God and the human are always found together. Discussing the incarnation, Brian O. McDermott suggests that the difficulty with accepting, for instance, the full humanity of Christ is often not an intellectual or a theological one. What may be required in order to accept the radical and total nature of God's self-giving is 'a healing of the heart concerning the value of one's own humanity in the face of God and before the tribunal of one's own self.'[5]

The human sciences can help in the 'healing of the heart' that is necessary if we are to find God where God has chosen to reveal God's self to us: in the fullness of our humanity. So this section begins with essays that invite us to reflect on our personal maturity and mental health, how we understand and live celibacy, how we exercise power and authority, and how we provide leadership. The third section also looks at how we relate to laypeople, fellow priests and bishops, and some of the difficulties that can arise in this regard.

The final section of the book invites us to reflect on how we celebrate the sacraments, as well as how we preach God's word, and the book concludes with consideration of the permanent diaconate as a new ministry in the Irish Church, and a quasi-poetic reflection on the priest as a servant of and witness to beauty.

In researching for this book I came across many similar volumes written since the Second Vatican Council. What they all had in common was a sense that the priesthood was and still is in crisis. For this reason I want to commend this book to you with this text from an essay by Karl Rahner entitled: 'What it means to be a priest today.'

There are people who yearn for the incomprehensibility and eternity of God. To these people the priest says that the most inconceivable optimism which you cannot even comprehend is actually your possibility, yes, even your most holy duty. You can be this because we have experienced the love of God in Jesus Christ.

I do not see why a priest of this vision could not overcome the crisis in today's priesthood. Naturally, all these things have been overshadowed by the triviality and the habitual nature of our life from which the priest also suffers. He is necessarily also the one who must constantly pray: I believe, Father, help my unbelief. He too must accomplish a breakthrough in hope – out of the banality of the mundane and into God's eternity. He cannot be a priest and be happy if he is not a spiritual person, if he does not always begin again – he need not do more than try. He must be a man of God, a man of experience with the Holy Spirit and a man of eternity. If he is not this, then the priesthood will be a terrible burden for him. But even if he is such a spiritually oriented person, it is also clear that he will experience disappointment in himself and in those to whom he preaches the word of God.

Of course, a priest's religious potential and dynamic force is going to depend upon his talents and personal history.

One should not turn up one's nose or look down upon even the smallest servant in God's kingdom who, true and faithful, proclaims the message of the New Testament through his priestly calling, even if this is done in a common, banal, traditional, and somewhat 'burnt-out' manner. Every priest should always say to himself: Within the limits given you by God, you should be truly a prophet, a man of God, one moved by the fire of God. You should love God and your fellow man. You should proclaim the message of Jesus Christ in our time, as Paul said, be it convenient or inconvenient.

In conclusion, I want to thank all of the contributors to the volume. I am grateful to my colleagues in the Department of Theology and Religious Studies at Mary Immaculate College, University of Limerick, for their advice, encouragement and cooperation. I want to thank my research assistant, Thomas Carroll, for his practical assistance. I also want to thank Donna Doherty and the staff of Veritas for their cooperation in bringing this project to fruition.

EAMONN CONWAY
The Feast of the Immaculate Conception
December 8, 2013

Notes

1. P. Zulehner and A. Hennersperger, 'Sie gehen und werden nicht matt' (Jes 40, 31), *Priester in heutiger Kultur* (Ostfildern: Schwabenverlag, 2001).
2. The full verse reads: 'but those who wait for the Lord shall renew their strength, they shall mount up with wings like eagles, they shall run and not be weary, they shall walk and not faint' (NRSV).
3. Gerald Arbuckle, 'The Call to Today's Church to Grieve in Hope', *The Australian Catholic Record* (October 1996), 387–93.
4. Pope John Paul II in an address to the European Council of Bishops' Conferences, 11 October 1985.
5. Brian O. McDermott, *Word become flesh: Dimensions of Christology* (Minnesota: Glazier Press, 1993), 202.

Section One

Ministering in a Time of Change

The Demands of Collaborative Ministry

MAUREEN KELLY

A window on a parish experience

Some time back, I was facilitating a meeting of a parish pastoral council in a rural area of our diocese. They began to look at the future shape of parish and ministry, and agreed that very likely there would not be a resident priest in the parish in the near future. Discussion focused on how the future ministerial needs of the community would be met in the absence of a priest. The pastoral council recognised that practically all the ministries in the parish were currently centred on the priest. They then began to see that many of the areas of ministry reserved for the priest were ones in which laypeople might fruitfully be involved. If a priest was unavailable to visit the sick, there were well-placed people in the local parish community to do this. Others had skills to help support faith formation of children and sacramental preparation. Some people within the parish had a special rapport with young people. The list went on. On Sundays when a priest was unavailable to celebrate the Eucharist, they saw themselves as continuing to gather for lay-led prayer, mindful of their call to be a praying community.[1]

As they reflected further, they recognised that, in reality, ministries were expressions of the whole Christian community and did not 'belong' solely to the ordained priest. The conversation opened a window for me on the future of Christian community, and on the shape ministry would take in the future.

The impact of a diminishing number of priests is now a crucial question for us as Church. It is obvious that the present way of being Church, based on every parish having its own priest, will not continue into the future. It seems evident, to me at least, that the only model on offer in five to ten years from now will be a collaborative one. Some years down the road, the question will no longer be whether we have priests but whether we have active Christian communities witnessing to the message of Jesus. This will only be possible with lay involvement in ministry and leadership, working alongside priests. What form working together will take is not yet fully in view. What is discernible is that the role of the priest in the future will not be as the provider of services (if it ever was) but to coordinate and animate all the other ministries within the Christian community. How can we prepare priests and an emerging lay leadership to work together fruitfully for that collaborative approach to ministry?

Examining assumptions

I believe that the first demand that collaborative ministry makes of us is that we examine the assumptions we work from; the habits of mind and heart so deeply engrained in us that shape our practice of ministry. We have deeply internalised models of ministry and often unconscious assumptions about the roles we take up as priests or laypeople. A full and free partnership between priests and people requires clear-sightedness about what prevents us from engaging as equals.

Most priests were formed for a style of priesthood that expected them to work on their own, with little reference to the ministry or responsibilities of laypeople. An individualistic formation prepared priests for self-sufficiency, and to provide for the spiritual needs of their parishes. In general, priests tend to operate with a high level of autonomy. The limitations of this model are becoming increasingly evident as the one-priest-one-parish model gives way to the development of pastoral areas and clusters of parishes grouped together for mission and ministry. Thinking, deciding and planning collectively as priests and with laypeople in a cluster of parishes or pastoral area can be challenging for priests trained to work independently. It can be a new job description taken up without much formation or training to go with it. On the other hand, laypeople were formed in a model of Church where their role was to 'help Father'.

Though we may speak about a theology which sees Baptism as the primary sacrament, it is not the operative theology among most laypeople on the ground in parishes.

Healing the legacy of unequal relationships

In his seminal work on the unconscious dynamics of groups and organisations, William Bion identified dependency as an emotional state to which the Church was prone.[2] In dependency, the leader is idealised and looked to for security. S/he is felt to be in a position to supply the group or organisation's needs and the dependent group looks to him/her to have their needs met. The dependent group, according to Bion, behaves as if it is stupid, incompetent or in need of rescue by the leader. Interestingly, when the leader fails to meet these impossible demands, the group may express disappointment and even hostility. In my experience, this dynamic is alive and well in the Church.

James and Evelyn Whitehead describe the journey which has to be made by priest and people in terms of a movement 'from parenting to partnership'.[3] How can this journey be facilitated? We first need to understand the journey that laypeople have to make before they can see themselves as partners. Hierarchical structures tend to heighten the sense of distance and separation between those who lead and those who are led. Those higher up in the hierarchical ladder are easily invested with superior status from those further down. Laypeople frequently defer to the priest, investing him with sole authority. There are also idealisations of priesthood as being holier, closer to God, more knowledgeable and wiser. In my experience of working with parish groups these dynamics are very much a reality. Laypeople can de-authorise themselves, and be reticent in assuming responsibility: 'We will wait to see what Father decides.' These deeply engrained attitudes and dynamics can only be healed by positive experiences of relationships based on mutuality and equality. It is vital therefore that in our parish structures, especially in leadership structures, experiences of Church based on co-responsibility and collaboration are available.

Effective parish pastoral councils where partnership is the predominant model, where decisions are taken by priest and people working together, give expression to a different experience of Church. They model a sharing of power and a belief in the ministry of the baptised. Working to this model will mean constantly encouraging laypeople to take up roles – even when it would be easier and faster to do something oneself. It means recognising the gifts of people in a parish, and calling them forth. It requires nurturing and walking beside laypeople as they grow in confidence in their own ability and willingness to take responsibility. It is not uncommon to hear laypeople say that they do not feel 'holy enough' or they don't know enough to take up roles in the parish. I consider formation of laypeople to be the single most important factor in helping them to let go of their reticence and their lack of confidence in assuming leadership roles. Opportunities for formation in theology and scripture, in spirituality and liturgy are needed to help people to become more self-assured. Then, as people come to know the language of Church and faith, they begin to feel less like outsiders in terms of ministry.

Pastoral areas or clusters of parishes are ideally suited as host sites for lay formation initiatives. My experience of involvement in that kind of programme is of witnessing laypeople on a journey of empowerment, letting go of dependency, growing in confidence and participation, leading to a willingness to take up roles and responsibility. A sustained period of formation is required if it is to be effective. It takes time for people to grow in the confidence needed to speak their own opinion and share ideas. A sustained period also allows for a process of group bonding where people build connection and support, which is more likely to result in future participation.

The politics of salvation and the politics of revelation

Organisations and institutions operate out of ingrained cultures and patterns of behaviour that become characteristic. W. G. Lawrence proposed that what is needed for 'distributed leadership' or shared leadership to emerge is a shift from what he terms the 'politics of salvation' to the 'politics of revelation'. The politics of salvation is defined by rescuing people from their situation, 'giving solutions to people and not allowing them to define their own situation for themselves or take their own authority to alter it'.[4] 'Salvation is linked to the idea that there is someone who knows all'. On the other hand the 'politics of revelation' is about working with people to enable them to find their inner authority to interpret their own situation, and to exercise that authority in all the dimensions of their lives including the spiritual.

The 'politics of salvation' has, I believe, been the dominant experience of the culture of our Church. We tend to look to some higher authority to inform our decisions and behaviour. It operates in local parish settings too. A priest recently told me of the frustration he experiences when people defer to him when it comes to decision-making in the pastoral council. It is an expectation of being told what to do. The 'politics of revelation' is a much messier business. It suggests there is no 'holier one' or expert to whom we can defer. We, priests and people, have to take up our own inner authority as responsible adult believers, trusting that God's Spirit is with us as we discern and work together on the ground. A community grows in the messy business of working things out together, finding the shared authority of the group or community. That is where God is revealed. I believe that this offers a potent metaphor for the journey we need to make as Church.

This question of authority is not an easy one. The models of authority we have internalised are often authoritarian. We learn to fear authority figures. Our Church structures can intensify this tendency. To work collaboratively requires a mature sense of inner authority which enables us to speak our experience truthfully, to say what we really feel. To work in partnership, laypeople may need to invite priests down from the pedestals where we have put them to begin to relate to them in freedom. Priests may need to do the same with their bishop. To be inner-directed is to have an appreciation that God's Spirit speaks in the depths of each of us. Deference to authority is not the same as respect. The latter is born out of freedom, the former out of fear.

What skills are needed for this journey?

Human skills, such as mature relating, a developed capacity for relationships based on respect, equality and mutuality. It means a capacity for self-reflection, an appreciation of one's own giftedness. It means an ability to reflect on one's own relationship with and exercise of power. Communication skills are crucial. We all know situations where poor communication has resulted in the erection of barriers and the development of resentment. At its most basic, good communication is the skill of honest conversation with each other. 'Partnership in ministry requires that we be available to each other and that we speak the truth.'[5]

We have all experienced groups that have been held back by the inability to speak honestly with each other. Conflict cannot be avoided in working with people. A natural part of the development of any group is to pass through a stage of conflict or 'storming'.[6] To develop the capacity to allow conflict without undue anxiety and to learn skills to enable working it through is a real necessity in a collaborative approach to ministry. In times of conflict, it is crucial to have supervision in place at a personal and group level so that issues can be resolved before they escalate.

Collaborative ministry involves priests and laypeople, men and women working together on the basis of mutuality and interdependence. A capacity to value the contribution that both genders bring to ministry, without threatening each other, is a *sine qua non* for working effectively together. The differences between men and women in their expectations and capacities for relationship need to be recognised, as well as issues of power. In a society where the exercise of power has generally been a male prerogative, this can be very challenging. To be a life-enhancing and growth experience we – women and men in ministry – need to be able to talk honestly to each other as issues arise.

Collaborative ministry has to be worked at. There is no other way to engage in listening, reflecting, visioning, planning, deciding, implementing and evaluating together except by engaging in deep conversation with each other. There is little point in opting for collaborative ministry if you are someone who is intolerant of meetings, if you can't sit long enough to really engage, if you are so consumed by the need for product that you cannot stay with the messy process of coming to an agreed decision. Meetings need to be productive and this will happen if they are well planned. Meetings do not have to be interminable. However, we need to learn the group work, facilitation and decision-making skills that are necessary to make them fruitful.

Parker J. Palmer points out that a 'leader is someone who can project either light or shadow onto some part of the world and upon the lives of people who live there'. A leader 'shapes an ethos as light-filled as heaven or as shadowy as hell. Some cast a light where growth can flourish; others cast a shadow where seedlings die'.[7] What Palmer says of leaders is true for all of us. We each have 'shadow casting monsters' in ourselves such as insecurity about identity and worth, the fear of failure, the belief that ultimately we are responsible for everything. If we are to engage in collaborative ministry we need to have spaces in our lives supporting our own inner work, where these demons can be named and integrated.

Collaborative ministry puts us in touch with our own humanity. The warp and weave of relationship is sometimes a crucible in which we identify unhelpful personal and interpersonal dynamics. This can be triggered at times of conflict. When there is sufficient safety and trust established, collaborative ministry can be deeply satisfying. However, we must not idealise it. A generosity of heart and spirit is needed to overcome conflicts and difficulties, and we need to be open to giving and receiving forgiveness and being reconciled. We need to be compassionate with ourselves and less ready to blame others. The gift and blessing of working at this level is that it enlarges our humanity.

A future of partnership

Collaborative ministry is still very much in its infancy in the Church in Ireland. As laypeople begin to flourish in local ministries, coming into the fullness of their own baptismal calling, supported by good formation and accompaniment, a more genuine partnership will emerge. The future will, I believe, see the emergence of ministerial teams of priests and laypeople working collaboratively in pastoral areas/clusters of parishes. Where a team works well together, where time is taken to clarify roles and relationship and expectations of each other, where team maintenance is as valued as the team's task, where a truly collegial way of working obtains, it will be an incredibly powerful experience, one that will school us in right relationship.

Belief in God's Spirit at work

We must do all that we can humanly to enable us to work together effectively. But we must also be mindful that it is God's work, not ours. Our purpose is to discover what God wants to do through us. To do this we need to listen deeply. What we are engaged in is God's work. Therefore, we need to ground ourselves in prayer, constantly discerning as a group where God's Spirit is leading us. This will challenge us to let go of our own agendas, so that we can come into the mature freedom required to allow God to be the guide.

Conclusion

Writing in the foreword to *The Sign We Give*, the final publication of the Roman Catholic Bishops' Conference of England and Wales on Collaborative Ministry, Bishop Crispian Hollis had this to say:

> I believe that it [*The Sign We Give*] contains the seeds of a revolution in the way in which we live and work in the Church today. The revolution is not simply one which will

affect radically our internal structures: it is a revolutionary insight into the way in which we exercise our mission, which is to proclaim the Good News in today's world.[8]

The language of revolution may appear overstated. The truth is, however, that collaborative ministry is not just a style, or technique or new approach we add to present practice. It is a way of being in ministry, whether priest or lay, which radically affects who I am and how I see myself. It is a radical shift from a model of Church based on a 'provided for' laity and a 'providing' clergy to an understanding that all are called and gifted by virtue of their Baptism. At is best, it represents a challenging, demanding but energising way of living out our Christian calling, one which will be deeply enriching at personal and community levels. It is an approach to ministry which is deeply consonant with the self-understanding of the Church as the People of God and as a communion of different vocations called to witness together to the presence and action of God among us.

I believe that the Church of the future will depend on our willingness and capacity to engage in collaborative ministry. As one way of being Church recedes, a more collegial and collaborative way is coming into view. Could it be that the seeds of the revolution identified by Bishop Crispian Hollis are beginning to germinate?

Notes

1. I understood this to represent a flowering of their baptismal priesthood. This is not to be confused with or diminish the sacramental role of the ordained priesthood.
2. W. R. Bion, *Experiences in Groups and Other Papers* (London: Tavistock Publications, 1961). Bion is one of the founding fathers of the Tavistock Approach to Group Relations.
3. J. Whitehead and E. Whitehead, *Promise of Partnership: A Model for Collaborative Ministry* (New York: Harper Collins, 1993), 4ff.
4. W. G. Lawrence, *Tongued with Fire: Groups in Experience* (London: Karnac Books, 2000), 170ff.
5. Ibid., 156.

6. B. W. Tuckman, 'Development Sequence in Small Groups,' *Psychological Journal* 63.6 (1985), 384–99.

7. Parker J. Palmer, *Let Your Life Speak: Listening for the Voice of Vocation* (San Francisco, CA: Jossey-Bass, 2000), 73–94.

8. *The Sign We Give: Report on Collaborative Ministry by the Roman Catholic Bishops of England and Wales* (London: Catholic Bishops Conference, 1996), 2.

Being a Priest in Contemporary Culture

EAMONN CONWAY

We know how important and useful a frame is in helping us to comprehend and appreciate a painting. A frame provides perspective; it defines a work of art, making it easier for the eye to take it in and make sense of it. In what follows, I want to put a 'frame' around secularisation as we are experiencing it in the contemporary Irish context for the same reasons as we frame a painting – in order to better interpret and appreciate it. Currently, many people, especially priests, believe that the 'mess' they see the Church in results from personal and communal failures in witness and leadership. To some extent this is true. But it is not the full story. We minister in challenging times culturally, so much so that it can be difficult to discern the right thing to do.[1] However, when we understand the challenges, and what is causing them, we can respond in a more measured and effective way.

At the World Synod of Bishops on the New Evangelisation (2012) there was a climate of urgency about proclaiming the Good News; but this was accompanied by an atmosphere of quiet joy rather than of pastoral panic, a sense that there is much work to be done, including the healing of past failure and wrongdoing, but also a humbling appreciation of the strength, power and richness of the Good News.

For two reasons panic has no place in the life of the Christian, especially the minister. The first is that the mission is Christ's. As St Paul reminds us, 'it is by God's grace that we are engaged in this ministry, and therefore we do not lose heart' (2 Cor 4). The second is that to profess an incarnate God is, as Jim Corkery has reminded us, to be disposed to be 'detectives' of God's grace, and not just of sin, present and active in people's individual lives and in cultures.[2]

Often in discussing secularisation we focus on how it distorts and damages people's relationship with God. But a damaged relationship with God also diminishes people as human beings. As French Jesuit Paul Valadier has said, the main concern of the New Evangelisation is not the future of the Church as such, but of humanity, as it seeks to fulfil is proper vocation.[3] There can be appropriate forms of secularisation, and Pope Benedict XVI spoke occasionally of 'positive secularity' where both civil and religious authorities respect their proper areas and realms of authority and competence, and religious freedom is guaranteed and respected.[4] At the same time, the human vocation is in jeopardy where secularisation results in a 'reductionist and curtailed vision of humanity'.[5]

Mapping secularisation

Secularisation as exclusion of religion from the public sphere, and purse

Charles Taylor provides a helpful threefold categorisation of secularisation. In the first instance, he speaks of it in terms of the recession of religion from the public square and the declining authority and influence of religion in public discourse. As society's confidence in science, technology and rationality grows, a religious worldview seems unsustainable and incompatible, and over time is expected to disappear. Whatever religious adherence or influence remains is considered a matter private to interested individuals.

In terms of the official relationship of the Irish State towards religious bodies, the tendency is not to exclude them but to be equally inclusive of diverse religious and atheist perspectives. This is reflected in the formal structured dialogue with the Churches and faiths, which also includes humanists and atheists. The Irish Constitution does not allow for any State 'endowment' of religion. Nonetheless, hospitals, schools and colleges owned and administered by Church bodies have been publicly funded. Increasingly, public and political bodies and interests are seeking control over how these institutions operate. While equality legislation in this country still provides for an exemption for religious, educational or medical institutions under the direction or control of a body established for religious purposes, over time this exemption will be diminished or removed.

Church leaders have to make important judgment calls as to whether to resist efforts to secularise publicly funded institutions that are still technically denominational or to let go of them. Important here is an assessment in regard to whether Catholic schools, hospitals and so on are 'fit for purpose' in terms of the mission of the Church today; that is, whether they can be 'agents' of evangelisation now. A middle-ground option might be to seek sufficient presence and influence within such institutions such that a 'culture of encounter' with Christian faith, a term already used several times by Pope Francis, can take place. In terms of evangelisation, this might be as important or even more important than control or ownership. It may also be all that is realistic in institutions paid for from the public purse, and it does not prevent the Church from developing its own institutions at the service of catechesis and evangelisation if resources permit. However, all of this requires careful discernment.

How does this kind of secularisation impact on priests? In parishes, especially rural and small urban areas where the local civil community and the ecclesial parish community still overlap, priests generally continue to hold public influence and there is still respect for the Catholic management of institutions. This is in spite of scandals in the Church, where we often hear of people's ability to distinguish between the failings of leadership and the valuable service provided by their local clergy whom they still support.

Generally, in fact, secularisation understood as the exclusion of religion from the public sphere is not progressing as rapidly as secularists would like. Since 9/11 there is a recognition that religion remains a potent force in society. In addition, even some secularists regard the loss of the values system and ethics which religion provided as leaving an undesirable moral vacuum and have called for religions to retain some public role and influence. However, we need to be alert to a dynamic that may be at work which seeks to exclude religion from the public sphere except for the aspects of it that are considered 'useful' from a public perspective. This is more problematic than outright exclusion because it represents an appropriation of religion in the public sphere on the State's terms, and not its own. In recent years, for instance, because of religious extremism, European Union member states were recommended to make provision for the training of Imams within their own countries in an effort to prevent radicalised Islamic leaders being trained overseas. Insofar as there is a public-sphere interest in religion, it is based upon the fear that it remains a potent force even in modern societies and it needs to be 'managed' and controlled.

Decline in adherence to religious beliefs and practices

In the second instance, Taylor speaks of secularisation in terms of the decline in adherence to religious beliefs and practices, which is taken as a measurement of decline in levels of belongingness to religious institutions. I am not going to delay here upon the findings of the many different surveys in regard to religious beliefs and attitudes – these are widely available elsewhere. The reality is that while the majority of Irish people still self-describe as Catholic, regular practice rates vary between one-tenth and one-half of the population, depending on whether one is looking at rural or urban areas. There are, however, a few points worth noting with regard to this form of secularisation.

The basis for a creative minority

When one views statistics longitudinally, for example, using the European Values Study data from 1991–2008, decline in Church practice would seem to be levelling off across age cohorts. In fact, practice rates are marginally higher among the current 18–29 year olds than the current 30–46 year olds. Speaking very generally, it would seem that one-fifth of the Catholic population in Ireland will continue to practice regularly, and this is true even of younger cohorts. One-fifth of those who self-describe as Catholic will probably never darken a Church door; for them the term coined by Grace Davie, 'believing without belonging', seems apt. The remaining three-fifths will be occasionally practising, semi-attached Catholics. In terms of adherence to Church beliefs, the pattern would seem similar, with only a minority accepting 'the full package', and a majority adopting a 'pick and mix' approach.

This landscape raises a number of questions for priests and those engaged in Church renewal. At one level, the expectation of a relatively sizeable practising minority is quite positive. It means that there will continue to be a core group of committed Catholics. Pope Benedict, for instance, spoke in terms of 'a creative minority'. How this core group views itself, and how it is led, however, will be very important. The emphasis among such a minority must be upon being an outward-looking, inviting and evangelising presence rather than a smug and self-contained sect that is entrenched and feels threatened by the wider secular milieu. It is important that it does not see itself as a diminishing faithful remnant, defining itself in terms of the exaggerated and idealised grandeur of what once was. Rather, if it is to be genuinely Catholic, then it will understand itself as a sacramental presence, providing a confident witness and exercising a sanctifying role on behalf of all of humanity, and confronting people, in a humble and inviting way, with the deep joy that the gospel promises.

Our own disposition as priests – confident, yet open and humble before the mystery and, at times, complex reality of human life as it is lived by people in very different circumstances to our own – will be key to providing leadership to Christian communities that will be genuinely creative and missionary, if even only a minority among the population.

Ministering to the semi-attached

At the same time, priests will continue to minister to 'occasional Catholics', or the 'semi-attached'. This is sometimes a source of frustration for priests. In part, this is because there does not seem to be any coherent strategy, not only at a national level but even within dioceses, for instance, with regard to admitting children who are from non-practising families to the sacraments of initiation and providing for sacramental marriage (more on this later). In other countries people are quick to register formally 'in' or 'out' of the Church. In Ireland, we tend to be pragmatic rather than to take principled stances, and so it is likely that many people will drift in and out of the Church. The challenge here is to get the balance right between providing pastoral care sensitively, on the one hand, and inviting people into fuller communion and conversion, on the other.

Effectively, every time priests celebrate a wedding or a funeral, they are not only ministering to 'the faithful' but also functioning as missionaries and in missionary territory. In any one congregation priests encounter older generations who were catechised into a form of Catholicism that some experienced as alienating and oppressive, leaving them hurt and resentful; at the same time they are addressing younger generations who have never been properly formed in Christian faith. Ministering in these circumstances is very demanding and this needs to be acknowledged and supported.

Focusing on 'deeper movements of spiritual sensibility'

The understanding of secularisation underpinning both of these forms was known as the 'zero sum theory', on the basis that modernisation and religion were considered incompatible with each other and effectively cancelled each other out. A society could not be both advanced and religious at the same time. Frequently, for example, sociologists point to the fact that the more educated people are, the less likely they are to adhere to religious beliefs and practices. As Taylor notes, there are problems with this approach to secularisation. The first is a pragmatic one. Religion, or at least religiosity, has not gone away. Instead, sociologists speak of 'the new visibility for religion in Europe' and the shift in the institutional location of religion but not its disappearance.[6] In fact, adherence to non-institutional forms of spirituality and religiosity seem to remain relatively constant.

Another problem is that it is only in the West that people think that an advanced or modern society means the demise of religion and religiosity. This view is part of a western way of looking at reality, and it is 'acultural' to assume that all advanced societies are or will be secularised.[7] For instance as many Asian countries show, a culture can be technologically and scientifically quite advanced, while also extremely religious.

However, the most serious limitation of these ways of looking at secularisation is that, as Michael Paul Gallagher has put it, they focus only on 'visible and measurable changes in social practice', rather than 'deeper movements of spiritual sensibility'.[8] This brings us to Taylor's third understanding of secularisation, and it is also the most useful. What we are experiencing is the emergence of a certain complex set of conditions which effectively shape or pre-determine, one might also say 'blinker', how we view ourselves, others, God, and so on. Taylor uses the term 'social imaginary' to describe 'the (complex) ways people imagine their existence'. What we are dealing with in the West is best understood, in his view, as a radically transformed cultural context where the impact of the whole, of technology, science, philosophy, rationality and religion, is more than the sum of the parts. The effect of these taken together is a transfigured understanding of what it is to be a human being not susceptible to superficial descriptors or scales of measurement.

We can clarify this by focusing on one issue that directly impacts on the work of priests: the authority which institutional religion claims. Taylor contends that there are fundamentally two different kinds of religious sensibility operative in the West today, and the fault line is in regard to whether or not people trust and effectively allow themselves to be guided by the navigational system that organised religion provides, or prefer to be guided only by their own inner spiritual compass.[9] This is because our transfigured sense of ourselves has affected our attitude to authority and so we are disposed to be suspicious of the authority and the truth claims of a religious tradition, or indeed any tradition, body or institution.

In the past no such fault line would have been conceivable: as Taylor says, 'no one ever thought that [their] own intimations were valid against the whole weight of Christian doctrine.'[10] However, the modern transformation in spiritual sensibility makes this entirely possible today. This means that the priest is no longer necessarily recognised as the representative of a tradition, and even where he is, this tradition is suspect to some, and effectively unknown to others. The priest has to stand far more on the basis of his personal authority and his personality as his role authority is considerably diminished. Apart from the pressure this can put on priests to 'perform' in public, this can also lead to an unhealthy cult of the personality.

In the spiritual marketplace, all truth claims are considered equally valid, regardless of the weight of tradition that may lie behind them. This places the priest in the position of being like a purveyor of fine spiritual products, with all the stress that having to be a competitor for people's attention entails.

Fleshing out the 'social imaginary': detraditionalisation and its impact

Lieven Boeve opts for the term 'detraditionalisation' to describe the transformation in spiritual sensibility to which Taylor refers. Boeve describes our cultural context as one of detraditionalisation because religious traditions, as living embodiments and communities of faith, no longer steer the process of constructing people's personal or religious identity.[11] This occurs in a context of pluralisation where competing worldviews and values are presented as equally valid life options. Instead, the cultural context in which we live provides what he calls 'an all inclusive consumer culture that presents itself as the intermediary par excellence between us and our cultural context'. In this context it has been noted that even 'bonds and partnerships are viewed as things to be consumed.'[12]

What Boeve, and, in the USA, Vince Miller, author of *Consuming Religion: Religious Belief and Practice in a Consumer Culture*, demonstrate is that increasingly people see religious beliefs and rituals, symbols and icons, as commodities to be assimilated into their lives and lifestyle, divorced from or devoid of the meaning and impact that they are meant to have in the context of the tradition in which they originate. In effect, for many people today, sacramental moments such as First Communion, Confirmation and church weddings are hardly different from other family occasions like birthday parties, stag parties or anniversaries, which they seek to customise, design and consume in accordance with their wishes and resources. Thus, they often find restrictions imposed on sacramental celebrations by parish priests or local communities, for instance in regard to appropriate dress, liturgical music or the use of photography, as simply incomprehensible. Such celebrations are viewed primarily as private family affairs. An understanding and acceptance of such celebrations as initiation in or further commitment to a living faith community with its traditions and beliefs is 'missing but not missed'. For example, how many couples getting married in church understand that by so doing they are placing their love for one another at the disposal of the Christian community in order to render present God's love for God's people? And where is the parish community, apart from being represented by the priest, to acknowledge this sign of love and experience it tangibly? Does the fact that we rarely celebrate church weddings in the presence of people other than invited family and friends not collude in the privatisation and commodification of the sacrament of marriage? And what of the fact that church buildings are often chosen primarily because they are near the hotel where the reception is being held?

We also need to consider if something valuable is being lost by celebrating baptisms privately or even collectively among a few families. Baptisms are the great sign of new life and energy in the Christian community, clear evidence that Christ is replenishing and building up his body, and ideally they should take place in the presence of the parish community.

We are required to celebrate sacraments so that they will be valid, lawful and also fruitful. This issue of fruitfulness needs serious consideration. It is dependent upon the proper formation and preparation of people receiving the sacraments, and at the heart of this is their understanding of them as key public moments of encounter with the living Christ in the life of the Church.[13] We need to be careful that our pastoral practice does not collude with the tendency towards the commodification of the sacraments in contemporary culture.

Responding to the contemporary openness to spirituality: the role of pilgrimages

While all this is important and true, Gallagher, following on from Taylor, points out that the starting point for many people today in terms of their journey into faith is not going to be on the level of concepts or ideas. Nor is it going to be in an overt sense institutional, but personal and subjective. And good pastoral practice must begin 'where people are at'. At the same time, we have noted that the contemporary spiritual quest may well be predicated upon what Taylor calls 'flattened' forms of authenticity; that is, upon truncated understandings of what it is to be human. Nicholas Lash has warned against spiritualities that merely 'smooth, rather than subvert our well-heeled complacency', and as such, dovetail too readily with our consumer approach to life in general. For instance, research in the USA has found that Moralistic Therapeutic Deism, common among young people, and which professes a fairly non-intrusive and mostly comforting deity, is de facto the 'new mainstream American religious faith for [our] culturally post-Catholic, individualistic mass-consumer society'.[14] The test of an authentic spirituality, according to Taylor, is the willingness 'to deny or sacrifice oneself' instead of merely 'to find oneself or fulfil oneself'. In the past, many spiritualities tended to see self-fulfilment as something to be expected only in eternity, and instead they focused on helping people to cope with 'this valley of tears'. Today, spiritualities are often only at the service of self-realisation here and now.

Perhaps here we have a criterion for discerning contemporary spiritual quests: an authentic Christian spirituality recognises that God's seeks our self-fulfilment, now and in the next life, but this only comes through self-sacrifice. The God of Jesus Christ tends to surprise us both in terms of the depths of unconditional love offered to us, but also the sacrifice of self-giving love that is demanded from us.

Conclusion

Given that faith journeys today tend to take the form of a more personal and individual seeking and searching that is innately suspicious of invitations to travel tried and trusted spiritual paths, we need to learn new ways of engaging with people. The challenge is to join the dots on their faith maps with the radical and gratuitous love of Christ, of which the Church is the sacrament. This love can be felt at its most intense in a vibrant Christian community and it is Christianity presented as such, and not merely as a system of ideas, which will appeal most in contemporary culture. Key, it seems to me, is that as priests we are also attentive to our own spiritual journey, and especially the contours of our own interiority and spiritual sensibility. If our personal Christian conviction and engagement remains merely at the level of service of a 'system', then in the present context we will convince very few. In the end, it is the quality of our personal relationship with Christ that will invite people into new depths of self-giving presence to God and to others.

Notes

1. Pope Benedict acknowledged this in his Pastoral Letter to the Catholics of Ireland (2010), 4. http://www.vatican.va/holy_father/benedict_xvi/letters/2010/documents/hf_ben-xvi_let_20100319_church-ireland_en.html (accessed 10/10/2013).
2. Jim Corkery, *The Irish Times*, 26 April 2005.
3. 'Le souci majeur de l'évangélisation n'est pas l'Eglise, mais l'humanite a faire advenir sa vocation humano-divine', unpublished paper presented to the International Congress of the European Society for Catholic Theology, Brixen (August 2013).
4. Pope Benedict as reported here: http://www.zenit.org/en/articles/benedict-xvi-favors-a-positive-secularity (accessed 10/10/2013).

5. Pope Benedict, Address to Young University Professors, Madrid (19 August 2011), http://www.vatican.va/holy_father/benedict_xvi/speeches/2011/august/documents/hf_ben-xvi_spe_20110819_docenti-el-escorial_en.html (accessed 7/10/2013).

6. See, for instance, Michael Hoelzl and Graham Ward, eds, *The New Visibility of Religion: Studies in Religion and Cultural Hermeneutics*, Studies in Religion & Political Culture (New York: Continuum, 2008).

7. Charles Taylor, 'Two Theories of Modernity, Hastings Center Report' (March–April 1995), 24ff.

8. Michael Paul Gallagher, 'Charles Taylor's Critique of "Secularisation"', *Studies*, 97.388, 433.

9. Charles Taylor, *A Secular Age* (Cambridge, MA: Harvard University Press, 2007), 510.

10. Ibid., 511.

11. Lieven Boeve, *God Interrupts History: Theology in a Time of Upheaval*, (London: Continuum, 2007), 22ff.

12. Z. Bauman, 'Europe and North America,' *Faith in a Society of Gratification*, M. Junker-Kenny and M. Tomka, *Concilium* 35 (1999/4), 6.

13. See Eamonn Conway, 'The Commodification of Religion and the Challenges for Theology: Reflections from the Irish Experience', *Bulletin ET* 17.1 (2006). Special Issue, *Consuming Religion in Europe? Christian Faith Challenged by Consumer Culture*, Lieven Boeve and Kristien Justaert (Peeters: Leuven), 142–63.

14. Thomas Rausch, *Educating for Faith and Justice: Catholic Higher Education Today* (Collegeville, MN: Liturgical Press, 2010), 146.

The Priesthood and Contemporary Society

DERMOT MCCARTHY

Being invited to offer some views on the role of the priest in secular society, from the perspective of the faith community and in the context of the impact on other social institutions, has prompted me to reflect on my experience of priests and how my own impressions of them were shaped: within the family, in my home parish, as a student at school and university and in my subsequent work and life, and not least as a reasonably active member of a parish community. My experience of priests, as family relatives, former schoolmates, colleagues and friends, is that as committed and caring pastors they have made a huge positive impact on society. Unfortunately, in the future, few people will have such direct and sustained contact with clergy and therefore such positive personal experiences are increasingly unlikely to rival media portrayals in shaping the image of priests, even among the faithful.

Reflecting on the attitudes and opinions of friends and colleagues towards priests, I was struck by the sense of paradox or ambiguity towards faith, the Church and priests themselves: on the one hand, familiarity and appreciation; on the other, some mild curiosity extending to indifference, resentment and even deep hostility. The range and strength of such views are a reminder that, as has been said, 'Christians today belong and don't belong ... The Church ... is in exile; people of faith are "resident aliens".'

Perceptions of priests

There is no doubt that the local priest is still viewed as an authentic representative and leader of the community, especially in times of difficulty. We see this in particular, even in the media, at times of local tragedy when very often the parish priest is among the first to be interviewed. Communities themselves continue to expect priests to function as key local resources, especially in service to those in crisis. Indeed, a recent BBC series *Catholics* portrayed priests as the embodiment of the Catholic community. As Cardinal Walter Kasper has said, 'it is above all through the priest that the concrete existence of the Church is perceived and made present in our towns and villages.'[1] However, there are distinct and divergent expectations of the priest within the community of faith: from those who demand rigid orthodoxy, who every morning 'read the rubrics before their Weetabix', to those who seek a democratisation of Church life, which would serve to undermine the traditional authority of the priest within the life of the parish.

As demographic change takes its toll outside the community of the faithful, and to some extent within, there is a sense of the passing of the priest, along with his authority and leadership. For some this is greeted with indifference; for others with eager anticipation, especially in the light of the devastating abuse scandal. In many instances, it is striking how overt hostility has replaced the former deference that at times bordered on the obsequious. At the same time, it is very clear that, increasingly, attitudes and behaviour vary sharply between the local or otherwise familiar individual priest and the clergy taken as a body, and indeed also the Church as an institution. In this respect it seems that knowledge and appreciation of individual priests protects them to some degree from the fierce anger which so many feel towards the institution.

Perceptions of the Church

The negative perception of the Church as institution cannot be downplayed. As Pope Benedict XVI acknowledged in his Pastoral Letter to the Catholics of Ireland (2010), the child abuse crisis has had a catastrophic impact.[2] In Irish society, the crisis compounded and accelerated the shift in the institutional role and influence of the Church in such areas as health and education; a shift which would, however, have come about over time as a result of demographic and social change alone.

The Church's defence of moral teaching and its resistance to legislative change that more accurately expresses social attitudes and behaviour has led to a strong perception in Ireland as elsewhere, that it is lacking in compassion, especially towards divorced people, homosexuals and others whose lives are widely seen to require acceptance and support in the context of respect for human rights and equality. This is readily expressed in accusations of fundamentalism, intolerance and rejection of democratic values directed at the Church. In particular, the views of the Church on significant moral issues and on the ordination of women have led to accusations of misogyny at the heart of the institution. As a result, the Church no longer occupies a preeminent role at the heart of Irish moral and civic life.

The insistence on priestly celibacy is seen as further evidence of the unreasonableness of the Church, with such insistence described as 'unnatural, impossible, even unacceptable.'[3] In some eyes, a perceived link to the abuse scandal compounds this hostility to the requirement for celibacy, while prompting sympathy for the individual priest subject to it.

More fundamentally, the plausibility of the Church's spiritual and dogmatic teachings has been widely challenged by the sense that scientific developments, ranging from evolutionary theory to neuropsychology, and the accumulation of sociological and philosophical reflection have undermined their credibility. In this context, Ireland is conforming to Taylor's assessment of the radically transformed cultural context in the West that has resulted in a transformed understanding of the self.[4] It is, however, the impact of the abuse crisis, and the sense that the reputation and interests of the institution were put above the safety of children, that amplified the hostility of those who rejected Church teachings and shook the support of the faithful to a degree that the centuries-old closeness of Church and people was fractured.

Comparisons with the public service

The pressures experienced by priests and the sea change in attitudes towards the Church are not the only evidence of a sharp critique of institutional performance and a collapse of public esteem, trust and support. The Irish public service, for instance, has experienced a similar fate. Clearly, the scale of the economic collapse and its impact, especially on employment, has generated widespread distress and anger. The view that this was largely a failure of domestic policy and delivery has resulted in a sustained negative public discourse regarding the public service. The failures of regulation are evident and contributed significantly to the crisis, as did the slow pace of adjustment of fiscal policy in advance of the international financial crisis. The understandable anger across society has led to an undifferentiated assault on the public service, its record, competence and values.

The legitimacy of the public service, the validity of public service values and the contribution of the public service to the achievements of Irish society have all been challenged. This has led to a sharp division and an opposing of interests: public sector v. private sector, frontline v. administrative staff, public agency delivery v. outsourcing and commercialisation. These reactions have in part been shaped into an ideology that impacts on views of the role of the State, the responsibility of the individual and the importance of competition in the market.

It is not as though there are no grounds for concern, reform and accountability. It is the sheer breadth and depth of the social transformation and the scope of institutional change which is noteworthy, with an interweaving of personal and institutional fates. The effect of social distress on the standing of institutions other than the public service, reflected in reported plummeting levels of trust, is evident from published survey results. The fall from grace across most institutions has been rapid and punishing. It is of interest that a distinction is drawn in public opinion between the failings of the institution and the merits of individuals whose particular work and commitment is seen and appreciated, just as the local priest is spared much of the hostility to the institutional Church. But the voice of the individual public servant, like the individual bishop or priest, is welcome in public discourse only if the content of the message is also welcome. Otherwise, there is little place for learning, forgiveness or redemption.

Factors underlying social change

The economic and social crisis is the proximate cause of the shift in social attitudes and the social standing of institutions. The leading role of the media in shaping and amplifying this cultural shift is also a significant factor. Public anger at institutions and individuals, including the Church and priests, probably also reflects some sense of guilt at the support for and participation of so many in what they now reject.

There are powerful underlying factors, some of which are particularly relevant to changing attitudes towards priests and the Church. These include the pervasive elevation of personal judgement over authoritative norms and the rejection of the concept of objective truth, such that 'competing worldviews and values are presented as equally valid'.[5] The abandonment of a shared sense of a moral community and core values has been called 'the suicide of the West'.[6]

Joris Geldhof has argued that in secular society, approaches to faith emphasise the epistemological over its content, such that faith has been reduced to a set of convictions or a system of ideas, to be assessed for their truth value first, and only then as a behaviour based on a personal reflection.[7] In this context, Taylor says 'we have moved from a world in which unbelief was virtually impossible to a world in which it is easy, even inescapable'.[8]

Even within the faith community, it has been said that 'individualisation makes religious people more critical of the institutionalised aspects of religion and deinstitutionalisation of religion will, in the long term, lead to a loss of religiosity'. As a result, Richard Rohr has argued that we are a faith community in exile – in exile from power, possessiveness and the prestige we once enjoyed – and we need to remember that all transformation begins in exile because that is the only time that God can get through to us. Our task ... is to stay with the pain long enough until it changes us.

A similar crisis of exile affects many of the pillars of the liberal democratic State. The alienation of voters, reflected in low turnout as well as opinion polls, the contested definitions of citizenship, and the hostility towards politicians for being 'all the same', suggest that there is a crisis of civic culture as significant as the crisis of faith. In a society where the faith tradition is 'missing but not missed', there is particular pressure on priests in the first instance, as Eamonn Conway says, 'to prove rather than celebrate the joy of Christian truth' and to market them like purveyors of spiritual products.[9]

There is also pressure on the State to approach the issue of religious freedom in a way that reflects a neutrality but adopting a philosophy of *laïcité* can lead the State, in the words of Cardinal Scola, to support 'a vision of the world which rests on a secular and godless ethos [such that] far from being neutral, in reality, [it] constructs its own specific culture, the culture of secularism'.[10] Nonetheless, a capacity and desire for the sacred remains in secular society. This is reflected in the turning to churches for consolation in times of distress, both communal and national. While this may well reflect a desire for 'momentary consolation and reassurance' rather than for a 'coherent package of beliefs to guide or challenge one's life', it confirms the potential for spiritual engagement.[11]

As Leonard Cohen put it, 'there is a crack in everything', even secularism, 'that's how the light gets in'.[12] It is through such cracks in contemporary society that the light of the gospel will get in. An indicator of this may be found in the vibrant character of the small Church in Scandinavia, where Norway was cited by Pope Benedict as an example 'where we see where we would not expect it, how the

Lord is present and powerful.'[13] In reflecting on this hope we must, however, recognise that 'the path to renewal in the first instance is the stony path of repentance for past wrongdoing.'[14]

Sources of optimism

Before turning to possible ways forward for priestly ministry in Ireland, it is appropriate to note some recent signs of hope for the place of the Church in today's society: the resignation of Pope Benedict, the process of election of his successor and the impact of Pope Francis.

The boldness of Benedict's decision to resign created a new dynamic and reminded us of the capacity for surprise in the life of the Church. As Paul Murray put it:

> [M]ay his abdication from the papacy in order to serve the healthy exercise of the office and effective governance of the Church inspire us more widely to discern that which we as a communion need to lay down, that which we need to prioritise, and the changes of life and structure to which we are being called.[15]

The process of electing the new pope was striking in the freshness and truthfulness of the engagement between the cardinals in the General Congregations. They discussed issues troubling 'ordinary' Catholics and parish communities as regards the disconnection between their lives and the high politics of the Vatican. That these topics were discussed by the cardinals in terms of the dysfunctionality of the Curia was reassuring. This was summed up in the reported comments of then Cardinal Bergoglio that 'the evils that, over time, happen in ecclesial institutions have their root in self-referentiality and a kind of theological narcissism'.[16]

The election of the new pope, beginning with the choice of name, has captured the imagination. In symbol, word and image, Pope Francis has conveyed a freshness, vitality and compassion that speak of the reality of Christ, the centrality of mercy in his message, and the excitement of the response to his call: 'stepping outside of ourselves, of a tried and routine way of living the faith, of the temptation to withdraw into pre-established patterns that end up closing our horizon to the creative action of God'.[17]

Priesthood in a secular age

In *Evangelii Nuntiandi* Paul VI distinguished between militant atheism and the 'just and legitimate secularisation which is in no way incompatible with faith or religion'.[18] Rolheiser argues that we should not view secularity 'as the enemy of our faith tradition but as largely our own child, the adolescent offspring of our faith tradition, historical Judeo-Christianity'. The challenge is to value the secular 'as a place where society gains independence from religious dominion' while developing a capacity to engage with those searching for meaning by 'inviting people into a community of faith, not merely a system of ideas'.

While the challenges of modern secularism are pervasive, we should take heart from the fact that the profane exists in every culture. It is no surprise that 'faith is likely to remain foolish for the Greeks and a stumbling block for the Jews'. As John Updike put it, 'the stumbling blocks have never dissolved. The scandal has never lessened'. The temptation is to withdraw to a safe space away from the fray. That would be to abandon the mission. Rather what is needed is a new perspective:

> [F]rom a focus on the weakness of the faith to its strength, from an apologetic attitude to an invitatory mood, from taking precautions to courage, and from a general sphere of mistrust to confidence.[19]

If we are to be 'a sacrament rather than a sect' we should live, as Conway put it, 'not threatened by other values but confidently expressing our own and looking for allies in the service of justice, truth and love'.[20] Reflecting along these lines, Geldhof has called for 'a truly visionary theology so that we don't silently agree to have our dreams smashed'.[21]

The Church needs to build a platform for the New Evangelisation that deploys its resources effectively in the encounter with secular society at national level. Such a context is necessary if the efforts of individual priests to build up communities of faith are to be effective. For example, it has been observed that whether the decline in the number of priests leads to a renewal of parish life or the collapse of it depends on the ability of dioceses to recruit, train, supervise, support and develop the gifts of laypeople in ministry. Such collaborative ministry 'involves investing time in dialogue and discernment to determine priorities, actions and responsibilities. It takes skill in planning, strategy formulation, personnel and task management. Decisions are taken jointly, responsibility is shared, accountability is recognised'. Second, we can challenge the supposed conflict between faith and the scientific understanding of the universe by recalling the Eucharistic approach to creation of St Francis which he termed 'a grammar of gratitude'. As shown by Brendan Purcell, we can present the diversity of the universe as a created echo of the Trinity.

Rolheiser has argued that 'intellectual disaffection with Christianity … needs to become cognisant and appreciative of the fact that the heritage that it has been so critical of is the very thing that has given it the freedom, insight and self-confidence to speak all those words of criticism'. In all of these challenges, there are parallels to those faced by civil institutions and lessons to be learned from the responses that they have developed. The disciplines of performance frameworks and strategic management, the cultivation of strategic agility in leadership, the military approach to developing and testing leadership capacity, the techniques of systematic consultation, impact assessment and integrated evaluation frameworks, the development and deployment of communications strategies – all have useful lessons to offer those faced with similar institutional and leadership challenges in an ecclesiastical context, as much from the failures as the successes of such approaches.

As regards Church–State relations, Scola argues that we need a State

> which, without appropriating any specific vision, does not interpret its own non-confessionality as 'detachment', as an impossible neutralisation of the world that finds expression in civil society. Instead, it should open up spaces within which people and institutions can bring their own contribution to the construction of the common good.[22]

In seeking to promote such an approach in Ireland, the vital task of ecumenical engagement and witness in building an effective presence is obviously central to engaging and challenging the secularist vision. At local level, the only way to extend credible invitations to people who are troubled by the fragility of the economy and the hollow rewards of affluence, concerned by social fracture and disturbed by the threats to the environment, to 'taste and see that the Lord is good' is through closeness.

Being comfortable with truth-telling in the Church, even when – especially when – the truth is uncomfortable is also vital. The liberating effect of facing up to unpalatable facts was demonstrated by the recent papal election. Furthermore, effective collaboration in ministry and a tangible reaching out to the poor and marginalised, constitute the most effective preaching. The priest will be respected for continuing to speak poetry in a world of prose, especially in this part of the world where Kavanagh showed that 'God is in the bits and pieces of Everyday'.[23]

The need for the mercy and healing offered by Christ is as great and urgent as ever in a world that Pope Francis has described as 'still divided by greed looking for easy gain, wounded by the selfishness which threatens human life and the family, selfishness that continues in human trafficking, the most extensive form of slavery'.[24] In short, while our society is increasingly hostile or indifferent to the institutional inheritance of faith, it is ripe for God's saving Word. The sense of the vigil which we are keeping in the Church in Ireland has felt like a wake, a death-watch. But it could just as well become a vigil for a new dawn, as anxiously awaited as it is certain in God's providence. As Pope Francis said at the Chrism Mass 2013:

> It is not a bad thing that reality forces us to put out into the deep, where what we are by grace is clearly seen as pure grace, out into the deep of the contemporary world, where the only thing that counts is unction not function.[25]

In demonstrating the power of symbol and image in witnessing to Christ, Pope Francis has emphasised that priests are anointed 'for the poor, for prisoners, for the oppressed'. His words on Palm Sunday are a fitting way to conclude: 'please do not let yourselves be robbed of hope! Do not let hope be stolen! The hope that Jesus gives us'.[26]

Notes

1. Walter Kasper, *A Celebration of Priestly Ministry* (New York: Crossroad, 2007), 17.
2. Benedict XVI, Pastoral Letter to the Catholics of Ireland (2010), http://www.vatican.va/holy_father/benedict_xvi/letters/2010/documents/hf_ben-xvi_let_20100319_church-ireland_en.html (accessed 1/4/2013).
3. See *The Tablet* (9 March 2013), http://www.thetablet.co.uk/article/163892 (accessed 1/4/2013).
4. Charles Taylor, *A Secular Age* (Cambridge, MA: Harvard University Press, 2007).
5. Eamonn Conway, 'With Reverence and Love: Being a Priest in a Detraditionalised Cultural Context', *50th International Eucharistic Congress: Proceedings of the International Symposium of Theology* (Dublin: Veritas, 2013), 389.
6. See James Burnham, *Suicide of the West: An Essay on the Destiny and Meaning of Liberalism* (New York: Random House, 1975).
7. Joris Geldhof, 'The End of the Mass for the Masses? Reflections on the Source and Summit of the Christian Life of Faith in Secular Cultures', *50th International Eucharistic Congress: Proceedings of the International Symposium of Theology*, 624–41.

8. *A Secular Age*, 25.
9. 'With Reverence and Love', 389.
10. Angelo Scola, 'The Edict of Milan: Initium Libertatis' (6 December 2012). http://www.oasiscenter.eu/articles/religious-freedom/2013/01/09/the-edict-of-milan-initium-libertatis (accessed 1/4/2013).
11. 'With Reverence and Love', 390.
12. Leonard Cohen, 'Anthem'.
13. Cited in Fredrik Heiding, 'Light from the North', *The Tablet* (19 January 2013), http://www.thetablet.co.uk/article/163699 (accessed 1/4/2013).
14. Eamonn Conway, 'The Path to Renewal', Homily at the Solemn Novena at Knock Shrine (23 August 2010), http://tuamarchdiocese.org/2010/08/novena-homily-rev-prof-eamonn-conway/ (accessed 1/4/2013).
15. Paul Murray, 'The Unfinished Business of Communion Ecclesiology', *National Catholic Reporter* (12 March 2013), http://ncronline.org/news/vatican/unfinished-business-communion-ecclesiology (accessed 1/4/2013).
16. See 'Bergoglio's Intervention: A Diagnosis of the Problems in the Church', http://en.radiovaticana.va/news/2013/03/27/bergoglios_intervention:_a_diagnosis_of_the_problems_in_the_church/en1-677269 (accessed 1/4/2013).
17. Pope Francis, General Audience in St Peter's Square (27 March 2013).
18. Pope Paul VI, *Evangelii Nuntiandi*, 55.
19. 'The End of Mass for the Masses?', 624–41.
20. Conway, 'The Path to Renewal'.
21. 'The End of Mass for the Masses?', 624–41.
22. 'The Edict of Milan: Initium Libertatis' (6 December 2012).
23. Patrick Kavanagh, 'The Great Hunger'.
24. Pope Francis, *Urbi et Orbi* (Easter 2013), http://www.vatican.va/holy_father/francesco/messages/urbi/documents/papa-francesco_20130331_urbi-et-orbi-pasqua_en.html (accessed 1/4/2013).
25. Pope Francis, Mass of Chrism (2013), http://www.vatican.va/holy_father/francesco/homilies/2013/documents/papa-francesco_20130328_messa-crismale_en.html (accessed 1/4/2013).
26. Pope Francis, Palm Sunday (2013).

The Role of the Laity: Reflections of a Priest

GERRY TANHAM

Since my seminary years and in the decades since the Second Vatican Council, my understanding of God, Church, priesthood, ministry, lay involvement, lay ministry and worldview have been continuously developing. I have come to understand that the laity *are* the Church and that bishops, diocesan priests, deacons and lay ministers exist to facilitate, collaborate and provide a Christian and collegial style of leadership for the vocation of all Christians. I now understand that the charism of secular priests is facilitating the mission and spirituality of the laity, adapting Augustine: 'with you a Christian, for you a priest'. I understand that ordained and other Church ministry is in service of the common priesthood of the laity. And that each Christian is called to allow Jesus Christ's radical values and spirituality to inhabit our hearts and minds as we go about our personal, occupational, social, cultural and political lives. Thus we act as salt (mixing in the complexities of living and serving) and light (encouraging, giving good example and witness) so giving meaning, purpose, love, good fruits and wonder to our lives. Being disciples of Jesus within the Church is our way of relating with God, all people and all things. Thus, the primary calling and the mission of all disciples is both sacred and secular – trying to live the values and ways of Jesus of Nazareth in our lives in the world, despite our real sins and real failings.

In my understanding, all ministry is a service and an office, role or duty which is publicly conferred by a Church community (eg.

parish, diocese, school, hospital) either formally (ordination or profession) or informally (celebration or contractual agreement). It is personally and publicly accepted by the minister. It can be remunerated or voluntary. The Church has historically exercised the freedom to create new forms of ministry and to modify and terminate existing ministry forms. Since the second century, the three ordained ministries of bishop (overseer), priest (elder) and deacon (caring service) have provided pastoral and juridical leadership in the Church. Bishops and diocesan priests have a general pastoral role in the Church. They are called to encourage, identify, enable, coordinate, support and integrate the gifts of the Christian community, connecting needs with resources and the gospel message, and to preach, teach, sanctify through sacraments and keep a holy order. Priestly ministry is by the few for the many on behalf of the Christian community – an activity with its focus and limits alongside other ministries, for the mission of the Church. The mission and ministry of the Church has always involved proclaiming (by witness of life, action and word); works of service and healing; eucharist, liturgy and prayer; and community building.

The focus of this essay is the role of the laity, and my experience is that the large majority of church-going laity participate in the Church at parish level by taking part at Mass and some of the liturgical, social, spiritual or caring activities of the parish, by keeping in touch with the life of the parish and wider Church, and by trying to pray in some way and to live their lives by the values of Jesus. They participate to some degree in whatever services the parish and Church provides. Their lives are usually preoccupied with family, employment, social, recreational, community and other commitments. Yet, they draw their meaning and understanding of life from the mystery of God revealed in Jesus.

Such laypeople, through their witness, deeds, service and word, represent the core activity of the Church on its mission in our world. In all the areas of their lives they live out their faith. And the parish, and the Mass in particular, is where they bring their lives to, and from which they are sent, regularly. It is within their funeral Mass that their lives are finally gathered, celebrated and commended to God. In each parish the vast majority of church-going people are welcoming and supportive, and a minority of parishioners give generously of their time and skills in providing various services and activities for the parish and wider community. Most of these are older, experienced people with a minority being under forty years of age.

This involved minority of laity can number hundreds in large active parishes. A quick recall of the activities led by laypeople in my various appointments include the provision of:

› youth clubs
› an addiction rehabilitation home
› a community centre abroad
› development of an orphanage abroad
› collaboration with state agencies in providing education and training for unemployed men and women
› a substantial educational project for young offenders
› literacy and second-chance education programmes
› the work of the Society of St Vincent de Paul
› care and activities for elderly parishioners
› collections for Church and other agencies providing emergency relief and human development programmes abroad, and much more.

Many laypeople are generously active in various caring, civic, recreational, sporting, business, political and cultural organisations outside the parish and Church in the wider community. All of this denotes 'the social gospel'. Another area of effective lay involvement is administration, which may include a paid secretary or manager, a finance committee, fund raising and development-project groups, church collectors and money-management groups, and parish pastoral centre management committees. A further essential area of involvement is in the area of prayer and liturgy with lay ministers of the Eucharist and the Word; Baptism, funeral and bereavement teams; liturgy groups; home, school and parish sacramental programme groups; prayer groups of various kinds; retreat organising groups; children's choirs and musicians; faith formation programmes; ecumenical activities; pilgrimages; church carers; altar-servers and sacristans.

Other obvious areas of lay involvement include the boards of management with the staff, parents and students of parish schools; hospitality and social groups; communications services (bulletin, newsletter, audio/visual, website); youth activities; justice and peace action. And, of course, there are significant lay Catholic organisations and movements of varied kinds at work outside the parish or diocesan structures.

Collaborative association of clergy and laity of nearby parishes in such matters as formation and support for lay involvement and ministries and joint pastoral activities is currently developing, and especially in light of the declining numbers and increasing age of clergy and religious. And, obviously, diocesan and local resources for good quality formation and ongoing support for all these ministries and church activities is essential to ensure their good quality and endurance.

Parish pastoral councils[1]

Parish pastoral councils strengthen and broaden the parish leadership, and provide a forum for prayerful reflection, planning, communication, initiatives and accountability for the parish staff. They can connect needs with resources and encourage involvement. They are the eyes, ears and heart of the parish and work towards a parish community which is spiritually nourished, challenged by the values of Jesus, socially bonded, inclusive and hospitable, caring and active. I have experienced them initiating and supporting parish services and activities of many kinds – not undertaking these themselves but seeing to it that they are done. They can connect and collaborate with other parishes, diocesan agencies and the various positive groups active in the wider community. They do not get involved in the day-to-day running of the parish, or finance or administration. They are a council who prayerfully reflect, plan, initiate and communicate. I have found that happy and fruitful parish council members of all sorts have things in common: they can listen; are willing to learn; can collaborate; are enthusiastic to see their parish develop; are involved in the life of the parish; are available to attend the council meetings; think in terms of the entire parish and Church; can proactively facilitate parishioners to get involved in the parish; are prayerful; and so on. This significant development needs to be introduced also at diocesan and all levels.

Lay pastoral ministry

The development and appointment of lay pastoral associates in recent years has been positive and significant. For example, some thirty of these trained and paid women and men have been appointed to work alongside priests in parish staff teams in the Dublin Archdiocese in recent years (this new ministry form emerged after consultations among priests and with endorsement of the Council of Priests). Their role, as with clergy, is to facilitate the mission of the baptised people where they are appointed. They facilitate lay involvement, support parish groups of all kinds, organise formation and support for ministry of various sorts in the parish, work to link parents, teachers and the parish, promote nourishing liturgy and catechesis, and promote prayer and Catholic action – the exact roles vary from parish to parish according to how the gospel addresses the local circumstances. These lay pastoral workers are accountable to the parish priest and work with the staff team and parish pastoral council. They are an appreciated 'work in progress' ministry.[2]

The Church, always developing for laity and all people

On a broader Church front, there is obviously a need for structures and the practice of collegiality at the universal Church level, and for reinvigoration in Church governance. This includes the selection and support of bishops as well as of popes, priests and other ministers. A proper and imaginative structured expression of collegiality of bishops using modern communications at all Church levels could also address many Church governance issues including the forms of ministry needed for the future – married and celibate, male and female, permanent and temporary, paid and non-stipendiary, full time and part time. The future will likely see old and new ministry forms and religious institutes different from but continuous with past tradition. And the hope is that our living tradition will take on a better expression of the Church as people of God: communio, scriptural, collegial, episcopal, primatial, prophetic, living-traditional, apostolic, ecumenical, holy, one and Catholic (rather than monarchic, imperial, feudal, patriarchic), with a curia which serves and administers rather than rules the Church.

Lay and priest alike

As we are considering priesthood today it might be appropriate, finally, to make a few summary remarks around ongoing formation and welfare and to link these with the laity for whom they exist and by whom they are supported. My sense is that most people want forms of liturgy and preaching that nourish and yet mediate the transcendent; parish staff who get on well together and know the people; a sense of belonging and identity, as well as warmth and a democratic style of leadership. I noted one survey when laity commented on priests[3] – saying they want them to be men of prayer who know God and people well, who dispense the sacraments, who collaborate with them, are emotionally balanced and at ease with themselves, approachable, in-touch community people, who affirm and promote, have a sense of humour and are not too self-serious, not too certain and dogmatic, are 'real people'. And it is said that the happiest priests are those who enjoy their work: flexibly relating to many people in the ups and downs of living; caretaking; leading; managing; counselling; presiding; preaching; managing to have some kind of private life and interests and recreation apart from their ministry; having a close relationship with God; keeping a certain detachment from careerism and institution; managing their intimacy issues positively through friends, family, prayer, interests and support. A bishop whom I respect and know tries to encompass many of these things. He tries to be competent, proactive, patient, to notice everything and turn a 'blind eye' to many things, to challenge a little, to know what is a matter of principal and what is not, and to encourage a lot – not a bad philosophy of life for a pastor who follows Jesus of Nazareth.

Leadership is also important. Perhaps it consists mostly in good influence rather than power – being an authority rather than in authority, as they say. It is certainly about listening more than speaking; encouraging and motivating; giving example; about relating well and respectfully; and involving, enthusing, delegating, reflecting and having a sense of direction. Among the qualities to be looked for in candidates for Church ministry are a sensitivity towards others, especially the weak and hurting; leadership; collaborative and social skills; a good and generous lifestyle; self-discipline; being attracted to groups dealing with human needs; being idealistic rather than materialistic; liking people; seeking meaning and spirituality in life; and being angry against injustice.

Ongoing formation and care

Most priests and ministers will participate in ongoing formation if it is relevant to personal and professional needs, if the participants feel ownership and control of what is being offered and if it is encouraged practically rather than imposed. It can take many forms: residential courses; workshops; seminars; mentoring; study tours; extended programmes; clergy only or wider participation; based on like-ministry or age or area; distance education; sabbaticals. It has many aspects – pastoral and leadership skills; personal development; spirituality; theological updating. These sessions provide opportunities for some fraternity, education and training, dialogue and pastoral planning. And of course a minority decline to participate for a variety of reasons, including poor health, anger, laziness, introversion and fear of being professionally exposed. Notwithstanding, such formation is most important, along with good personnel and pastoral care policies for priests and paid ministers. Such policies should also including care for the minority who are experiencing acute difficulties of various sorts requiring sensitive support (mental health, faith, vocation, conflict, addiction, psychosexual, boundary issues).

A common spirituality

It strikes me that diocesan priests and laity have much in common concerning spirituality. Spirituality is the spirit and morality of how you live your life – how you relate to yourself, others and God – your true motivations and values. It is not something apart from your daily life. It is less spiritual exercises and more your diary. Thomas Aquinas defined spirituality as 'God working in the human soul as the inward responsiveness to the indwelling of God', which leads to service, witness and holiness, including prayer and discipleship. The spirituality of Jesus is seen in his life, actions, relationships and encounters with people, in his words, thoughts and values. And actions speak louder than words. In a narrower sense we can speak of kinds of spirituality: monastic (seeking God in community, obedience, prayer, choir, study, manual work and pastoral charity), Franciscan (poverty, detachment, mission to the poor, love of nature, community), Jesuit (seeing God in the ordinary, discerning, learning, contemplation in action, spiritual exercises), Benedictine, Dominican, Carmelite, Pharasaic, Ascetical and even non-Christian kinds such as Buddhist. Secular priestly and lay spirituality is a 'street spirituality' – surrendering yourself to your role in life and the Church – borne out of your Baptism and discipleship of Jesus. It is both active and contemplative. Priests find their roles as leaders among the laity, allowing themselves to be enriched by people by handling the issues involved in being a shepherd. They must know the things of God and of humanity, being true to the Church while being in tension with it. And laity live their faith in all aspects of their lives, including prayer and their rightful involvement in the Church. This is the spirituality of the everyday, and it touches eternity.

Notes

1. Since 2005, all parishes in the Archdiocese of Dublin are required to have a parish pastoral council to enable people, priests and other parish staff to work together to build up a dynamic Christian community characterised by faith, mission, worship and service. Guidelines, formation, resources, support and ongoing evaluation have been features of this positive development. (The work of a Forum of Pastoral Agencies in Dublin Archdiocese during the 1980s led to the establishment of a Parish Development & Renewal Agency with full-time staff, which into the 1990s conducted research and pilot programmes in parishes concerning lay involvement, young adult involvement, pastoral resources and continuing formation and care of clergy. This, along with new diocesan leadership, has led in the 2000s to the introduction of parish pastoral councils and lay pastoral workers, and in the 2010s to continuing reorganising and developing of diocesan administrative and pastoral resources and strategies – in very challenging circumstances.)

2. The lay pastoral workers initiative began as a four-year pilot project in the Dublin Archdiocese in 2008. It involves a one-year pastoral formation postgraduate course and qualification, followed by employment with a parish staff team. Candidates are required to possess a primary degree in theology or religious education, or equivalent qualification and experience. The project is being evaluated positively to date and continues.

3. From a survey conducted in 1990 by the Irish Episcopal Commission for the Laity.

Professional Lay Pastoral Ministry: Preserving Integrity and Quality of Practice

AOIFE MCGRATH

A growing number of parishes, parish clusters and dioceses throughout Ireland are embracing the reality of greater lay involvement in the life and ministry of the Church. The Second Vatican Council affirmed the authenticity of this involvement in several of its teaching documents.[1] For instance, in its Decree on the Laity, the Council confirmed that the lay faithful 'have their own share' in the Christian vocation to carry out the mission of the People of God 'in the Church and in the world'.[2] The Council Fathers described this activity, like all activity directed to the attainment of this goal, as the 'apostolate'.[3] In the decades following the Council, the lay apostolate in Ireland has flourished. A significant 'share' of this apostolate is embodied in the daily Christian living of all the lay faithful. These people transform 'the world' according to Christian values. They witness to their Christian faith through their everyday activities in familial, social, economic, political and cultural settings. In addition, many laypeople also undertake spontaneous ministerial roles within our Church communities.[4] Laypeople in these roles are highly committed to serving their communities, but their activity is largely occasional: they balance their activity in the Church with their daily familial, occupational and societal responsibilities. For the most part, they do not receive payment for their activity in the Church; their livelihood is earned elsewhere.

More recently, and at an increasing rate, laypeople are responding to the call to 'stable' or 'professional' activity in their Church communities, and are being appointed to pastoral leadership roles. These individuals are employed on a full-time or part-time basis to dedicate all their energy to ministerial activity.[5] This type of activity forms a significant part of their identity as Christians, and redefines their relationship with the communities they serve: they enter into a public relationship with their respective communities, they are held to a high moral and ministerial standard, and they are expected to have the necessary formation and education for the roles they perform. These roles involve increased responsibility for leading the other members of the faithful, in collaboration with ordained and religious leaders within these communities:

> By virtue of their preparation, leadership, close collaboration with the ordained, and authorisation ... [they] are called into a new set of relationships, a new position within the ecclesial community: they minister in the name of the Church.[6]

Their roles thus involve a formal public service within the ecclesial community, on behalf of the Church, in a public and professional way.[7] These public and formal roles involve a continuous commitment to activity in the ecclesial community. It is difficult for laypeople to make this type of commitment while earning a living elsewhere. Lay pastoral leaders need to dedicate all their energy to ecclesial labour. Therefore, their primary source of income is often their work in the Church. A steady income provides the means, opportunity and motivation for them to seek formal education and preparation for the pursuit of excellence in their leadership roles.

In this chapter the designation 'professional pastoral ministry' is used to describe this form of the lay apostolate. It indicates the level of dedication, engagement and responsibility required of the laypeople involved. By focusing on this professional form of the lay apostolate, this essay engages with the task of discerning the pastoral structures and interrelationships that are most conducive to preserving integrity and quality in ministerial practice. This exercise is valuable for pastors who are engaging in the process of appointing laypeople to professional ministerial roles, and for laypeople discerning their vocation to such roles. It also has broad implications for the ministerial practice and the life of the Church community more generally.

Preparation and formation

It is of the utmost importance that time and effort is given over to preparation in particular communities where laypeople will be active in pastoral leadership roles. Without such preparation, much of the lay pastoral leaders' time and energy will be dedicated to explaining their role, promoting the forms of service they can provide, or, in the case of negative reception, justifying their position. This is far from ideal because their role should be other-focused: their time should be spent on caring for the welfare of the people within the community; and their energy should be used in actively listening to them, enabling them to grow in faith, supporting them in their own apostolate and encouraging them to be active and co-responsible in the Church's mission.

Clarity in this area would serve a number of purposes. First, it would help improve the quality of service provided to communities by informing them of the many services lay pastoral leaders can provide, and by addressing their preconceptions, misgivings and expectations. Second, it would encourage laypeople to embrace their co-responsibility in the Church, by leading them to a greater awareness of the vocation and gifts they received through their sacramental initiation. Adult faith formation programmes would be instrumental in this context. These would need to specifically address lay pastoral leadership and its relationship with other forms of ministry in the Church. These programmes could continue once the lay pastoral leader has begun his or her ministry in the community.

In addition to the general formation needed for ecclesial communities, in-depth formation is needed for both the laypeople entering into pastoral leadership and the other leaders and ministers within their communities – namely the ordained and religious pastoral leaders as well as 'spontaneous' lay ministers.[8] In order to build a good working relationship between these individuals, it is desirable that this formation should be shared or undertaken jointly. Such formation should be both general in terms of outlining accepted collaborative practices, but also specific in terms of developing interpersonal relationships. This latter form should directly address the personalities, preconceptions and rapport of the individuals in question, since difficulties in these areas can adversely affect the quality of ministerial practice:

> Sometimes relationships among those working collaboratively break down. It is caused by poor communication, misunderstandings, different temperaments, sensitivity and other human weaknesses. Priests and laypeople, men and women, are equally prone to behave in these ways. When this happens, whether in a parish or in a team, a great deal of energy and time can be absorbed in sorting matters out.[9]

Therefore, 'collaborative teams in particular need formation planned to meet their particular requirements as a team and not just a collection of staff'.[10] This form of preparation pre-empts difficulties that may arise, contributing to the stability and sustainability of professional lay roles.

Discernment and authorisation

A distinctive aspect of preparation for professional pastoral ministry is the discernment of the need in the particular community for this type of leadership and of the layperson's call to this form of the lay apostolate. This process of discernment needs to begin well in advance of the appointment of the layperson to a leadership role. The discernment approach will differ somewhat depending on the community in question. For example, in some situations, a layperson may emerge from within the community as a potential candidate for a leadership role; in others, a need for lay leadership may develop and a suitable candidate will be sought from within or outside the community.

In any case, the appointment of a layperson to such a role should not be done arbitrarily. Rather, in terms of the person's vocation to this form of ministry, the process of discernment 'requires prayer, dialogue and evaluation. It is both personal and communal, involving family [including spouses and adolescent children] and friends as well as colleagues and mentors'.[11] In other words, this discernment is personal and ecclesial: it is personal in the sense that the layperson may 'feel called' by God to be involved in pastoral leadership; it is ecclesial because, in the best interests of the community, it needs to be discerned whether the layperson's desire for public ministry is actually rooted in a divine calling.[12] Sacramental initiation, which is the source of the person's sense of calling, is not an individual occurrence. Each Christian is initiated into the community of the People of God, and the call to serve must therefore come through this community:[13]

> The community tests the personal discernment of the individual to ascertain that the personal desire for ministry is accompanied by the appropriate human and spiritual characteristics essential for public service and that the individual has acquired the necessary formation and education.[14]

Therefore, God calls through the discernment of the community.

In addition to discerning the personal and ecclesial vocation of the layperson, the needs of the community need to be assessed vis-à-vis the gifts of the lay candidate. The appointment of a lay pastoral leader should not be an arbitrary imposition on a community: the gifts of the layperson need to correspond with the needs of the People. Moreover, the positive reception of the layperson depends on the openness of the community to both the person and the role. This openness will have emerged during the process of preparation and formation. It is during this process that members of the community can participate in the discernment process. The preparation process will also indicate the perception of existing pastoral leaders and spontaneous ministers on the appointment of a layperson to public service. This perception is immensely important, because professional lay pastoral ministry in collaboration with other forms of ministry 'will not work if those involved do not really want to do it, or feel it has been imposed':[15]

> If people do not desire to collaborate, or do not find that desire in those with whom they must work, directives or policy alone will not be sufficient for collaboration to work.[16]

Therefore, the introduction of professional lay pastoral ministry should not be imposed, but chosen. There will be instances where the needs of the community are clearly evident, but the pastoral leaders or spontaneous ministers are less amenable. These individuals

> may feel threatened or inadequate alongside skilled or expert laypeople, and there may be tensions as both together learn how to make use of different skills and knowledge … Tensions can also arise from different financial situations; when one is full-time and professionally paid, another is full-time but has living costs supplied and a very small salary, and others are voluntary.[17]

It is important to build up good interrelations between these individuals despite these tensions. It may be 'a gradual and mutual evolution of new patterns, new attitudes and new self-understanding'.[18] Yet, such a process is necessary if ordained, religious and lay pastoral leaders are to work effectively in partnership. This form of collaboration is needed to maintain the integrity and quality of ministerial practice.

The discernment process is incomplete without appropriate authorisation. The diocesan bishop has ultimate responsibility for authorising the layperson to begin public ministry. This authorisation can only be given if the candidate meets the standards required 'to consideration for service within the diocese'.[19] These standards should include criteria for professional and academic preparation, personal qualities, ministerial skills and previous ecclesial participation. In many cases, however, the bishop is only involved indirectly: he entrusts the responsibility of appointing people to pastoral leadership teams to the pastor of a parish. Where this occurs, the pastor authorises the minister.

In this context, there may be a question of accountability: are members of the pastoral team accountable to the pastor who has authorised their ministry? Is there any sense in which he is accountable to them as a co-member of such a team? In situations like this, great care is needed to establish structures that will safeguard the individual members of the pastoral team, as well as build strong interrelationships between them. The object of these structures should be to create a supportive environment wherein team members are mutually accountable to each other. The pastoral practice of these pastoral teams is significantly enhanced when members interact in this way. The vision is one of bringing 'together into partnership' people who have different vocations, gifts and offices arising out of different sacraments in the Church.[20] This collaborative ministry 'does not blur the distinctiveness of each vocation or gift. Rather it enables the identity of each to be seen and expressed more fully'.[21] It would be useful in this context, to ensure supervision is provided by an external and independent facilitator for all members of the pastoral team. This form of supervision would provide team members with a suitable person to whom all parties can be accountable for the appropriate management of their ministerial partnership.

Ecclesial organisational practices

In Ireland, the practices whereby laypeople are authorised and appointed to pastoral leadership roles are quite diverse. In some instances, bishops and pastors have a deliberate selection, formation/education, ritualisation and employment structure, while others are more informal in their approach. This diversity has been caused by the gradual movement of laypeople from spontaneous to professional roles, in response to the needs perceived within communities, and in line with the availability of resources in specific regions. A certain amount of diversity is inevitable, and indeed preferable, in order to respect the particularities of individual communities and situations. However, excessive diversity in the appointment of laypeople to professional ministerial roles can have adverse consequences. It can cause uncertainty about the sustainability of individual posts, the adequacy of ecclesial working environments, the quality of resulting ministerial practice, and even the authenticity of such lay positions within the Church.

In order truly to nurture professional lay pastoral ministry, the Church in Ireland will need to evaluate these overly diversified patterns of employment. The goal should be to establish a measure of consistency: pastoral structures will need to adhere to the same values and principles, preserving the same standards of quality across ministerial practices. Benedict XVI recently espoused two primary values that should be preserved by pastoral structures. These are promoting the co-responsibility of all the faithful for the being and activity of the Church, and strengthening a mature and committed lay faithful. He observed:

> [I]t is necessary to improve pastoral structures in such a way that the co-responsibility of all the members of the People of God in their entirety is gradually promoted, with respect for vocations and for the respective roles of the consecrated and of laypeople. They must no longer be viewed as 'collaborators' of the clergy but truly recognised as 'co-responsible', for the Church's being and action, thereby fostering the consolidation of a mature and committed laity.[22]

In addition, the United States Conference of Catholic Bishops stated that pastoral structures should share 'both characteristics of a faith community of co-workers, as described by St Paul, and the characteristics of a modern organisation'.[23] That is, the employment practices used by the Church should 'integrate gospel values and best organisational practices'.[24] The ministerial workplace should be characterised by 'respect for persons, justice, integrity, efficient use of resources, successful accomplishment of mission and goals, and an environment in which committed and skilled workers are treated fairly'.[25] Therefore, one can name three requisite principles for the establishment of adequate ecclesial employment structures: a) a commitment to the co-responsibility of all the faithful; b) a faithfulness to realising gospel values (in particular, love and justice); c) a responsibility for maintaining best organisational practices.

In accordance with these principles, appropriate ecclesial organisational practices should, first, provide structures for the discernment of the vocation and the determination of the candidate's suitability. This determination includes 'references, background checks, and various screening instruments'; an extensive application form; psychological screening instruments, personal interviews; evaluations; and the development of formation plans.[26] Second, they should involve the appointment of the layperson to the position in writing, including the title of the position, the rights and responsibilities attached to the position or office, relevant employment and personnel policies, any limitations on the term of the appointment, transitions and terminations (especially in terms of a change in pastor or the end of a pastor's term in office), and grievance proceedings.[27] Third, they should entail the blessing or ritualisation of the appointment.[28] These liturgical ceremonies or rituals 'can underscore the importance of this person's role in the life of the community and provide opportunity for the lay ecclesial minister and the community to pray together'.[29]

Fourth, they should ensure that laypeople receive orientation during the initial stages of their appointment, and that they are mentored and supported throughout their ministry.[30] Fifth, they should provide lay pastoral leaders with a formal opportunity to reflect on their own performance in ministry and to receive feedback from their supervisor, mentor, colleagues and people served.[31] Finally, they should ensure that laypeople involved in professional lay pastoral ministry receive fair compensation for their work: 'The Church has a long history of speaking about the dignity of work and the proper recognition of people's service. In a comprehensive personnel system, this area includes salary plans that may establish ranges through which individuals may progress, as well as benefit plans (e.g. health insurance, family leave, childcare assistance, funding for ongoing education).'[32] The process of determining fair compensation for professional lay pastoral ministry will include some discussion of the scheduling of ministerial activity and the resultant expectations on the pastoral leader.

Conclusion

The many laypeople who are involved in professional lay pastoral ministry bear witness to the reality of the lay vocation to public and formal ministry in the Church. These laypeople remain active in the Church, and persevere in their ministry, despite any uncertainties about the value, quality and sustainability of their ministerial roles. They strive to serve the mission of the Church when the people they serve do not always fully comprehend their duties and responsibilities, when relationships with colleagues are strained, and when inadequate employment structures leave them susceptible to isolation and burnout. This reality poses a direct challenge to the Church community to preserve integrity and quality in its ministerial practices. In meeting this challenge, several issues need to be addressed: an adequate understanding of this form of the lay apostolate; personal and ecclesial discernment of the vocation; preparation of candidates, colleagues and members of the community; and appropriate structures of selection, authorisation, ritualisation, orientation, evaluation and compensation. It would greatly enhance the development of this form of the lay apostolate if parishes, parish clusters and dioceses adopted a shared approach regarding each of these issues.

Notes

1. See, for example, Second Vatican Council, *Lumen Gentium* (1964), 3ff.; *Apostolicam Actuositatem* (1965); *Ad Gentes* (1965), 15, 21, 41; *Presbyterorum Ordinis* (1965), 9. http://www.vatican.va/archive/hist_councils/ii_vatican_council/index.htm (accessed 25/4/2013).
2. *Apostolicam Actuositatem*, 2.
3. Ibid.
4. The term 'spontaneous' is used here as an alternative to 'voluntary'. The term 'voluntary' fails to capture the ecclesial and vocational aspects of this form of lay involvement in the life of the Church. Volunteers can be found in the secular sphere, where voluntary activity is not readily recognised as having its source in a call from God. One can be a non-believer and still wish to engage in voluntary activity. However, the term 'spontaneous' embraces the understanding that laypeople are being called by God to be active in the mission and life of the Church, freely cooperating with the divine grace they have received in the sacraments of initiation to empower them for this activity.
5. These laypersonnel have different job titles depending on the context: parish/diocesan pastoral workers, parish/pastoral assistants, pastoral team coordinators, etc.
6. Edward P. Hahnenberg, 'Serving in the Name of the Church: The Call to Lay Ecclesial Ministry', *In the Name of the Church: Vocation and Authorization of Lay Ecclesial Ministry*, William J. Cahoy, ed. (Collegeville, MN: Liturgical Press, 2012), 47.
7. Ibid.
8. See footnote 4.
9. Catholic Bishops' Conference of England and Wales, *The Sign We Give* (1995), 26, http://www.cbcew.org.uk/document.doc?id=64> (accessed 25/4/2013).
10. Ibid., 26–7.
11. United States Conference of Catholic Bishops, *Co-Workers in the Vineyard of the Lord: A Resource for Guiding the Development of Lay Ecclesial Ministry* (Washington DC: United States Conference of Catholic Bishops, 2005), 29. http://old.usccb.org/laity/laymin/co-workers.pdf (accessed 25/4/2013).

12. Gula, *Just Ministry: Professional Ethics for Pastoral Ministers* (New York: Paulist Press, 2010), 5.

13. Hahnenberg, 44–5.

14. Susan K. Wood, SCL, 'A Theology of Authorization of Lay Ecclesial Ministers', *In the Name of the Church*, 100.

15. *The Sign We Give*, 24.

16. Ibid., 10.

17. Ibid., 21.

18. Ibid., 24.

19. *Co-Workers in the Vineyard of the Lord*, 56.

20. *The Sign We Give*, 12.

21. Ibid.

22. See Pope Benedict XVI, Opening Address of the Pastoral Convention of the Diocese of Rome on the theme 'Church Membership and Pastoral Co-Responsibility' (2009), 7. http://www.vatican.va/holy_father/benedict_xvi/speeches/2009/may/documents/hf_benxvi_spe_20090526_convegno-diocesi-rm_en.html (accessed 25/4/2013).

23. *Co-Workers in the Vineyard of the Lord*, 61.

24. Ibid.

25. Ibid.

26. Ibid., 32.

27. Ibid., 32, 64.

28. Ibid., 59.

29. Ibid.

30. Ibid., 62. 'An experienced Church minister introduces the prospective lay minister into the ministerial workplace. A mentor passes on more than skills. He or she presents an understanding of the particular culture in which the ministry will take place, including the challenges and the opportunities. The mentor helps the prospective minister to develop realistic expectations about ministry, including the limits of what can be accomplished' (ibid., 29).

31. Ibid., 63.

32. Ibid.

Going to God Together: Priests in Ecclesial Movements

BRENDAN LEAHY

American journalist and analyst of the Catholic Church John Allen has commented that seen as part of expanding lay roles in the Church, the new ecclesial movements 'can be understood as incubators and laboratories for new approaches to the lay vocation.'[1] It is true that membership of the new communities in the Church such as Charismatic Renewal covenant communities, Communion and Liberation, Cursillo, Focolare, L'Arche, Legion of Mary, Neo-Catechumenal Way, Regnum Christi, Sant'Egidio and Teams of Our Lady are made up primarily of laypeople, but not exclusively. As Allen also points out, the movements carry implications for virtually every member of the Church, including priests. And indeed many priests are members of these new 'ecclesial' communities.

In what follows, I would like to offer a few brief reflections on the phenomenon of priests in ecclesial movements. My focus is primarily on the involvement of diocesan priests in movements though I will refer to some distinct issues in relation to priest members of religious orders in movements.[2]

An overview
It is useful to begin with a brief overview of what movements are and who joins them. In its *Directory of International Associations*

of the Lay Faithful, the Pontifical Council for Laity provides concise descriptions for 122 new movements. They are to be found from North America to Australia, from Brazil to Sweden, from Ireland to Nigeria. There is a great variety among them in terms of self-understanding and spirituality, external structures and procedures, training or formation methods, goals and fields of work.

Although it is sometimes felt they are marginal to the main life of the Church, the statistics do not bear that out.[3] Take the US for instance. It is estimated that more than one and a half million Americans have benefitted from a Cursillo weekend while more than five million Catholics' lives have been impacted by the Charismatic Renewal's Life in the Spirit seminars. The Marriage Encounter weekends have enhanced the vocations of around three million couples and priests. More than 30,000 people are currently deeply committed to the Neo-Catechumenal Way's catechesis in nine hundred US parishes. Seven new seminaries are animated by the Neo-Catechumenal Way, while 30 per cent of current US seminarians cite the Life Teen movement as an important catalyst that got them thinking about a priestly vocation. It is estimated that some 700,000 Catholics attend Life Teen liturgies in 1,700 parishes each week.

Those who belong to a movement or community often say it wasn't so much that they joined an association or group but rather met a person who changed their life. It was an encounter for the first time or a new form of encounter, in the power of the Spirit, with Jesus Christ. In many ways, the expression 'Baptism in the Spirit' is accurate. For those who were already Christian by Baptism, Christian faith suddenly comes alive for them in a new way.

Referring to the Franciscan movement of the thirteenth century as probably providing 'the clearest instance of what a movement is', the then Cardinal Ratzinger affirmed:

> [M]ovements generally derive their origin from a charismatic leader and take shape in concrete communities, inspired by the life of their founder; they attempt to live the Gospel anew,

in its totality, and recognise the Church without hesitation as the ground of their life without which they could not exist.[4]

According to this definition, movements are linked to 'charisms' that are communicative in the sense that others are attracted by what the charismatic leader is doing (or has done) and promoting, saying and writing. This, in turn, leads to a spiritual affinity between persons that develops into friendships based on the gospel and a way of living out evangelisation.

The term 'ecclesial movement' is general enough to cover a wealth of forms produced by the life-giving creativity of the Spirit.[5] Blessed John Paul wrote that movements represent 'a powerful support, a moving and convincing reminder to live the Christian experience to the full, with intelligence and creativity'. This also provides a basis 'for finding adequate responses to the challenges and needs of ever changing times and historical circumstances'.[6]

Movements and priests

To explore the significance of the presence of priests in movements, we need to recall some of the major features of the Second Vatican Council. The Council's ecclesiology was one of communion with a new focus on the Church as People of God, Body-Spouse of Christ and Temple of the Spirit.[7] In the light of this ecclesiology, the Council emphasised the reciprocity of all the vocations in the Church's Catholicity.[8] A particularly significant rediscovery was the charismatic profile of the Church as 'co-constitutive' along with the hierarchical-sacramental dimension of the Church.[9] The acknowledgement of the universal call to holiness that emerged so powerfully at the Council brought a new understanding of the relationship of laity, religious, priests and bishops.[10] Along with that, the common baptismal missionary calling came to the fore. The Church's Marian profile emerged as the fundamental dimension of the Church and the ultimate goal of the Council in the sense of promoting the conditions in our time for letting the Christ event become history.[11] Within this broad horizon, while affirming the ontological distinction between the ordained and lay faithful,[12] the Council presented priestly identity in relational and dialogical terms.[13]

On the basis of the Conciliar event and texts, in the enthusiasm of the years immediately after Vatican II, a lot of religious, priests and seminarians came into contact with movements and it was for many a very positive encounter. Admittedly, it was a time of great crisis in vocational and apostolic identity (in part due to an insufficient initial reception of the Council's teachings on issues like laity, mission, universal call to holiness). There are many today who would say that belonging to a movement saved their vocation. In recent years, however, there has been a tendency to say something like 'we are grateful for what you did for us in times of crisis but now we want to reclaim our own identity'.

It is certainly true that diocesan priests are incardinated in a diocese with a specific identity, religious orders have their own formation itinerary shaped by the charism of that order, and seminaries have their own formation programme. But the Holy Spirit brought new movements to life not just as a stopgap for a crisis after a council but for a longterm purpose. Perhaps there is a need now to recognise that movements aren't just for times of crisis. They are an expression of what the Spirit is saying to the Church also in terms of how the Spirit wants the Church to be today and how it can get there.

In brief, we can summarise the benefits to priests as follows. On the basis of a common charism and spirituality, movements provide a vibrant, lived experience of the ecclesiology of communion among vocations – married people, priests, young and old. Belonging to a movement provides priests with a spiritual pathway that can nourish their spiritual life, promote holiness and prompt zeal in pastoral commitment. The new communities and movements put forward significant suggestions for the New Evangelization. Priests' ongoing formation is enriched by contact with a movement. Priestly fraternity is helped by priests sharing a common spirituality. Being in contact with a movement can be a help and support for seminarians along their formation journey.

Priests contribute greatly to the life of a movement. Their very presence at the community's gatherings is itself a sign of encouragement for many. Celebrating the liturgy, hearing confessions and offering spiritual advice are the most obvious manifestations of a priest's contribution. But priests also bring with them particular experience and wisdom linked to their own insertion in to a diocese or religious order. They offer enriching perspectives from history, theology and philosophy. The insight and judgement gained from pastoral charity can also be shared with the movement as it makes its way forward in fidelity to its charism. In all of this, however, priests find the movements provide them with an experience of *being with* others rather than *being in charge.*

Issues that arise

While many priests are members of movements, most are not. After all, there is salvation outside movements. It can be that a priest simply hasn't yet met a movement that particularly attracts him. There are a variety of charisms, movements and communities and not everyone will feel equally attracted to all of them. It can be that a priest has had a negative experience of a community and that has turned him off.

Whether or not a priest belongs to a movement, he is called to value the variety of charisms, movements and communities he meets in his pastoral ministry. Among his tasks in community building is that of discerning and esteeming the charisms in the parish or diocese. This should not mean trying to squeeze movements into a straight jacket of a parish or diocese's pastoral programming. Each movement has something to say and can prompt ideas if a priest is attentive. Saint Bernard already recognised that in the twelfth century.[14] Priests, respecting the specific goal of each charism, can always benefit from the presence of a movement in a parish or diocese.

Apart from the general issue of the usefulness of movements within a parish or diocese, there is the more personal issue of *belonging* to a movement. Some priests can be hesitant because they are not clear about how to reconcile being in a movement with being a member of a diocesan presbyterate or religious order. A question that can arise, for instance, is whether diocesan priests need the help of other spiritualities. After all, a priest has already many aids for his spiritual life – the breviary, celebration of the sacraments, pastoral charity, the rosary, devotions and prayer. That would seem sufficient. There is truth in that. The key spiritual practices are already a great basis for the spiritual life. Furthermore, by the very fact that a priest belongs to a particular diocese, a priest's spirituality and ministry take on a specific hue – each diocese has its traditions, stories, sacred places and times, way of doing things. A parish community can provide opportunities to grow in love of neighbour.

And yet, when we consider so much of what priests value for themselves and for their pastoral ministry, we have to recognise that much of it came from charisms linked to movements and communities of the past – the breviary comes to us through the Benedictine tradition, the Rosary through the Dominicans, the Spiritual Exercises through the Jesuits, the Stations of the Cross through the Franciscans, the devotion to the Sacred Heart through the Jesuits (and First Fridays with Margaret Mary Alacoque), missions and novena days through the Redemptorists and Vincentians, and so on. It should come as no surprise, therefore, that the Holy Spirit in our day offers new spiritual pathways. The new thing in our day is that the communities coming to life provide an experience of the Spirit to be shared with other priests, religious and laity.

English scholar and expert on John Henry Newman, Ian Kerr, has pointed out that the model of priesthood lived up to Vatican II was to a large extent the product of the Council of Trent but was deeply influenced by the many spiritualities that came to life after Trent, especially the Jesuit spirituality. Today, the new movements offer inspiration for the exercise of priesthood in the light of the Second Vatican Council's ecclesiology of communion, focus on the gospel, dialogue and missionary dynamic.[15]

Another issue can be the question of a priest's role vis-à-vis laity. It is true that as an ordained minister, the priest stands 'before' (i.e. in front of) the lay faithful in the sense that he is in the Church as a visible continuation and sacramental sign of Christ in his own position before the Church and the world. And yet in *Pastores Dabo Vobis* we read:

> The ministerial priesthood conferred by the sacrament of holy orders and the common or 'royal' priesthood of the faithful, which differ essentially and not only in degree, are ordered one to the other – for each in its own way derives from the one priesthood of Christ. Indeed the ministerial priesthood does not of itself signify a greater degree of holiness with regard to the common priesthood of the faithful; through it Christ gives to priests, in the Spirit, a particular gift so that they can help the People of God to exercise faithfully and fully the common priesthood which it has received. (PDV, 17)

Priests and religious certainly have to help lay faithful in their formation. This is very much the traditional role we are accustomed to. Yet, in the living out of their ministry, and in recognition of the universal call to holiness, priests can also learn from lay faithful. In *Christifideles Laici* we read how 'the lay faithful themselves can and should help priests and religious in the course of their spiritual and pastoral journey'.[16] Involvement in movements can be for priests a significant access point to this spiritual maternity of the Church expressed also in lay men and woman, companions along the faith journey. Ian Kerr puts it like this:

> The sacrament of holy orders does set apart in the sense that the one who receives it shares in the ministerial priesthood – but it does not set apart the priest in the sense that somehow he no longer shares in, because he has risen above, the common priesthood of the baptised.[17]

Pope John Paul II saw the value of movements for priests also in this regard. Attracted by the same charism, sharing in the same story, inserted into the same group, priests and laypeople in a movement share an interesting experience of co-fraternity, building each other up mutually without confusion.[18] The paradox is that in living a strong experience of baptismal communion together with lay faithful – married, young people, consecrated – on the basis of a charism, priests emerge strengthened in their own specific ministry. This experience is also important today when very often priests feel they are dedicated publicly to a cause (religion) that is seen increasingly as limited to the private sphere. It is no surprise that Pope Benedict, in his letter to priests for the Year of Priests, invited them to welcome the new springtime which the Spirit is now bringing about in the Church also through movements, adding that these movements can be of help not just to lay faithful but to clergy as well.[19] An important point here too is that the experience in a movement reminds priests not to view the Church primarily in terms of being built up around the clerical state as its centre.

A priest can sometimes feel that belonging to a movement is an 'extra' duty on top of what is already a very busy schedule. Here we can think of the story of Cardinal John Henry Newman. At a time when he was particularly busy, his secretary was concerned for him and suggested to the cardinal that he review things. The cardinal took his secretary's advise on board by commenting, 'Yes, you're right. Add in a half an hour's prayer every day to my schedule'. There will never be a shortage of things to do. But the wisdom of the Church has always recommended we give priority to nourishing the roots of our faith commitment. Instead of viewing involvement in movements as an extra duty, it is wise to recognise involvement in them as a form of modern spiritual spiritual exercises.

Double belonging and alternative formation?

For priests who are members of religious orders, there is the question of 'double belonging'. Can you be a member of a religious order with its distinct charism and spirituality while also belonging to a movement? The 2002 instruction issued by the Congregation for Institutes of Consecrated Life and Societies of Apostolic Life, *Starting Afresh from Christ: A Renewed Commitment to Consecrated Life in the Third Millennium*, encourages opening to others beyond one's own institute in order to build up communion with other religious families and institutes. Doing so facilitates a rediscovery of common gospel roots and a deeper grasp of the beauty of one's own identity as well as the beauty of the variety of charisms. In referring to new forms of evangelical life, the instruction specifically mentions movements:

> Finally, a new richness can spring from an encounter and communion with the charisms of ecclesial movements. Movements can often offer the example of evangelical and charismatic freshness such as the generous, creative initiatives in evangelisation. On the other hand, movements as well as new forms of evangelical life can learn a great deal from the faithful, joyful and charismatic witness of consecrated life which bears a very rich spiritual patrimony, the many treasures of experience and wisdom and a great variety of apostolates and missionary commitments.[20]

So there is mutuality between 'old and new charisms' as it puts it. Older charisms provide the wisdom distilled from years of experience. But they can also gain spiritual perspectives, formation methodologies and renewed expressions of apostolate that they can then integrate into the patrimony of their own religious order or seminary programme.

Members of religious orders belonging to a movement are, therefore, not engaging in a 'double belonging' or parallel formation, but rather opening to an expression of communion and mutual enrichment that today's ecclesiology of communion encourages and in forms provided by the Holy Spirit. We can learn from Thérèse of Lisieux who, being love, and faithful to her contemplative vocation, wanted to live all the ecclesial vocations. As already stated, a consecrated person (and by analogy a priest or seminarian) has, of course, to be well inserted into his or her religious order.

Conclusion

In conclusion, I want to mention a topic that is gaining increasing attention today – the relationship between charism and priesthood within a religious order or movement. Many of the new movements have witnessed some of the consecrated men become priests while remaining within the community. While the general theology of priesthood is valid for all priests, there is room for reflection on what is specific about priests who are ordained and remain primarily linked to their religious order or movement. It is not a topic that can be pursued here. Some valuable lines of reflection on this theme are to be found in a number of *Sequela Christi* dedicated precisely to this topic.[21]

This essay has reviewed some of the significance, especially for diocesan priests, of belonging to ecclesial movements and communities. Along with all the lay faithful, priests too have the right of association. With today's need, as Blessed Pope John Paul put it, to make the Church a 'school and home of communion', we can be grateful to the Spirit for offering movements as an experience also for priests that helps realise this goal.

Notes

1. John L. Allen, *The Future Church: How Ten Trends are Revolutionizing the Catholic Church* (New York: Doubleday, 2009), 425.
2. Priests belonging to religious orders number some 300,000 in the world today. On the involvement of diocesan priests and seminarians, see Brendan Leahy, *Ecclesial Movements and Communities* (New York: New City, 2011), 150–60. See Pope John Paul II's Apostolic Exhortation, *Pastores Dabo Vobis*, 68.
3. I am grateful to William Neu for these statistics which were prepared for a November 2011 workshop for Bishops of the United States entitled 'Catholic Ecclesial Movements and New Communities in the US in Conversation'.

4. Cardinal Joseph Ratzinger, 'The Ecclesial Movements: A Theological Reflection on Their Place in the Church,' Pontificium Consilium Pro Laicis, *Movements in the Church* (Vatican City: Pontificium Consilium Pro Laicis, 1999), 23–51, at 46–47. This article was also reproduced as 'The Theological Locus of Ecclesial Movements' in *Communio* 25 (Fall 1998), 480–504. See also Ratzinger's *New Outpourings of the Spirit* (San Francisco: Ignatius Press, 2007).

5. It should be pointed out that the Charismatic Renewal is not a single unified worldwide movement but rather a common experience of sharing the fundamental experience of the empowering presence of the Holy Spirit. See Charles Whitehead, *What is the Nature of the Catholic Charismatic Renewal?* (Locust Grove, VA: Chariscentre, 2003).

6. 'Message of His Holiness Pope John Paul II,' *Movements in the Church*, 13–19, at 18.

7. See *Lumen Gentium*, 1.

8. See *Lumen Gentium*, 13 and John Paul II's Apostolic Exhortation on the Laity, *Christifideles Laici* (30 December 1988), 55.

9. See especially *Lumen Gentium*, 4 and 12. This rediscovery was underlined by John Paul II in both his message and homily in the context of the 1998 meeting of the movements. See *Movements in the Church*.

10. See *Lumen Gentium*, 6.

11. See *Lumen Gentium*, 8. See Brendan Leahy, *The Marian Profile in the Ecclesiology of Hans Urs von Balthasar* (New York: New City Press, 2000).

12. See especially *Lumen Gentium*, 10.

13. See *Presbyterorum Ordinis*, 7 and 9; and also John Paul II's Apostolic Exhortation on the Formation of Priests, *Pastores Dabo Vobis* (25 March 1992).

14. See St Bernard, *Apologia to William of Saint Thierry*, 4.8, cited in John Paul II, Apostolic Exhortation, *Vita Consecrata*, 52.

15. See Ian Kerr, 'The Priesthood and the New Ecclesial Movements,' *Louvain Studies* 30 (2005), 124–136, at 126.

16. *Christifideles Laici*, 61.

17. Ibid., 134.

18. John Paul II, Letter to Cardinal James Francis Stafford, President of the Pontifical Council for the Laity on the occasion of a pastoral meeting organised by the Focolare Movement at Castelgandolfo (June 2001), entitled 'Ecclesial Movements for the New Evangelization' (21 June 2001). See also John Paul II, *Pastores Dabo Vobis*, 31.

19. See Letter to Priests Proclaiming a Year for Priests on the 150th Anniversary of the '*dies natalis*' of the Curé d'Ars (16 June 2009).
20. Congregation for Institutes of Consecrated Life and Societies of Apostolic Life, *Starting Afresh from Christ: A Renewed Commitment to Consecrated Life in the Third Millennium* (2002), 30.
21. See *Sequela Christi: Periodica Congregationis Pro Institutis Vitae Consecratae et Societatibus Vitae Apostolicae* 2 (2009) [new series].

Priests and the Clustering of Parishes: A Theological Reflection

EUGENE DUFFY

The reality of one priest serving multiple parishes is something with which many Catholics worldwide are familiar. It is gradually becoming a reality in Ireland and will become much more common in the coming years. Currently, nearly 40 per cent of the active diocesan clergy are over sixty-five years of age; in a number of dioceses this figure is higher than 50 per cent. So, over the next ten years it is inevitable that a large number of parishes will no longer have a resident priest and will have to be joined to another or several parishes for the provision of pastoral care, liturgy and sacraments. While practical arrangements have to be made, it is important that they are done in a way that is pastorally sensitive and grounded in a sound theological framework. The purpose of this essay is to explore some of the key elements of that framework and to demonstrate that a changed configuration of ministerial provision can be comfortably aligned with the best insights of the Second Vatican Council. It is important, therefore, that those who are involved in planning for the clustering of parishes do so not just with an eye to the practicalities but also with an eye to a proper theological underpinning.

A definition of 'cluster'

A 'cluster' is a group of parishes committed to the long-term relationship of collaboration to plan and provide for the spiritual, sacramental and pastoral needs of their respective communities. It involves the sharing of personnel, resources, programmes and facilities so that the needs of the constituent parishes or communities can be addressed without straining the resources of individual parishes. It contributes to the strengthening rather than diminishment of the life and ministry of each individual parish or community.

Theological foundations

Any worthwhile pastoral initiative must have a solid theological foundation and this is true for the process of parish clustering. It will be considered here under five headings: images of God; an ecclesiology of communion; an inclusive theology of the priesthood; a spirituality of collaboration; and a renewed vision of parish.

Images of God

An older generation was formed on an image of God as a remote figure, omniscient and omnipotent, presiding over the affairs of the world. Contemporary theology has recaptured a more biblical approach to imaging God, leading to a greater appreciation of the Trinity. Our images of God condition our outlook and behaviour more than we sometimes realise. Leonardo Boff remarked:

> Sticking only with faith in one sole God, without thinking of the Blessed Trinity as the union of Father, Son and Holy Spirit, is dangerous for society, for political life and for the Church … It can lead to totalitarianism, authoritarianism, paternalism and machismo.[1]

This is a useful reminder in the context of a call to work more collaboratively with others in clustering arrangements.

Any language about God is inadequate. However, the New Testament gives us the least inadequate language when it says 'God is love'. Love is a dynamic between persons in a relationship. It suggests mutuality, vulnerability, goodness, truth and integrity. The doctrine of the Trinity captures something of these characteristics as they pertain to God. The doctrine is an attempt to give a coherent statement of how God is best understood in the light of the human experience of the Divine interaction with humankind. Reflection on the life, death and resurrection of Jesus leads one to see that he is the Son of the Father, that he embodies the compassion of God for humankind and that his mission is kept alive and active through the power of the Holy Spirit. In his public life Jesus reveals the extent of the Divine love that is prepared to empty itself in compassion for humankind, willing to embrace even death in the desire to embody that love as concretely as possible. This love is given a fully human expression, showing what the human person is capable of when fully responsive to God's initiative. The Spirit that empowered Jesus in his life is then given to his disciples after his resurrection so that God's love can continue to be experienced and expressed by them until his return. The opening paragraphs of the *Dogmatic Constitution on the Church* show how each of the Divine Persons plays a role in drawing humankind into the circle of their love and friendship. In fact, this is the mission of the Church, to draw people into a fellowship of love with Father, Son and Spirit.

The Trinity acts as a model for all those involved in ministry. It is particularly apt for those being called to work in greater collaboration with other ministers and other communities. It is a reminder that all are called to a life of communion, mirroring the communion of life that is at the heart of the Trinity. It challenges all systems of dominance and individualism. So, if the older image of God was reflected in the rather monarchical approach to Church structures, a consideration of the Trinity demands a much more relational and participative approach to ministry and governance. This is the only approach that will work in the context of clustering parishes.

An ecclesiology of communion

Since Vatican II the Church is understood more as a communion of communities than as a monolithic static institution. This communion of life at the heart of the Church is experienced in very concrete ways at the local level. Whenever a community assembles to celebrate the Eucharist, it is already sharing in the Banquet of Life prepared by the Triune God. It is an assembly of people continually striving to grow in communion of life among themselves, through their common worship and their efforts to support one another in various social and material ways. Those gathered for the Eucharist are reminded that they are also in communion with all those other communities that comprise their diocese under the leadership of the bishop and even beyond this to include the whole Church. The ordained ministry in the Church is a visible agent of ecclesial communion, ensuring that each local celebration of the Eucharist is a bonding of those present with one another under the presidency of their presbyter who is in communion with his bishop, who in turn guarantees unity with the universal Church. This is a sacramental foundation for collaborative relationships in the Church.

The very nature of the Church then demands that people work in a spirit of partnership that reflects the dynamic of love and mutuality that characterises the Triune God. No minister can serve a community as if he or she were an isolated individual. The minister, lay or ordained, is always in relationship with others. This is as true for the pope as it is for the pastoral assistant in the most remote parish. In fact, when Vatican II spoke about the collegiality of bishops it was simply giving concrete expression to this ecclesiology of communion. There is a collegial dimension to all ministry. Just as the bishops are called to cooperate with one another under the leadership of the pope, so are the priests of a diocese called to cooperate with one another under the leadership of their bishop. Similarly, those who serve in other ministries are called to work collegially with one another under the guidance of their pastors.

An ecclesiology of communion can remain an abstraction unless it is practised at the most local level. It is not something that applies only to the ministry of the Church; it applies to communities as well. Each community is in relationship with all other Christian communities, in a sacramental way through the Eucharist, but this needs to be expressed in concrete ways if the eucharistic communion is to bear full fruit. Communities are called to share their resources with one another, to support one another so that all are built up to be more credible signs of the reality of Christ's presence in the world. Clustering provides an ideal opportunity for this to happen.

An inclusive theology of the priesthood

If previous generations laboured with an image of God as one who was aloof and isolated, this was mirrored in the popular perception of the ordained priest. Vatican II helped to retrieve a richer understanding of the ordained ministry by situating it in relationship to the entire community of disciples and also by accenting the collegial nature of the diocesan priesthood.

A number of key decisions at the Council determined a richer approach to membership of the Church. First of all, Baptism was presented as the foundational sacrament. It brings one into communion with the Triune God; it brings one into relationship with all the other members of the Church; it gives one a mission to be an ambassador of Christ. This community of people called together by Baptism is a priestly people. This people offers the sacrifice of praise and thanksgiving to God by the witness and conduct of their lives and bring this with them to the Eucharist. This principle was amplified in a second decision, namely, to treat of the whole people of God before speaking of the hierarchy. Thus, the ordained ministry in the Church is at the service of the entire community, ensuring that it is structured and equipped to fulfil its mission as the community of disciples. Therefore, any planning in the Church must focus on the needs of the community in the first instance, not on the needs of the ordained ministers. This should be a guiding principle for any decisions about the clustering of parishes: how can each community be enabled to become the priestly people of God?

The Decree on the Ministry and Life of Priests, *Presbyterorum Ordinis,* again situates the ordained ministry in the context of the whole people of God, all of whom are called to offer their lives in a sacrifice of praise to God. The ordained minister enables this offering to be made, in the first instance, through the preaching of the Word. This dimension of the priestly service is given prominence, because it is foundational to the celebration of all the sacraments. It evokes and supports the faith of the Christian community so that it can more consciously offer a worthy sacrifice to God:

> Priests should carefully study liturgical knowledge and art, to the end that through their service of the liturgy the Christian communities entrusted to them may ever give more perfect praise to God, the Father, and Son, and Holy Spirit.[2]

The focus is on enabling communities to grow in faith, to be more conscious of their vocation to know, love and serve God in their daily lives, in common worship, especially in the Eucharist. The goal is to ensure that all God's people are equipped to realise their true vocation and that each local community becomes a genuinely priestly community.

Collegiality was a notable feature of the ecclesiology of Vatican II. While it was expounded primarily in respect of the episcopate, it also has implications for the way in which all authority and leadership are exercised in the Church.[3] It is a term, then, which can be applied analogously to the diocesan presbyterium and its bishop. The very first document issued by the Council makes this quite clear. It states:

> They should all be convinced that the Church is displayed with special clarity when the holy people of God, all of them, are actively and fully sharing in the same liturgical celebrations – especially when it is the same Eucharist

– sharing one prayer at one altar, at which the bishop is presiding, surrounded by his presbyterate and his ministers.[4]

Lumen Gentium also points in the same direction when it says:

> The individual bishops, however, are the visible principle and foundation of unity in their own particular churches, formed in the likeness of the universal Church; in and from these particular churches there exists the one and unique Catholic Church.[5]

The implication is that the local Church is not a mere subdivision of the universal Church but is that Church in its local manifestation.[6] At an early stage in his pontificate, John Paul II spoke of collegiality as

> the adequate development of organisms, some of which will be entirely new, others updated, to ensure a better union of minds, intentions and initiatives in the work of building up the Body of Christ.[7]

Lumen Gentium speaks clearly of the collegial nature of the priestly ministry of the presbyterium:

> As prudent cooperators of the episcopal order and its instrument and help, priests are called to the service of the People of God and constitute along with their bishop one presbyterium though destined to different duties ... Under the authority of the bishop, priests sanctify and govern the portion of the Lord's flock entrusted to them, in their own locality they make visible the universal Church and they provide powerful help towards the building up of the whole body of Christ (cf. Eph 4:12).[8]

Among themselves, 'priests are bound together in a close fraternity, which should be seen spontaneously and freely in mutual help both spiritual and material, both pastoral and personal, in reunions and in the fellowship of life, work and charity'.[9] Priests are also called 'to unite their efforts and combine their resources under the leadership of their bishops'. *Christus Dominus* states that 'moreover, all diocesan priests should be united among themselves and fired with enthusiasm for the spiritual welfare of the whole diocese'.[10]

So, the conciliar teaching is very clear that the ordained priesthood is a genuinely fraternal and collegial ministry. Its reception is crucial to the success of the clustering project. The practice of fraternity and collegiality will begin in the immediate pastoral area or cluster. It is in this concrete situation that priests will most easily begin to cooperate with one another, sharing the burdens of the ministry with one another. Such a collegial spirit will mean that each priest will be open to offering the benefit of his own resources to neighbouring presbyters and their communities and he will be equally open to accepting their gifts. What applies to the ordained priests applies to all other ministries as well.

A spirituality of collaboration

The ecclesiology of communion guides the spirituality of all those who are engaged in the ministry of the Church, not just those in the ordained ministry. All ministers are called to act in a collaborative fashion because by its very nature the Church is a community graced with a variety of complementary gifts so that it may grow in unity and charity (1 Cor 12). As Richard Gaillardetz comments on St Paul's theology of community, it 'is dynamic and organic. It conceives of Christian community as constituted by a shared life in Christ begun in Baptism and nurtured in the Eucharist'.[11] To be a member of the Church is to be part of an interdependent community of people, where the bonds are both spiritual and concrete. Saint John speaks eloquently of how one's love of God has to be expressed in interpersonal relationships (cf. 1 Jn 4:20-21). The New Testament is more helpful in providing a spirituality for ministry than providing clear guidelines for its structure. In this respect, too, it is more concerned with a spirituality for communal living and ministering than in providing a spirituality for the individual. It is quite clear in the New Testament that the call to holiness is not a private affair but a call to be in relationship with God through a pattern of loving, respectful relationships with all those in the community.

A spirituality that is rooted in Baptism takes the centrality of *kenosis* seriously. It is in self-surrender and self-giving that we really rise to new life with Christ. We recognise our own poverty and helplessness and grow in appreciation of the fact that all we have comes from God and not from our own resources. Not only do we depend on God, but we depend on other human persons too for all that enables us to flourish. God's gifts are at work in them not just for their personal well-being but for the benefit of others as well. This means that not only are we challenged to show great generosity in the service and love that we show for one another, we are equally challenged to be humbly receptive to what others can offer us in our poverty and weakness.

All of these considerations bear on the demands that the clustering of parishes will bring to individuals and communities. Unless this kind of spirituality begins to percolate through to all involved in the process, no amount of new structures or arrangements will enable the full benefits of the opportunity to be experienced. A spirituality of collaboration is the only antidote to the inevitable temptations of distrust that often beset individuals and communities who try to work together. All those involved in the process of clustering are invited to relinquish some of the possessiveness that they may have had towards their own community and be willing to accept the gifts of others or to offer some of their own resources to enable others to thrive and flourish.

A renewed vision of parish

Parish loyalty is a deeply rooted dimension of Irish life, so much so that 'parish' is often used as a synonym for local community. John Paul II said: 'The parish is not principally a structure, a territory, or a building, but rather, "the family of God, a fellowship afire with a unifying spirit", "a familial and welcoming home", "the community of the faithful".'[12] The focus here is on community and relationships. The pope went on:

> We believe simply that ... the parish has an indispensable mission of great contemporary importance: to create the basic community of the Christian people; to initiate and gather the people in the accustomed expression of liturgical life; to conserve and renew the faith of the people of today; to serve as the school for teaching the salvific message of Christ; to put solidarity in practice and work the humble charity of good and brotherly works.[13]

In the context of clustering, this vision is still important. The emphasis is on building Christian communities, not safeguarding territory or securing financial support for a priest.

Clustering parishes is a delicate and sensitive pastoral agenda. It is not a rationalisation process appropriate to industry. It is rather an attempt to ensure that local communities are in the best possible relationship with one another in their efforts to be communities of the disciples of Jesus Christ. The process is profoundly relational and grounded in the reality of the Church as a communion of communities. This is not a purely human achievement but is also the work of God's Holy Spirit whose gifts are generously given to lead all the disciples of Jesus into a deeper unity with one another and with the Triune God.

Conclusion

We are rapidly facing into a situation that is unfamiliar to most Irish priests. As their numbers diminish the demands on them increase dramatically. The old patterns will not serve them or their communities. New configurations will have to be imagined. The ministry of deacons and lay ministers will have to be more actively encouraged. It will have to be accepted that not all communities will have a Sunday Mass and that other forms of liturgy will have to be provided. The clustering of parishes is just one element of major shifts that will have to occur if the Word is to be preached and celebrated amidst all God's people and all of these shifts need to be grounded in the theological vision offered by Vatican II.

Notes

1. Leonardo Boff, *Holy Trinity, Perfect Community* (Maryknoll, New York: Orbis Books, 2000), 7.
2. *Presbyterorum Ordinis*, 5. All translations from Norman Tanner, ed., *Decrees of the Ecumenical Councils*, Vol II (London: Sheed & Ward, 1990).
3. Although the noun 'collegiality' is not used in the documents of Vatican II, episcopal governance is described as 'collegial' (fifteen times) and the hierarchy is described as a 'collegium' (thirty-seven times). See Michael Fahy in *The HarperCollins Encyclopedia of Catholicism*, Richard McBrien, ed. (New York: HarperCollins, 1995).
4. *Sacrosanctum Concilium*, 41.
5. *Lumen Gentium*, 23.
6. See Joseph A. Komonchak, 'The Local Church and the Church Catholic: The Contemporary Theological Problematic', *The Jurist* 52 (1992), 416–47.
7. *Insegnamenti di Giovanni Paolo II*, I (Vatican City: Libreria Editrice Vaticana, 1978), 15; quoted in Charles M. Murphy, 'Collegiality: An Essay in Better Understanding', *Theological Studies* 46 (1983), 41.
8. *Lumen Gentium*, 28.
9. Ibid.
10. *Christus Dominus*, 28.
11. *Ecclesiology for a Global Church: A People Called and Sent* (Maryknoll, New York: Orbis Books, 2008), 22.
12. *Christifideles Laici*, 26
13. Ibid.

The Role of the Priest in Regard to Pastoral Councils and Finance Committees

PAT FARRAGHER

The purpose of this essay is to explore the role of the priest in regard to parish pastoral councils and finance committees, and in particular the importance of permanent and ongoing formation. Over the past four years I have worked as a diocesan resource person for pastoral councils. Among the insights that have crystallised for me during that time is the need for an underlying ecclesiology on which to ground the development of structures such as a pastoral council or a finance committee. Two central components of such an ecclesiology are communion and co-responsibility. When understood in this context, ongoing and permanent formation is not something the priest undertakes alone but rather as part of the faith community where he is pastor and as member of a presbyterate in a local diocesan church. Such formation requires a disposition of openness on the part of council members including the priest. It requires a willingness to learn new ways of ministry while at all times being faithful to the mission of the parish in forming faith and in forming the faith community.

As we gain a clearer understanding of communion and co-responsibility, it becomes evident that both the parish pastoral council and the finance committee, of which the priest is a member, are structures by which this ecclesiological vision is worked out and realised at local level. Ongoing formation for both the priest and members of pastoral councils and finance committees is essential to this process. Among the avenues of ongoing formation, we include training for the members of parish pastoral councils and finance committees at parish and at pastoral area level. Diocesan in-service courses for priests, which include attention to the spiritual, human, intellectual and pastoral dimensions, also offer opportunities for ongoing formation. Regular pastoral supervision as a means of ongoing formation has been shown to bear fruit for those who take part. Before we focus on ongoing and permanent formation in relation to parish pastoral councils and finance committees, it is necessary to look at elements of an ecclesiology which undergirds both structures.

Communion and co-responsibility

Among the significant changes that took place in the Second Vatican Council was a shift in the Church's self-understanding. In the Constitution of the Church the Council Fathers state that 'the Church has been seen as "a people made one with the unity of the Father, the Son and the Holy Spirit".[1] Eugene Duffy summarises this transition in the following terms:

> Vatican II then speaks of a communion of life which is grounded in the heart of the Trinity and which finds genuine expression in the concrete life of the Christian Community. The Church is to be a sign and an instrument through which the Spirit affects the union of all people with God and of all people with one another.[2]

Following the Second Vatican Council the Church understands itself more in terms of a pilgrim people of God and community of communities rather than in terms of an institution, which held sway in previous decades.

What is the role of the priest in such a Church? In *Pastores Dabo Vobis*, the late Pope John Paul II proposes the following answer:

His consciousness of this communion leads to a need to awaken and deepen co-responsibility in the one common mission of salvation with a prompt and heartfelt esteem for the charisms and tasks which the Spirit gives the believers for the building up of the Church. It is above all in the Pastoral Ministry, directed by its very nature to the good of the people of God, that the priest must live and give witness to this profound communion with all.[3]

It is clear that part of the role of the priest is to recognise the charisms which the Spirit gives to believers for the building up of the Church and to animate these gifts for the good of the local Christian community. The word John Paul II used in 1992 to describe the relationship among the community of believers, including the priest, is 'co-responsible'. This theme is echoed by Pope Benedict XVI in his May 2009 address at the opening of the Pastoral Convention of the Diocese of Rome, when he reminded priests that the laity 'must no longer be viewed as collaborators of the clergy but truly recognised as co-responsible for the Church's being and action, thereby fostering the consolidation of a mature and committed laity'.[4] To see the faithful as co-responsible with the priest for the life and mission of the local Church calls forth different leadership skills in the priest. This involves a style of leadership very different to that instilled in seminary formation prior to the publication of *Pastores Dabo Vobis*. This is a participatory style which involves inviting people to assume various ministries, promoting group discussion, listening, clarifying the significant issues, identifying a lack of information and reminding the group of its mandate. This leadership style will involve a deep respect for each person, and openness to new learning. My belief is that both the parish pastoral council and the finance committees are structures by which this sense of communion and co-responsibility, this new leadership style, can be built up and actualised at parish level.

Finance committees and parish pastoral councils

Both parish pastoral councils and finance committees are recognised as representative bodies through which the faithful are empowered to be co-responsible along with their pastors for the building up of the local Church. The finance committee is referred to in the *Code of Canon Law* in the following terms: 'In each parish there is to be a finance committee to help the parish priest in the administration of the goods of the Parish.'[5] In practical terms, parish finance committees are composed of four or five laypeople who assist and advise the priest in the administration of the temporal goods of the parish. The responsibilities of the finance committee include the efficient and transparent management of the parish finances and the putting in place of financial systems and controls to ensure the sound management of all aspects of the parish finances. While their focus is on financial matters, members of the finance committee must recognise that the purpose of the committee is to manage the finances in association with the priest so as to contribute to the stability of the parish as it supports the ongoing conversion of all its members through evangelisation and catechesis. Pastoral councils are referred to in the *Code* in the following terms:

> If after consulting the Council of Priests, the diocesan Bishop considers it opportune, a pastoral council is to be established in each parish. In this council, which is presided over by the parish priest, Christ's faithful, together with those who by virtue of their office are engaged in pastoral care in the parish, give their help in fostering pastoral action.[6]

Pastoral councils are representative bodies made up of members of the faithful and attend to the spiritual and pastoral needs of the parish. Frameworks for developing diocesan norms and parish guidelines in relation to pastoral councils have been issued by the Irish Episcopal Conference and have been adapted locally in many dioceses. We will now look at some of the forums in which the ongoing and permanent formation in relation to both of these bodies takes place.

Means of ongoing formation

Formation at parish level

The focus here is specifically in the area of pastoral councils and finance committees. One of the first tasks in the formation of a pastoral council is to raise levels of awareness within the community regarding the council's role, the qualities needed in members, and the vision of the Church which underpins its work. The Pauline image of the body (cf. 1 Cor 12:4-21) consisting of the various parts, each with its own role to play, is helpful to our understanding of the pastoral council as the group which animates the various members in the formation of faith community and in the formation of faith.

As president of the pastoral council, the role of the parish priest in its initial formation, and in its continued effectiveness and smooth running, cannot be overstated. The corollary is also true in that the pastoral council will flounder, will suffer a lack of energy and direction if the leadership from the president is not forthcoming. *Grouping Parishes for Mission* puts this well when it states that 'the ongoing formation and training of priests is therefore essential in order to equip them with the outlook and skills that nurture a sense of co-responsibility, and to enable them to adopt a style of ministry that is consistent with that sense of co-responsibility with all of the People of God.'[7] There are numerous aids available to guide the recruitment and formation of a new pastoral council.[8]

In his role as president, the priest is part of the formation process from the outset, both guiding and directing it. However, the priest cannot understand himself only as an agent of formation; he is also a participant in the formation process.

While the theory of what constitutes a pastoral council or a finance committee is relatively clear, how this is actualised at a local level can have its difficulties and problems. Clarity of terms of reference as well as a specified term of office are helpful in maintaining energy and a sense of direction in both groups. This clarity is provided in part from an overall shared vision of what a pastoral council is but also in terms of the goals identified at the start of its term of office. Formation in a 'spirituality of communion'[9] and an understanding of the central place of prayer are foundational in the training of council and committee members. Allocating a time of prayer prior to discussion, decision and action, as modelled in the Acts of the Apostles (cf. Acts 2:42, 44-47, 6:1-6), is the guiding example for the meetings of the council.

One of the common pitfalls for any pastoral council is to try to take on too much during its term. This can lead to a sense of despondency and frustration. The pastoral council will do well to recognise that it will not change the world (the parish) during one term of office. What a council can hope to do is to build on the efforts of those gone before in this role and to lay good foundations for those who will follow in their footsteps. Regular two-way communication between members of the council and parishioners will enhance the work of the council. This is particularly true at the time of formation of a new council or committee. At such a time, it is important to highlight the work of both bodies and to open the invitation to all members of the community to have their say in the membership of the new council or committee. Formation for members of both bodies at the outset of their term of office will bear fruit in terms of purpose, spirituality and clarity of role. Such formation will also enhance a sense of ownership among members of the council and thereby cultivate a sense of co-responsibility.

At local and diocesan level, there is need for ongoing and regular training and formation for new and current members of parish pastoral councils and finance committees. The priest, as a member of both these bodies, often co-ordinates and participates in such training and this is an important element in his own ongoing formation.

Pastoral areas

Recent developments throughout dioceses in western Europe and in the English-speaking world have seen the grouping of parishes so that their pastoral needs may be met with a declining number of ordained ministers. These developments have brought many challenges as the priest is now called to minister to more than one parish community, thus affecting the traditional bond between the priest and people. Pastoral area leadership teams and area pastoral councils can provide the structures through which pastoral leadership is exercised in these groupings of parishes. These initiatives can seem like a journey into the unknown for both priest and people as communities seek to respond to the spiritual and pastoral needs of the parishes involved. Ongoing formation for members of these teams, including the priest, is necessary so that the group will be clear about its purpose, understand the challenges involved, and be unified in its approach. As *Grouping Parishes for Mission* states, 'challenges for clergy may include frustration resulting from an increased number of meetings, a struggle with Team Ministry, or irritation at having responsibilities outside of one's own parish'.[10]

In light of such changed understanding and expansion in the pastoral demands being placed on the priest, ongoing formation must address the changing nature of priesthood itself. For many dioceses the medium which presents most opportunity for such ongoing formation are the residential diocesan in-service days for priests.

In-service days

In-service days are valuable opportunities for priests to meet as part of a diocesan presbyterate to reflect on the pastoral challenges to be faced and to receive ongoing spiritual, human, intellectual and pastoral formation. They are usually organised by priests themselves in association with their bishop and provide a forum to reflect on pastoral challenges but also on the manner in which priesthood itself is changing. In an era when the number of priests available to minister is declining, discussion often focuses on what is essential about priesthood in this changed pastoral landscape. Is it the celebration of the sacraments? Is it the animation of the local community to take responsibility for the handing on of the faith? Is priesthood sufficiently concerned about the spiritual leadership the priest provides and about building the rapport and relationship between the priest and the community he seeks to serve? Recognising the co-responsibility of the faithful in the mission of the Church, many dioceses involve members of pastoral councils and finance committees in pastoral planning and in identifying what is to be legitimately expected from priests in today's changed pastoral landscape. *Grouping Parishes for Mission* affirms this when it states that 'the formation of priests in this area can be very effective when it takes place together with other members of the people of God.'[11] Along with all these aspects of ongoing formation, diocesan in-service days can provide an opportunity in which to meet and socialise with fellow priests in a relaxed atmosphere.

Pastoral supervision
Another forum for ongoing formation is pastoral supervision. Supervision can be undertaken either at individual or peer-group level. With the trust developed in the context of pastoral supervision, the priest can share the challenges he encounters, whether in relation to his work with the pastoral council or finance committee or other challenges he meets in ministry. Supervision can provide the priest with an excellent opportunity for ongoing and permanent formation where the disorienting dilemmas of ministry can become positive opportunities for transformative learning.

Conclusion
This essay has considered the centrality of the themes of communion and co-responsibility in undergirding a vision of Church today. Both the pastoral council and the finance committee are means by which this vision is realised in the parish and are means by which members of the parish community can assume

leadership and co-responsibility. *Pastores Dabo Vobis* alerts us to a serious danger:

> The multiplication of responsibilities and services, the complexity of human life in general and the life of the Christian communities in particular, the activism and anxiety that are features of vast areas of society today often deprive priests of the time and energies they need to 'take heed of themselves' (cf. 1 Tm 4:16).[12]

The need for ongoing formation in such a context becomes all the more pressing. This formation takes place alongside members of the finance committee and pastoral council as well as at pastoral area and diocesan level. In this changed environment, there is need to address the changing understanding of priesthood both by priests themselves and members of the communities they serve. Experience shows that there may be resistance to these changes both by priests and by parishioners but this should not deter those involved from partaking in ongoing training. Just as the Church itself is always in need of reform, so too the priest can never see himself as fully formed but always in the process of being formed both by the people among whom he ministers and by the opportunities for formal training of which he avails. Frances Ward puts this well when she writes, 'I suggest that to minister is to refuse to understand oneself as ever "formed", but always open to growth, to the encounter with new ways of doing things and to interpret the given practices and traditions of faith in new ways.'[13]

Notes

1. *Lumen Gentium*, 4
2. Eugene Duffy, *Parishes in Transition* (Dublin: Columba Press, 2010), 104.
3. John Paul II, *Pastores Dabo Vobis: On the Formation of Priests in the Circumstances of the Present Day* (London: Catholic Truth Society, 1992), 74.

4. Pope Benedict XVI, Address at the Opening of the Pastoral Convention of the Diocese of Rome (May 2009), http://www.vatican.va/holy_father/benedict_xvi/speeches/2009/may/documents/hf_ben-xvi_spe_20090526_convegno-diocesi-rm_en.html (accessed 1/2/2013).

5. *Code of Canon Law*, 357.

6. Ibid., 536.

7. Irish Catholic Bishops' Conference, *Grouping Parishes for Mission* (Dublin: Veritas, 2011), 43.

8. J. Ferguson, *A Handbook for Parish Pastoral Councils* (Dublin: Columba Press, 2005); D. Harrington, *The Welcoming Parish* (Dublin: Columba Press, 2005); J. C. Doherty, *Think Big, Act Small, Working at Collaborative Ministry Through Parish Pastoral Councils* (Dublin: Veritas, 2005); D. Snoddy, J. Campbell and A. McNally, *Parish Pastoral Councils: A Formation Manual* (Dublin: Veritas, 2010).

9. John Paul II, *Novo Millennio Ineunte* (Quebec: Médiaspaul, 2001), 43–5.

10. *Living Communion*, 37.

11. Ibid., 43.

12. *Pastores Dabo Vobis*, 78.

13. Frances Ward, *Lifelong Learning: Theological Education and Supervision* (Norwich: SCM Press, 2005), 17.

Digital Media: A Version of the Pulpit

PAUL TIGHE

In this essay, I would like to consider how the emergence of the so-called 'new' or 'digital' media invites priests and pastoral leaders to think through the implications for their efforts in evangelisation. It is clear that the use of new media can greatly enhance our efforts to communicate and make known the Good News, but we must be careful that our reflection on this topic does not remain at the technical or instrumental level. Traditionally, the new means and technologies of communication have been understood as instruments to be put into the service of the transmission of the Word. In 1975, Paul VI characterised the new means as a 'modern and effective version of the pulpit'.[1] The challenge today is to realise that the new technologies are not just instruments of communication but are profoundly affecting the very culture of communications. It is not enough to ask how we can use the new media to evangelise; we must begin with a reflection as to how we can most effectively make present the Word of God in a media and communications environment that has been radically transformed.

Exponential change

The last twenty-five years have seen an exponential rate of development in the capacities of the technologies available to support and facilitate human communication. The combination of these developments in mobile telephony, computer technology, fibre optics and satellites mean that many of us now carry with us devices that allow us instant access to an extraordinary range of information, news and opinion from around the globe and that enable us to communicate by word, text or the sharing of images with people and institutions in every corner of the world. This revolution in information and communication technologies, however, cannot be adequately understood merely in mechanical terms: it is not simply a question of communication and the exchange of information growing in terms of volume, speed, efficiency and accessibility but rather that we are also witnessing concomitant changes in the ways in which people use these technologies to communicate, learn, interact, relate and associate. We are living through a change of paradigm in the very culture of communication. Pope Benedict stated that: 'The new technologies are not only changing the way we communicate, but communication itself.'[2] A recent study sponsored by the British government focusing on personal identity concluded among other things that 'particularly among younger people, their view of themselves is shaped increasingly by online interactions of social networks' and it further indicated that the elements that traditionally would have been considered most important in forming a person's identity, such as their religion, ethnicity, job and age, are less important than they once were.[3]

The new culture of communication requires that those of us who wish to make present the gospel must rethink our approach. We cannot simply do what we have always done, albeit with new technologies. In 1990, John Paul II had already identified the particular challenge to those who wish to make known the message of Christ:

> It is also necessary to integrate that message into the 'new culture' created by modern communications. This is a complex issue, since the 'new culture' originates not just from whatever content is eventually expressed, but from the

very fact that there exist new ways of communicating, with new languages, new techniques and a new psychology.[4]

I would like to identify some of the more obvious features of this new culture and tease out the implications that follow for evangelisation. I do not intend to offer definitive solutions – the cultural transformation is still ongoing and my observations are necessarily tentative – but I offer some ideas in order to stimulate further debate and to encourage others to take up this reflection.

The reality of digital space and the need to learn the language

The first and most basic point is that the digital space is a reality in the lives of many people today. We must not think of it as a 'virtual' space that is somehow less important than the 'real' world. If the Church is not present in this space, if the Good News is not proclaimed 'digitally', then we risk abandoning the many people for whom this is where they 'live': this is the forum in which they get their news and information, form and express their opinions, ask questions and engage in debate. Benedict XVI spoke of the digital arena as a 'continent' where believers would seek to share their faith but he also identified the need for an appropriate 'inculturation':

> In the early life of the Church, the great Apostles and their disciples brought the Good News of Jesus to the Greek and Roman world. Just as, at that time, a fruitful evangelisation required that careful attention be given to understanding the culture and customs of those pagan peoples so that the truth of the gospel would touch their hearts and minds, so also today, the proclamation of Christ in the world of new technologies requires a profound knowledge of this world if the technologies are to serve our mission adequately.[5]

I am convinced that a particular task for priests, in collaboration with others who are involved in evangelisation, is that of helping the Church to find a language appropriate to the new media environment created by the technologies and the social networks. This is especially important if we are to be faithful to our mandate to speak to those who are not members of our community – to other Christians, to those of other religions, to non-believers and to those who are now distant from the life of faith having parted from the Church for various reasons. In speaking of language, I am thinking of our styles of engagement, our means of communication and our vocabulary.

It is commonplace to observe that the style of engagement of the digital forum, especially of the so-called Web 2.0, is conversational, interactive and participative:

> In the digital world, transmitting information increasingly means making it known within a social network where knowledge is shared in the context of personal exchanges. The clear distinction between the producer and consumer of information is relativised and communication appears not only as an exchange of data, but also as a form of sharing. This dynamic has contributed to a new appreciation of communication itself, which is seen first of all as dialogue, exchange, solidarity and the creation of positive relations.[6]

As a Church, we are more used to preaching, to teaching and to issuing statements. These are important activities but the most effective forms of digital discourse are those that engage people individually, that seek to respond to their specific questions and that attempt to dialogue. We need to understand better how our message is being heard and understood by different audiences. We have always, and rightly, focused on the content of our teaching; today we must listen more attentively to our audience, or the multiple audiences we address, and understand their concerns and questions. We need to understand better, and take account of, the contexts and environments in which they will encounter the Word of God. The emergence of the internet as an interactive medium, where users seek to engage as subjects and not just as consumers, invites us to develop more explicitly dialogical forms of teaching and presentation.

It is a basic truth of communications that our witness – our actions and our patterns of behaviour – is often more eloquent than our words and proclamations in expressing who we are and what we believe:

> To proclaim the gospel through the new media means not only to insert expressly religious content into different media platforms, but also to witness consistently, in one's own digital profile and in the way one communicates choices, preferences and judgements that are fully consistent with the gospel, even when it is not spoken of specifically.[7]

In the digital arena, 'a particularly significant way of offering such witness will be through a willingness to give oneself to others by patiently and respectfully engaging their questions and their doubts as they advance in their search for the truth and the meaning of human existence'.[8] Engagement with the questions, and more importantly with the questioners, opens up the possibility of a more profound dialogue. One can discern concerns about the ultimate questions of human existence. What can we know? What ought we do? What may we hope? A careful listening, rooted in respect for the questions and the questioner, is required to allow these deeper concerns to emerge. Adapting a more dialogical style is demanding but when we reply to blogs, comment on articles and posts and explain our positions in different social media we are not just engaging our direct interlocutors but, given the nature of social media, wider publics and audiences.

Within the Church, we are accustomed to the use of texts as a normal mode of communication. Many of the websites that have been developed by different Church institutions continue to use that language. One can find on the web many wonderful homilies, speeches and articles, but it is not clear if they speak to a younger public that is fluent in a different language, a language rooted in the convergence of text, sound and images; a public that is used to clicking quickly through pages and material unless its attention is captured. We need to rediscover the capacity of art, music and literature to express the mysteries of our faith and to touch minds and hearts. Just as the stain glass images of the medieval cathedrals spoke to an illiterate audience, we must find digital forms of expression that are appropriate to a generation that has been described as 'post-literate'. We have long being accustomed to telling our story; we can now aspire to show who and what we are. We need to learn to show how we celebrate our faith, how we seek to serve and how our lives are graced and blest.

We are required to be more attentive to our vocabulary. Much of our religious and ecclesial language is unintelligible even to believers. Many of our religious icons and symbols need to be explained for our contemporaries. We can no longer presume that young people, even in countries with a long Christian heritage, are familiar with our most basic beliefs. Those who are concerned that the language of the digital culture is too banal or ephemeral to translate the profundity of the Christian message should remember that it is not a language that will substitute the precise language of dogma and theology or the rich language of homiletics or liturgy but rather will serve to establish an initial point of contact with those who are far from faith. Those who respond to this initial contact will be invited to more profound forms of engagement, where they will learn these other languages in their proper context.

Proclaiming a challenging message faithfully

For the Church, a further challenge is to find a language that is appropriate for this new forum but that does not betray the depths and nuances of the message that has been entrusted to it. The Church's efforts to make present the Good News of the gospel in the digital arena mean that it will have to challenge some of the features of the culture of social media. It is important that our reflection on social media would be critically aware of these considerations, if our engagement is not to be naïve. The Church speaks of truth in an environment where scepticism is the norm, it seeks to speak to all in a milieu where the focus is often on niche markets and interest groups and it invites people to commitment in a world where novelty reigns.

The single greatest challenge to those forms of meaningful dialogue where we can best share out faith is the often unarticulated relativism that is so prevalent in western culture, and the refutation of which was a key element in the teaching of Pope Benedict. If there is no such thing as truth, as right or wrong answers, then dialogue becomes meaningless. It is a shared commitment to searching for truth which gives human dialogue and debate their ultimate value; otherwise, they become exercises in coercion and manipulation in which each seeks to assert his or her own view without any reference to the claims of truth. The generalised and uncritical social reception of the tenets of relativism finds particular expression in the digital world where the sheer volume of information and opinion, much of it contradictory, can lead to an almost resigned acceptance that it is meaningless to speak of truth and objectivity. A commitment to promote the values of reason and logic in public debate should be the hallmark of the contributions of those who wish to share their faith in social media. An insistence on these values will both foster the possibility of dialogue in the public forum and address the prejudices of those who seek to relegate religion to the private or subjective realm.

One common response to this phenomenon of relativism is that people turn only to sources of information and opinion that they judge to be trustworthy. Often the judgment as to what sources are trustworthy is rooted in the person's pre-established worldview and serves only to confirm people in their opinions rather than leading to a real search for truth and understanding. In the political arena, there is the risk that people will only engage with media that they know to support their particular views and they will not be exposed to alternative positions or to reasoned debate or discussion. This is turn will create increasingly polarised and confrontational forms of politics where there is little room for the voices of moderation or consensus. A similar phenomenon is emerging in the world of Catholic media, especially in the blogosphere, where often it seems not enough for protagonists to propose their own views and beliefs but where they tend also to attack the arguments, and even the person, of those who disagree with them. It is natural that debates about faith and morals should be full of conviction and passion but there is a growing risk that some forms of expression are damaging the unity of the Church and, moreover, are unlikely to draw the curious and the seekers to a desire to learn about the Church and its message. Even though the social networks often seem to give greater attention to those who are most provocative or strident in their style of presentation, we should insist on the importance of reasoned debate, logical argumentation and gentle persuasion.

There is a particular challenge to the possibility of the new media serving as channels for dialogue and growth in understanding between peoples. The extraordinary range of words and images generated by these media, the speed with which they are produced and the fact that there is a constant stream of news and information means that there is very little room and time for a sustained and considered engagement and that there is real danger that our cultural discourse becomes superficial. American archbishop Charles Chaput expressed this risk succinctly in 2009:

> Visual and electronic media, today's dominant media, need a certain kind of content. They thrive on brevity, speed, change, urgency, variety and feelings. But *thinking* requires the opposite. Thinking takes time. It needs silence and the methodical skills of logic.[9]

The gradual loss of the boundary between the provision of information and entertainment witnesses, and further contributes, to a loss of a social appetite for serious engagement with important issues. Media attention can also be very fickle and one seemingly compelling issue is abandoned as another is judged more likely to engage audiences. Some commentators speak of the risk of new media leading to shallowness in human reflection and to the alienation of people from meaningful engagement with ideas and each other. In this context, I would suggest that an essential dimension of the Church's communicative activity must be to provide occasions and opportunities, both physical and digital, for people to learn the arts of silence and contemplation, to recover an appetite for solitude and interiority. This would undoubtedly be a fruitful starting point for our proclamation of the gospel but it would be invaluable also as a service to meaningful human communication.

The social media and the ministry of priests

In his Message for World Communications Day in 2010, *The Priest and Pastoral Ministry in a Digital World: New Media at the Service of the Word*, Pope Benedict directly addressed the question of the involvement of priests with social media. What is most striking about the message is that it is an exhortation rather than an instruction: the message, although it mentions the importance of images, videos, animated features, blogs and websites and takes for granted the need for adequate formation in the use of the new technologies, cannot be read as a technical manual but rather as a profoundly theological reflection on the enormous potential of the technologies to enhance and enrich the ministry of priests. The insistence is more on the spiritual formation of the priest than on his technical capacity. Pope Benedict insisted that 'all priests have as their primary duty the proclamation of Jesus Christ, the incarnate Word of God, and the communication of his saving grace in the sacraments'. In the message we are told that priests should be 'witnesses' to the gospel. They should be in 'constant dialogue with the gospel of which they will be enthusiastic heralds'. They should come with the 'gospel in hand and heart'. What the pope is saying to us here is that the priest's communicative ministry must begin with his own profound listening to and meditation of the gospel. Such meditation allows the gospel to shape our being and ministry. We must strive to be people of the gospel who will be more 'notable for our priestly hearts rather than for our technical savvy'.[10]

If priests take up the invitation of Pope Benedict and enter into dialogue with those, who in their browsing and searching of the internet, are ultimately in pursuit of truth, hope and meaning in life, and if they can further introduce them to the Good News of the gospel, they will serve not only the gospel but the good of humanity. If priests bring their deepest convictions with them as they go online, and encourage others to debate the ultimate questions, they, as Pope Benedict says, 'will not only enliven their pastoral outreach, but also will give a "soul" to the fabric of communications that makes up the "Web".[11]

Notes

1. *Evangelii Nuntiandi*, 45, http://www.vatican.va/holy_father/paul_vi/apost_exhortations/documents/hf_p-vi_exh_19751208_evangelii-nuntiandi_en.html (accessed 1/4/2013).

2. Message for World Communications Day (2012), http://www.vatican.va/holy_father/benedict_xvi/messages/communications/documents/hf_ben-xvi_mes_20120124_46th-world-communications-day_en.html (accessed 1/4/2013).

3. Government Office for Science, Foresight, *Future Identities: Changing Identities in the UK* (2013), http://www.bis.gov.uk/assets/foresight/docs/identity/13-523-future-identities-changing-identities-report.pdf (accessed 1/4/2013).

4. John Paul II, *Redemptoris Missio*, 37, http://www.vatican.va/holy_father/john_paul_ii/encyclicals/documents/hf_jp-ii_enc_07121990_redemptoris-missio_en.html (accessed 1/4/2013).

5. Message for World Communications Day (2009), http://www.vatican.va/holy_father/benedict_xvi/messages/communications/documents/hf_ben-xvi_mes_20090124_43rd-world-communications-day_en.html (accessed 1/4/2013).

6. Message for World Communications Day (2011), http://www.vatican.va/holy_father/benedict_xvi/messages/communications/documents/hf_ben-xvi_mes_20110124_45th-world-communications-day_en.html (accessed 1/4/2013).

7. Ibid.

8. Message for World Communications Day (2013), http://www.vatican. va/holy_father/benedict_xvi/messages/communications/documents/ hf_ben-xvi_mes_20130124_47th-world-communications-day_en.html (accessed 1/4/2013).

9. Archbishop Chaput, 'Catholics and the 'Fourth Estate' (8 July 2009), http://www.archden.org/index.cfm/ID/2265 (accessed 1/4/2013).

10. Message for World Communications Day (2010), http://www.vatican. va/holy-father/benedict_xvi/messages/communications/documents/ ht_ben_xvi_mes_20100124_44th-world-communications-day-en.html (accessed 1/4/2013).

11. Ibid.

Priesthood Today Within Evolving Church Structures

ANNE CODD

In this essay I will offer observations and reflections on some of the challenges facing priests within our evolving Church structures, and on the possibilities I see in these very challenges. I will also identify some of the bridges that, in my view, have yet to be crossed if these possibilities are to be realised. In this context a radical revision of initial formation and ongoing transformative processes of pastoral reflection are vitally important for all in ministry. Within the limits of this piece and given my particular topic, I will focus mainly on the priest in the parish, and specifically on the parish priest, though hopefully the outcome will be relevant to others. It will also be evident that my contribution relates primarily to the Irish context.

The priest in the parish community

A parish priest today may be the one priest where previously there were two or three, he may be structured into a network of parishes in a pastoral area, bringing an additional layer of meetings and other commitments. Or indeed he may be assigned the responsibilities of parish priest in two or more parishes. At the same time, he may face expectations in these communities that he continue to provide the same services of pastoral care as was 'always done'. In this situation it is vital that he gives the time and attention that are needed to 'step back and take the long view'.[1] This critical review, I suggest, requires historical, socio-cultural and pastoral-theological lenses. We now live in a socio-cultural context which is increasingly pluralist and largely secular. While it would appear that religious sensibilities endure, attitudes to the Catholic Church are highly critical and levels of participation in Church life have fallen quite dramatically, particularly since 1992.[2] However, surveys have consistently found significant contrasts between public attitudes to Church and Church leaders on the national and wider fronts and people's appreciation for priests in the local community context.[3] The recognition of the priest as a responsible and benevolent representative of the local community is remarkable when the media, for example, need a spokesperson regarding a local tragedy.

The theology of ordination highlights the essential connection which exists from the beginning between the one designated to act 'in the person of Christ the head' and the community which he will serve. The gradual erosion over time of this connection in the understanding of ordained priesthood is well documented.[4] The resultant absolutising of ordination – its attribution to the person of the priest in isolation from community or indeed from ministry – has had far-reaching consequences.

When Vatican II established that the commissioning of a bishop to be head of a diocese amounted to 'the fullness of the Sacrament of Holy Orders'[5] it heralded a renewed emphasis on the priest as ordained to an analogous relationship with the faith community of the parish or parishes 'entrusted to his care'.[6] This relationship is characterised, in continuity with the ministry of the bishop, by the three-fold task of enabling (teaching) faith, nurturing holiness and facilitating life-giving order in the community. Within this theological paradigm, the priest in the parish is head of that faith community in communion with the bishop and his fellow priests, called to exercise his ministry in collegial relationships with them within the framework of diocesan planning and policies. There is an implied shift here away from the canonical paradigm which would ascribe to the parish priest a significantly higher degree of autonomy.

Forming faith community

The universal call to holiness and the participation of the baptised in the threefold mandate of Christ to be priest, prophet and king at the service of God's mission are the foundational principles which inform the ministry of the priest as head of the faith community of a parish. The interpretation of his ministry as service is entirely valid in this sense: the priest is charged with serving God's mission by sponsoring the growth of that community in its life of faith, fellowship, worship and justice.[7] To preside at Eucharist, the summit and source of Christian life in community, is integral to this ministry of service.

However, the popularity among pastors of the concept of 'servant leadership', developed by Robert Greenleaf in the 1960s, has to be interrogated critically. Any reduction of the ministry of the priest to simply taking care of the pastoral needs of 'his flock' is unacceptable. While reflection on Jesus washing the feet of the apostles is of immense spiritual and social significance, I argue consistently that this biblical vignette is essentially a paradigm for discipleship: 'you also ought to wash one another's feet.'[8] In light of Church documents beginning with *Lumen Gentium*, the priest, in the manner of a master-disciple, is charged with enabling the discipleship of the entire community,[9] discipleship which serves nothing less than the totality of God's mission, bringing God's reign progressively to light in the world, through living the kingdom values of truth, holiness and grace, justice, love and peace.[10]

Service through strategy

Traditionally, pastoral ministry has been understood as serving the spiritual and certain corporal needs of those in the pastoral care of the priest. Under pressure to deliver the next 'service' there is every danger that the priest in parish pastoral ministry can put off repeatedly the call to 'come aside' – to rest awhile but also to take that long view. This is understandable but detrimental. Transformations in the Church's understanding of salvation and of her 'salvific' ministry, as well as a rapidly changing social context, call the priest to raise critical and strategic questions.

What purpose is my ministry serving, not just here and now but in the longer term? How does this parish need to be formed in faith, built up as a community, celebrate the liturgy and honour its call to live justly? To lead the parish along this path, what next steps do I need to take? Who are the people with the gifts and the calling at this time to collaborate with me in this work, and how may we organise ourselves to be effective? Most importantly, another question seeks an answer: what do I need so that I can live this ministry wisely and sustainably?

The work done to resource this kind of reflection in clergy conferences and in longer residential *fora* for priests is, I suggest, vitally important. Having been invited from time to time to collaborate in this work (and also from having been centrally involved in similar processes in my own and other religious congregations), I have learned that planning and preparing a conference requires diligent attention. The particular purpose of a conference or forum needs to be located, from the outset, within the whole life-mission, as well as the ministry of participants, the structures and methods, the substantial 'input' have to be expertly designed and the focus maintained throughout the event. Moreover, responsibility for follow-up when the event is closed needs to be clarified and agreed. I can also personally vouch for the constructive engagement that can happen when priests, religious and laypeople participate together in well-organised conferences, seminars and workshops.

A commitment to pastoral reflection is essential to wise and sustainable ministry. I have often facilitated priests in revisiting ministerial encounters. By re-membering a scenario with liberal use of aesthetic and affective associations, by replaying with care the exchanges of words, messages and meanings, and by paying attention to the impact of this exercise in the present, the significance of ministry can be perceived at new depth, the qualities which are worth developing become clear and pitfalls can also be revealed. It is not unusual to hear comments such as 'I had no idea what a graced moment that was.' I have also heard men say, 'That experience was far more stressful than I realised at the time. I wonder now what I did about it.' Surely ministry which drains the spirit of the minister is unlikely to be fruitful?

Reflective review can also illuminate and critique both the experience and practice of the priest in the context of the wider community of life within which the parish resides. While his relationships within that community offer scope for witness to gospel vision and values at every turn, the call to be missionary there can slip to the edges of consciousness. As well as pastoral-theological resources, processes of personal renewal and upskilling for ministry, a school of thought I firmly believe to hold huge potential is the 'living system' model of organisation. I have explored the dialogue between ecclesiology and systems theory at some depth in my practice over the last ten years and continue to experience its ability to liberate and empower. I have found several points of correlation between Church envisaged as a communion of life and an organisation viewed as a living system.[11]

The model provides bases for integration between part and whole, between local and global, and between inner and outer dimensions of life and work. It highlights the fact that transformations in the ministry of the priest and development of the whole community of the parish are mutually inclusive. The 'living system' imagery cultivates a vision of leadership that is attentive to changing environments and calls the 'system' to be responsive. Studies such as the interrelatedness of person, role and system and the dynamics of power and authority within systems are highly relevant to the priest who is negotiating the task of living well as a human being, a disciple and an ordained minister in the Church.

Forming faith

Share the Good News, National Directory for Catechesis in Ireland is unequivocal: the bishop is the chief catechist in the diocese.[12] While he exercises his responsibility through various structures, notably the diocesan faith development services, which support, facilitate and train[13] others for the tasks of faith development, the bishop's immediate delegate in relation to faith development in the parishes is the parish priest. It is he who directs the catechetical activity of the parish. *Share the Good News* calls for a comprehensive faith development plan in the parish, ensuring a diverse range of activities – and reaching appropriately all the members of every age, including those at the margins.[14] Parish priests are asked to take up this responsibility effectively in a time when the task of sharing faith has becoming increasingly specialised.

The work of faith development coordinators in bringing the faith-development plan to life in the parish(es) is variously described in the *Directory,* but their appointment, deployment and accountability structures are properly the responsibility of the parish priest, or one of the parish priests with the cooperation of the others where a person is appointed for a group of parishes.[15]

Clearly, there is now an onus on the parish to provide the wider community setting within which children and young people may not only grow in faith but also grow into faith community beyond the confines of the experiences the school can offer. The faith development coordinator is to work with the parish priest in building up the parish/school relationship.

The contribution of pastoral councils to this task is characterised by notably secondary functions of research and support. The parish priest is, as he always was, the one with primary responsibility for the work of programmatic and comprehensive faith development in the parish. And to fulfil this aspect of parish ministry, even availing of the expertise of others, requires significant investment of time and energy. This will only ever be possible if other members of the community of disciples are called, formed and mandated to 'wash one another's feet' in well-structured ministries matching the wide array of other services which are needed.

The priest, member of diocesan presbyterate

Having mapped some elements of the 'long view', I return briefly to the parish priest in the context of the diocese. From my perspective, the critical questions which must be asked include: is this man alone as he tries to discern his way forward? Are there directions within the diocese to guide his planning? Have structures for participation, notably pastoral councils, become normative? Are there resources to enable him to develop the parish community accordingly? Are there programmes to support the growth within the parishes of those men and women who are gifted and called to become co-workers in development as well as in the provision of services?

The community of a parish is not merely a collective of those to be served by its pastor. The community is, as Pope Benedict XVI stressed, co-responsible for the being and action of the parish, the being and action of the Church. And the parish priest is the one charged with enabling that community to become what it is called to be, living Church within diocesan, universal and trinitarian communion. How may he be accompanied, as pastor, in his journey in ministry, including indeed his painful transitions, so that he will live well, serve effectively and find the 'great joy' which we are assured comes with the Good News which we share?

Notes

1. From a text composed by Bishop Ken Untener of Saginaw, in 1979, often ascribed to Archbishop Oscar Romero.
2. The 2008 European Values Systems survey findings suggest that almost 64 per cent of the population believed in a personal God and 60 per cent prayed either daily or once a week (outside of religious services). However, this study also noted that 36 per cent of Catholics stated that they had their own way of connecting with the Divine apart from the Church or religious services.
3. Andrew M. Greeley and Conor Ward, 'How Secularized Is the Ireland We Live In?', *Doctrine & Life* (December 2000).
4. See for example Paul Bernier, *Ministry in the Church, a Historical and Pastoral Approach* (New London, CT: Twenty-Third Publications, 2006).
5. Vatican II, *Christus Dominus*, Decree Concerning the Pastoral Office of Bishops in the Church, 15.
6. Canon 515 §1.
7. Acts 2:42-45.
8. The liturgical use of this text in the Mass of the Lord's Supper (celebrating disciples in mutual service) and not the Chrism Mass (in which the focus is on ministerial priesthood) supports this view.

9. See, for example, United States Conference of Catholic Bishops *Co-workers in the Vineyard of the Lord* (2005), www.usccb.org (accessed 1/4/2013).

10. See Preface for the Feast of Christ the King.

11. See my 'The Pastoral Context as a Living System: Implications for Theology and Practice', *Pastoral Ministry for Today*, Tom Grenham, ed. (Dublin: Veritas, 2009), 64–89. The 'living system' is understood as activities (happening live) within a boundary (i.e. for a purpose) in dynamic relationship with the wider context. The metaphor clearly has its origins in biology.

12. *Share the Good News: National Directory for Catechesis in Ireland*, Irish Episcopal Conference (Dublin: Veritas, 2010).

13. Ibid., 136.

14. Ibid., 135.

15. Ibid., 71.

Section Two

Spiritual and Theological Foundations

Ignatius of Loyola: An Imagined Message for Today

MICHAEL PAUL GALLAGHER

Being a priest was central to my life, but my love for priesthood is not easy to explain to people nearly five centuries later. Even the facts of my life will seem surprising. For instance, after my ordination I did not celebrate my first Mass for nearly a year, and then I celebrated it with great devotion at the altar of the manger in the Basilica of St Mary Major in Rome. You see, I had a childlike (you might think childish) passion for the realities of Our Lord's earthly life. When I visited the Holy Land I wanted to stay there forever, but providentially the Franciscan Superior threw me out on pain of excommunication. If he had not done so, the Jesuits might never have existed. But back to priesthood: in your eyes I will seem a strange kind of priest, at least in terms of ordinary ministry. I never worked in a parish. I seldom preached (partly because I was so bad at Italian and most of my priestly life was in Rome). I rarely heard confessions. I celebrated Mass usually without a congregation, which was just as well because I often had to have long pauses when I used weep with fullness, caught up in the presence of the Trinity.

So what on earth can I say that would be of use for priests today? Looking back now, in all humility, I had an unusual gift for talking to people, for what I called 'spiritual conversation'. It meant listening deeply to their desires, identifying the genuine movements of the Spirit in their lives and mirroring that back to them, helping them to recognise God in their human experiences, as well as in their times of prayer. Notice that I said 'genuine movements'. In my own inner life I had painfully learned about deceptions, the subtle temptations to opt for evil under the appearance of good. Many people need priests to help them make important decisions, and so you need to be able to 'discern' what will lead them towards God, unmasking some clever trick of the one I called the Bad Spirit.

Roots and discoveries

Let me tell you something of my own discoveries in this respect and why I think a priest of today could be at home in this area of fostering religious experience and helping people to make wise decisions. You have probably heard that my life changed when my leg was broken in battle. In fact, the real change came weeks later when I was getting better. I was bored and wanted to read romance stories. But they had nothing like that in my family home – books were still a fairly recent invention – all they had were some lives of saints and passages from the gospel. For want of something better to do I began to browse them, and then I passed the time with two different fantasies. What would it be like to go back to my old life in the court, dancing, romancing and so on? Or, in a separate moment, what would it be like to imitate the saints and follow Christ? Years later, in a kind of autobiography-interview, I looked back on this time and said (in the third person): 'One day he noticed a difference, and wondered about it. One topic left him dejected afterwards, while the other left him joyful. This was his first insight into spiritual things.' I found that you could recognise the roots by the fruits, and that the Spirit was guiding me through my deeper feelings. There is much more I could say about all this but I am convinced that being able to help people to discern their inner movements is vital for priestly ministry. I came to insist that it is never wise to decide anything important in desolation: wait for dawn. Even to offer this nugget of wisdom could protect people from hasty and rash choices.

But more than this: it is also a question of recognising God in our experience. Karl Rahner (who was partly under my influence) said famously that believers of the future will have to be 'mystics' or they will not be believers at all. He did not mean that everyone would have special contemplative ecstasies, but rather that in today's complex culture people need to ground their faith in experience – which he called 'experience of God'. I would simply say that faith is best nourished through learning to pray personally. And yes, that prayer, if it becomes a regular part of a person's life, amounts to a gradual experience of God.

The Magi journey

In this spirit let me propose a way of meditating on a well-known gospel text. At first sight the story of the Magi might seem to have little to do with priesthood, but I want to suggest that it evokes some important dimensions of priestly ministry in the complex context of your world – so different in many ways from the one I knew. To begin with, those Magi set out on a journey into the unknown, their desire awoken by a new light. Is that not true of each priest? It is good to look back at the roots of your vocation, even though they can seem far back and so much has changed since then. You are still trying to live faithful to the light that guides your life.

Did you ever notice that the light goes out for those Magi? The Gospel of Matthew does not tell us so explicitly, but we are told that when they saw the original star again they were filled with joy. So it seems that it was there at the beginning but that it did not guide all their journey. On the road towards Jerusalem they seem to have been somewhat in the dark. Faith is like that, a light-on and light-off experience as someone has said. We should not be surprised if we experience a certain pendulum between what I call consolation and desolation. Consolation is when you find yourself in the light, confidently guided by the good Spirit. Then you sense the movement of your life and ministry as towards love, towards God. From God we come, to God we go, with Christ. But desolation happens to everyone, bringing non-movement or paralysis. You can run into some really disturbing times, moments of doubt and emptiness, times when prayer is either a painful struggle or just seems impossible. In desolation you may regret and resent the whole road and role of priesthood. What am I doing here at all?

As mentioned earlier, I discovered a crucial bit of spiritual wisdom about desolation. It is simple but important for priests and indeed for everyone. Indeed it can be fruitful when trying to help people in situations of difficulty. The golden rule, so to speak, is never to make a major change in desolation, never to decide anything important without a sense of light. If we go back to the Magi, we see them in danger of falling into that trap. When the light seemed to have disappeared, they looked in exactly the wrong direction. They consulted the wrong man, the most deceptive person around, Herod.

Discerning the dangers

At a key moment in my *Spiritual Exercises*, I ask people to pray about the contrast between genuine and false desires. It is a meditation called the Two Standards, in the sense of two flags or loyalties to choose between. Our faith can be too innocent if we do not know the battleground in each heart and also in the pressures of the culture around us. It is not enough to think about this: we need to experience it prayerfully. Herod can symbolise the attractive but ultimately destructive solution. He was charming to the Magi, inviting them to afternoon tea or something stronger, saying that he wanted to adore this new king too. Later in their journey they were to have the joy and surprise of real adoration. But they had to be warned in a dream not to return to Herod with their news. More of that later. For the moment I am inviting you to pray to be able to recognise the difference between true and false fulfilment. Every priest needs that wisdom, for his own life, and as a skill in his ministry to others.

Before leaving the scene of Jerusalem, note an ironic fact – one that may point to a professional hazard for priests. The experts in religion knew where the Messiah should be born. These 'chief priests and scribes' had all the right answers in their head. But, interestingly, they made no move to go to Bethlehem themselves. We can be so involved in religion as a system that we fail to move towards Christ, towards our transformation. Our words can be correct but cold, unfruitful in our own lives. We know the answers for others but our own fire burns low. Saint Augustine once remarked about those scribes of Jerusalem that they were guides for others but immobile in themselves.

And so the journey of the Magi continues. One expression is strong: they were filled with 'great joy' on finding the star again. We need moments like that, especially when the going has been tough. When people do 'spiritual exercises', in my experience, they will run into a series of ups and downs. In fact, if they don't, I would usually ask them if they were entering fully into the adventure of prayer. I came to believe that even in ordinary life (as distinct from the more intense times of retreat) we will encounter this kind of variation. You can swing from dullness and tired emptiness towards peace and fullness. Sometimes it is the sheer wonder of people that you meet in ministry that triggers the change and opens the door to gratitude. Sometimes the pain of others puts your own complaints in perspective. Or again, you can glimpse the mystery of their strength as they live generously with difficulties. Or the life-giving times of birth or love or reconciliation. I am convinced that priests need both to seek out and to protect their consolation. Without it the road can be dangerously dry or undernourished. The consolation I am thinking of is a spiritual grace: 'the God of all consolation comforts us in all our sorrows so that we can offer others the consolation we have received' (2 Cor 1:4).

Consolation as normal

But let us not forget the more human blessings that come our way: relaxing with friends, contact with families, the privilege of being trusted, an outing for sport or a meal, and especially needed for our vocation, soul friendship, some kind of *anam cara* as you say in Ireland. It can be a small group of trust or it can be a particular person: we need spaces to express our selves with openness and even intimacy, to be known and understood in our *gaudium* and *spes* as well as in our vulnerability and disappointment. Without consolation the star becomes dim and we can return to or be taken in by the deceptions of Herod. I came to believe that 'consolation' is not a matter of rare or blessed times of grace. If we are living a generous life of service, God's consolation is normal, not in a bubbly or emotional way, but simply as a quiet sense of rightness, harmony and the presence of God.

The Magi travelled on in the light and arrived at the goal of their journey. Their encounter with Jesus was the climax of their search and a surprising one at that. They brought their gifts but in a moment of adoration they discovered that they were receivers. How much did they understand of the identity of Jesus? That's an open question. But they surely glimpsed that here was more than an earthly king. Perhaps they knew, in ways that could not be put into words, that they were in the presence of God. That is the heart of all prayer. When such graced moments happen, we are invited to take rest, and find strength for the remainder of our journey.

In fact, the story of the Magi involves two other details that seem important to me and that can be meditated upon personally. There is no indication in the gospel that the Magi would not have gone back to Herod. To protect them, and to protect the baby, there had to be another grace. They were 'warned in a dream' to take 'another way'. I believe that God continues to guide us in our depths if only we would pay attention, first protecting us from deception and then teaching us a different way of living. Indeed that little expression 'another way' may well be a summary for the whole adventure of faith and for how priests can help people to have the courage to be different.

Translating for your world

Standing back from that rich gospel text, I have to recognise that your world is utterly different to that which I knew. Herod has so many faces. Searchers are plentiful but journeys of adult faith are more difficult (and basically the Magi story is a great example of the ingredients of adult faith). In my time, it was practically impossible not to be a Christian, not only in the sense of growing up with the sacraments of the Church, but with what seemed a natural or obvious sense of God around us. Life was often short. Death was frequent, even for children and young people. I came very close to death when I was about thirty and that was the background music for my conversion. With life so fragile, we easily believed in angels and devils, in sin and judgement. But all that has faded in your culture, even for believers. You live with very different assumptions about life and about God. Your people are more secularised, as they say. Not just in the sense that many no longer have regular contact with the Church, but in a deeper sense that the images they live from focus on the self in the here and now. They often feel themselves perfectly at home in the world, as if there were no God. They are surrounded by complexity, like a forest in which it is hard to find one's path. Faith is seldom inherited: instead it was to be something of a journey and decision. But, to draw towards a conclusion, exactly on this point I think I have something to offer.

I would start by remembering that we are not left alone by God. Grace is at work everywhere and in everyone. Even outside the Church: that is an insight that I did not grasp in my time. It does not mean that priests can simply trust in the Spirit and do nothing to make the gospel real for people. We are meant to know the love of God. For that, Christ came. For that, Christ died. For that, priests are ordained. So how can we help people towards a faith worthy of today, a faith rooted in decision and not just in 'cultural Catholicism'? For me the key is simple: teach them the art of personal prayer. People say that I founded an order to combat the Reformation. Not true. The first Jesuits came together by coincidence or providence because we found ourselves transformed by prayer, and we saw great needs around us to renew people's faith in a time of crisis. I never advised people to fight against the Reformation but to respond to the challenge with a ministry of inner rebirth. When people can meet Christ in personal depth, they decide to say yes to his yes. In your image-soaked culture, my old insight might still be helpful: I learned that the mysteries of the gospel came alive when I could enter them by 'imagining Christ our Lord present' and putting myself personally into the scene.

Each one of you has his own gift. 'What I do is me: for that I came,' Hopkins was to say.[1] Find your own wavelength of inner nourishment and of pastoral service. There you will find your thread of harmony, in spite of times of struggle. As I once said of myself: 'I seek to offer God all the good I find in myself, see that all are his gifts and to thank him for them.' Amen.

Note

1. Gerard Manley Hopkins, 'As Kingfishers Catch Fire', *Gerard Manley Hopkins: Poems and Prose* (London: Penguin Classics, 1985), 51.

Letter to Priests, from Brother Francis, the Little Poor Man of Assisi

CAOIMHÍN Ó LAOIDE

> In the name of the Father and of the Son and of the Holy Spirit, Amen.
>
> Brother Francis, their servant and subject, sends esteem and reverence, true peace from heaven, and sincere love in the Lord to priests – whom he esteems above all, since they touch the Lord in the Eucharist with their hands, receive him in their hearts and mouths, and offer him to others.[1]

Over eight hundred years have passed since I walked from Assisi to Rome with my first companions. We were a group of people who were young, passionate and aflame with a desire to serve the Lord, and to do so with the blessing of our mother, the Church. (I know that there are similar young people today too, if one has ears to listen to their dreams!) We went to ask approval of Pope Innocent III, the greatest man of his age – a glorious man, prolific in learning, brilliant in speech, burning with zeal for justice in matters which the cause of the Christian faith demanded.[2]

The Spirit moved powerfully in this man of great authority and high sophistication and, against the expectations of many, he had the vision to see the Lord at work in the ragtag band of simple brothers standing before him. I told him about the Lord's words to me from the cross in the church of San Damiano: 'Francis, go repair my house which, as you see, is falling completely to ruin.'[3] He, in turn, spoke about the vision he had had of the church of St John Lateran threatening to collapse, and of a man, small and of shabby appearance, supporting it on his shoulders.

For my brothers, in my time no less than in yours, the Church was in a ruinous state and we feared for it. But the Lord sustained her through many a dark and confusing hour and he will continue to do so in ways that we can never predict or imagine. Could I ever have thought that there would appear a pope called Francis from the land of the silver river, far in the west – a place totally unknown to me or anyone I ever met? Could I have foreseen that the Lord Bishop of Rome would one day have no standing army, or hardly any territory? That he would dream of a humble Church of the poor and realise that the Church will only be prevented from collapse by a return to the gospel way of simplicity, communion and joy? And yet, by God's grace, so it has come about in your day. But first let me speak about the joy I have in being a Christian and about the graces the Most High God has given to me, and through me to others.

The brotherhood and sisterhood of all creation

The Lord gave me a deep sense of brotherhood with all created things – not just human beings, but everything created by God the Creator. Once the Lord revealed this to me, then so many things made sense to me. It can be so too for you, pastors whom the Lord calls first of all to be brothers to all God's creatures, in virtue of your brotherhood with Christ, through whom all things were made. In the early days of our Order very many priests joined us and lived joyfully as simple brothers, with no distinction between cleric and lay. We did this because we wanted to express the reality that every created thing – human beings, plants and animals, even inanimate things – have a kinship with one another. Being conscious of this fundamental brotherhood and sisterhood leads us away from competition, greed and exploitation, and invites us towards reverence, community and simple living. It is this that will save our beautiful planet from the destructive forces that threaten it.

Every one of God's creatures has a unique quality, and each praises God by doing what God has intended it to do and be. Brother sun gives praise to God, by being beautiful and radiant with great splendour; the earth gives praise to God by sustaining and governing us, producing various fruit with coloured flowers and herbs.[4] Men and women praise God by being in the image of Christ, the one who has reconciled all of creation in his humble and obedient death. And for you priests, the sure sign of living out your God-given call is to be a person who reconciles – a peacemaker, forgiving and loving, enduring all things so as to bring God's peace, love and joy to a broken world.

> Praised be You, my Lord, through those who give pardon for Your Love,
> and bear infirmity and tribulation.
> Blessed are those who endure in peace
> for by You, Most High, shall they be crowned.[5]

Everyone who comes to you must encounter the compassion of Christ. *I wish to know in this way that you love the Lord: that there is not anyone who has sinned – however much they have sinned – who after they have looked into your eyes, would ever depart without your mercy, if they are looking for mercy!*[6]

'Where there is poverty with joy ...'

People said that I was too much in love with poverty – as if I could ever love the grinding destitution which robs people of their dignity. I fought against that kind of poverty when I went among the lepers and tried to bring them back from misery and exclusion into a more human way of life. No, what I love, by the grace of God, is a way of life which acknowledges that we all live without anything of our own.[7]

We cannot *own* anybody or anything because everything comes as undeserved gift from a bounteous God. When we realise this, then we know that seeking riches and power is an illusion – or worse, a trap! So much of your world is built on the notion that the more you have, the happier you will be. But brothers, where there is poverty with joy, there is neither greed nor avarice.[8] The market economy, which is now the arbiter of all things, depends on stimulating your desire to have more and more – thus reducing men and women to consumers in competition rather than brothers and sisters in community. This automatically means that the world is divided into those who are powerful and those who are powerless. The priest must always walk with those who are the 'little ones'; he must renounce power and live in the power of the poor Christ.

Christ's humility in coming to us — in the flesh and in the Eucharist

Let us consider this Christ who became poor for us, who chose to be born in a stable, of a poor woman. I have spoken of the praise given to God by his creatures, who are a token of his divine presence. But remember, God was not satisfied with this; he wanted to be present in human form, in the world he had created, by being born into human history at a particular time and place. This condescension and extraordinary generosity is in the nature of God.

I always wanted to live in imitation of that Christ, to walk in the footprints of the poor man of Nazareth. So when an opportunity arose to experience something of the life of Christ, I said to my friend John of Greccio:

> Make ready the things I tell you. For I wish to enact the memory of that babe who was born in Bethlehem: to see as much as possible with my own bodily eyes the discomfort of his infant needs, how he lay in a manger, and how, with an ox and ass standing by, he rested on hay.[9]

And so it happened, and those of us who stood around the crib that night felt in our hearts the wonder of God's entry into human history in circumstances of utter humility and simplicity. *From the womb of the Virgin Mary he received the flesh of our humanity and frailty. Though he was rich, he wished, together with the most*

Blessed Virgin, his mother, to choose poverty in the world beyond all else.[10] That the creator of the universe should humble himself in this way indicated to me that it is in living simply and humbly that we can most surely encounter the Lord, receiving him in our hearts and sharing him with others.

The humility of the Incarnation is matched by the charity of the Passion. Christ humbled himself and became obedient even unto death, death on a cross. Throughout my life I wept for the sufferings of the Lord – tears of sorrow for his anguish and agony, and for my part in causing it; tears of joy that we have a Saviour who loved us even unto death. On the mountain of La Verna, God's grace was given to me so that I could experience in my own flesh the Passion of Christ, and so come to some understanding of the great love which led to the saving Passion. During my lifetime I rarely spoke of my mysterious encounter with the six-winged seraph of Divine Love, and of the wounds impressed upon me. I will not do so now, save to beseech you priests to immerse yourselves in the saving Passion and to do your utmost to live in mystic union with Christ crucified.

Brothers, the unbounded love and humility of Christ continues to this day, and you priests encounter it every day of your lives!

Let everyone be struck with fear,
let the whole world tremble,
and let the heavens exult
when Christ, the Son of the living God,
is present on the altar in the hands of a priest!
O wonderful loftiness and stupendous dignity!
O sublime humility!
O humble sublimity!
The Lord of the universe,
God and the Son of God,
so humbles Himself
that for our salvation
He hides Himself

under an ordinary piece of bread!
Brothers, look at the humility of God,
and pour out your hearts before Him!
Humble yourselves
that you may be exalted by Him!
Hold back nothing of yourselves for yourselves,
that He Who gives Himself totally to you
may receive you totally!

See your dignity, my priest brothers, and be holy because he is holy. As the Lord God has honoured you above all others because of this ministry, for your part, love, revere and honour him above all others. It is a great misery and a miserable weakness that when you have him present in this way, you are concerned with anything else in the whole world!

Listen, my brothers: if the Blessed Virgin is so honoured, as is becoming, because she carried him in her most holy womb; if the Baptist trembled and did not dare to touch the holy head of God; if the tomb in which he lay for some time is held in veneration, how holy, just and fitting must be he who touches with his hands, receives in his heart and mouth, and offers to others to be received the One who is not about to die but who is to conquer and be glorified, upon whom the angels longed to gaze.[11]

The Lord gave and gives me still such faith in priests who live according to the rite of the holy Roman Church because of their orders that, were they to persecute me, I would still want to have recourse to them. And if I had as much wisdom as Solomon and found impoverished priests of this world, I would not preach in their parishes against their will. And I desire to respect, love and honour them and all others as my lords. And I do not want to consider any sin in them because I discern the Son of God in them and they are my lords. And I act in this way because, in this world, I see nothing corporally of the most high Son of God except his most holy body and blood which they receive and they alone minister to others.

You live in a time when the priest is not held in great esteem, where vocations to the priesthood have fallen away, where the concept of a life of self-sacrifice is considered foolish, and where the crimes of a few priests are associated with all priests. Nonetheless, you must have a deep sense of your own dignity and that of your ministry, while never losing sight of humility and a reluctance to acquire power.

I too, like you, lived in a time of change and reform following a great council. The Fourth Lateran Council, to my great joy, decreed that greater care should be taken of the sacred mysteries we celebrate. As I wrote at the time, 'Let all those who administer such holy mysteries consider how very dirty the chalices, the corporals and altar-linens are upon which the Body and Blood of our Lord are sacrificed. It is left in many dirty places, carried around unbecomingly, received unworthily, and administered to others without discernment.'[12]

> I want to have these holy mysteries honoured and venerated above all things and I want to reserve them in precious places. Whenever I find our Lord's most holy names and written words in unbecoming places, I want to gather them up and I beg that they be gathered up and placed in a becoming place. And we must honour all theologians and those who minister the most holy divine words and respect them as those who minister to us spirit and life.[13]

The grace of God in unexpected places

In 1219, during the disasters of the Fifth Crusade, I went to the Holy Land and there I met and conversed at length with Sultan Malik al-Kamil. This man, nephew of the great Saladin, impressed me by his faith and his wholehearted submission to Allah, the one God, almighty and eternal. Although I could not convert him to the Christian faith, he and I could see in each other a search for the Divine, and a desire to do the will of God and live in peace. Here was a better way than warfare, than suspicion and resentment. Surely the same applies now to your world where, on the one hand, faith of any kind is being pushed out of daily life, and where also a fatal opposition between Christian and Muslim is being fomented.

Therefore we must be open to the possibilities of reconciliation even in the midst of warfare and hate. So often we can find an ally where we had expected to find an opponent. People of faith of every kind can come together to declare the primacy of God in our world rather than spending their energies in divisions. How wonderful it is to see the place of my birth, Assisi, become synonymous with a new-found and fragile Catholic respect for other faiths, and for their expressions of prayer and unity with the Divine. What joy it is to me to see so many people of so many faiths come to visit Assisi and there find a living, breathing expression of God's love and mercy. So many people of good will, all over the world, can pray with me the prayer I wrote so long ago – a prayer that can be shared by all who seek understanding and common ground between faiths:

> You are the holy Lord God who does wonderful things.
> You are strong. You are great. You are the most high.
> You are love and charity; you are wisdom, you are humility
> You are patience, you are beauty, you are meekness,
> You are security, you are rest,
> You are gladness and joy, you are our hope, you are justice,
> You are moderation, you are all our riches to sufficiency.
> Great and wonderful Lord, Almighty God.[14]

Conversion through your relationship with the 'little ones'

> The Lord gave me, Brother Francis, thus to begin doing penance in this way: for when I was in sin, it seemed too bitter for me to see lepers. And the Lord himself led me among them and I showed mercy to them. And when I left

them, what seemed bitter to me was turned into sweetness of soul and body.[15]

Brothers, never tire of going among the lepers of your day. Be converted every day through your relationship with those whom the Lord loves in a special way. You will find sweetness where once you found only bitterness, as I can testify. If you follow the example of the Lord Jesus who delivered himself into the hands of his enemies, who loved and forgave them, then you will indeed be converted and experience the mercy of God. Be firmly focused on Jesus Christ and always be the servant of the holy mysteries which you alone administer to others.

May the Lord bless you and keep you. May he show his face to you and be merciful to you. May he turn his countenance to you and give you peace. May the Lord bless you![16]

Notes

1. From the opening of St Francis's Letter to the Faithful (2LF) and from the Letter to the Entire Order (Lord), 22. All quotations from the writings of St Francis are taken from *Francis of Assisi: Early Documents*, Regis J. Armstrong, J. Wayne Hellmann, William J. Short, eds (New York: New City Press, 1999).
2. Thomas of Celano, 1228 (1 Cel 1, XIII, 33).
3. *Legend of the Three Companions* (L3C, 13 & 51).
4. From *The Canticle of the Creatures*, written by Francis in 1225.
5. Ibid.
6. *A Letter to a Minister* (1221–1223).
7. Francis uses the term *sine proprio*, also used in the Franciscan formula of Profession which includes the phrase, '[to live] without anything of my own'.
8. From *The Admonitions* (27), an undated writing of St Francis.
9. *The Life of St Francis* (1 Cel 84).
10. Second version of the *Letter to the Faithful* (1220).
11. *A Letter to the Entire Order* (1225–1226).
12. *Exhortations to the Clergy* (later edition 1220).
13. *The Testament of St Francis* (1226).

14. *The Praises of God* (1224).
15. Opening words of *The Testament*.
16. *A Blessing for Brother Leo* (quoting Num 6:24-27).

Bringing God to the World and the World to God: The Priest in the Twenty-First Century

JIM CORKERY

'By having mercy and by choosing him' (*Miserando atque Eligendo*) is the motto of Pope Francis, chosen when he first became a bishop in 1992 and retained on his election as Bishop of Rome. The words are taken from Homily 22 of the Venerable Bede, prepared for the feast of Saint Matthew. Bede writes of the gospel scene describing the call of Matthew: 'Jesus therefore sees the tax collector, and since he sees *by having mercy and by choosing*, he says to him, "follow me".[1] In his own life, on the feast of St Matthew in 1953, when Jorge Mario Bergoglio (now Pope Francis) was seventeen years old, he felt both the touch of God's tender mercy and the call to religious life. His experience reveals, at once, something universal and something particular. Everyone is in need of God's mercy and no one can move forward as a disciple of Jesus, as Matthew did, without receiving and accepting the mercy of God. According to the words of St Bede, God's seeing involves being merciful and choosing. This expresses the situation of all of us before God: sinners, yet forgiven and called; wretched, yet loved and chosen. Anyone seeking to live a life of discipleship of Jesus Christ will know something of this experience. Yet it will come to each individual in a unique way, deeply embedded in his or her own particular life story.

'Reading' the divine invitation

In this essay, my focus is on that form of discipleship that is the Christian priesthood. It is often referred to in terms of vocation and it is an important, but by no means the only call received in the Church. No one can follow a call from God unless he or she has become a kind of 'reader' of the presence and actions of God in the world and in their own life. Five years ago, when gathered at a meeting with Jesuit companions from all over the world, it was through the telling of our 'vocation stories' that we were able to find what we had in common and work together on a shared project. We came to see that despite all our differences in character, culture and personal circumstances, we shared an eye for how God had 'touched into' our everyday lives and invited us to join with Jesus in the work of building up the Kingdom of his Father, God's reign 'on earth as it is in heaven'. Just like the many accounts of calls in the scriptures, we too had somehow heard God's voice in the ordinary circumstances of our lives and it had taken these lives in a specific direction, a direction that made all the difference.

Without noticing it, believers operate implicitly with an idea of how God and the world relate, and anyone who says 'yes' to a call already has a sense of how it is that God can be encountered in our human world. All such encounters are grace, which is not a thing but a relationship: 'the history of two freedoms, the meeting of two loves.'[2] As an expression of God's love, deeply embedded in the concrete circumstances of our everyday lives, grace can often be present unnoticed – to be recognised later, perhaps, as when Jacob exclaimed: 'Truly, the Lord is in this spot, although I did not know it' (Gn 28:16). If anyone who is reading this is trying to live out a vocation, they already know what I am talking about. The Lord calls, nudges, whispers to us, at the heart of our experiences and activities, and, like the young Samuel perhaps, we gradually manage to respond: 'Speak, for your servant is listening' (1 Sm 3:10). Such experiences are rarely overwhelming, although they can occasionally be somewhat dramatic. They are almost always gentle, like that of Samuel, or like that of the prophet Elijah, who recognised the voice of the Lord in the 'tiny whispering sound' that followed the wind, the earthquake and the fire (cf. 1 Kgs 19:12-13). Without bowling us over, the Lord knocks gently: 'Behold, I stand at the door and knock' (Rv 3:20). The important thing is to be able to read the signs of the divine presence in the world – a presence that is the hidden, yet ultimately transformative, gift of grace of a living, divine-human relationship!

Once a person has known, thought about and begun to live out such an experience as I have been describing, they have a view of what theologians call the relationship between nature and grace, the human and the divine, the world and God. There are different ways of thinking about this relationship – different *theologies* of nature and grace, you might say – and they make a difference to how one lives in fidelity to God's call to live according to the gospel. What I am concerned about in this essay, mainly, is how the person who has discerned a call to the priesthood today – who has heard the voice of God amid the ordinary circumstances of life – comes to understand what has happened and how to live it out in the service of God and of others.

Grace, nature and the Incarnation

Once we are thinking about how God and the human world interact – how the human and the divine are *related* – we are thinking about the theology of nature and grace. 'Nature', an abstract term though it is, refers to *all* that God has created and rejoices in as being 'very good' (Gn 1:31). 'Grace', in itself an abstract term also, refers to no less than *God*, but God as 'us-focused', bent on encounter, oriented to human reality in unending forgiveness and love. One can think about 'nature' and 'grace' conceptually – and it is even good to do so in order to allow the distinction between God and creatures to remain clear; but, concretely, the two (nature and grace) always interpenetrate in our world. Humans are created graced – oriented to the divine, gifted with a 'God-towardsness'.[3] And God, Father, Son and Spirit, has an undoubted 'us-towardsness' that leads the divinity to spill out into the world in the loving missions of the Son and the Holy Spirit. Thus the whole created world (and every human life in this world) is created with a view to God being with, loving and saving it. And, in the concrete, nature and grace, the human and the divine, the world and God, interpenetrate, following the pattern of their most excellent interpenetration in the divine-human Jesus himself. When we pray, when celebrating the Eucharist, that we may 'come to share in the divinity of Christ who humbled himself to share in our humanity', we are asking to receive this existence of God-made flesh, so that we can come to say with Saint Paul, 'I live, no longer I, but Christ lives in me' (Gal 2:20). This is the oneness of love; it is divine-human relationship, grace and nature together – expressing what the Incarnation is and makes possible.

In the Incarnation, heaven and earth, the holy and the human, God and humanity, meet. And so we have a (delightful!) difficulty. This is to detect, to uncover, to find the earthed presence of God in the manner in which it 'occurs' or comes to be, in an interpenetrating kind of way that does not permit us to neatly identify 'grace' here and 'not-grace' there. The two become one, remaining distinct but not separated. Here the predominant insight is – to borrow an idea from Leonardo Boff – that grace turns up in the world in tandem with something created, something that becomes transparent of God to the world.[4] Here one sees that Jesus Christ himself is grace[5] and that in him, God-made-flesh, the divine-become-human, there is made visible for us the God who is invisible.[6] Thus the best word to describe the way God touches humanity is 'incarnational': flesh is taken by God, a form is adopted by God that is human in character, God speaks an 'abbreviated word'[7] that we, limited beings of sense, can understand. In and through the things of creation – suffused as they are with the drenching of grace – God's own presence is detected and, like the poets, we too 'see His blood upon the rose and in the stars the glory of his eyes' (Joseph Mary Plunkett). Gerard Manley Hopkins comes to mind at this point also, as he speaks of how 'Christ plays in ten thousand places, lovely in limbs, and lovely in eyes not his to the Father through the features of men's [that is, our] faces.'[8]

A vision with implications

The insight here is that grace – the forgiving, healing, restoring, up-building love of God – does not reach us unalloyed; it arrives in tandem with the things of God's own created and beloved world. It arrives personally, but mediated through the circumstances, situations, experiences and encounters of our lives; that is, it arrives in our histories and relationships, our worship and prayer, our struggles and growth. When Ignatius of Loyola urged us to try to find God in all things, this is what he had in mind. The vision of the divine-human relationship presented here is one that does not put divinity on one side of a line and humanity on the other, as if they did not somehow belong together in God's intent but were only later coupled, like two carriages of a train (that look nice together but that are really quite self-sufficient and would more or less do fine if they were not together at all). It was an older, more 'mechanistic' but less 'relational' way of thinking about nature and grace that envisioned things in this way. However, it was largely set aside at the Second Vatican Council, thanks to theological work carried out at and before that council by such theologians as Henri de Lubac, Karl Rahner and others. After the council, then, their thought was built upon by the next generation of theologians.

The 'newer' vision of the nature-grace relationship that I have been talking about is aware that, concretely, there exist only human beings who are destined, from the beginning, for a relationship with God throughout this life and eternally. From the outset, the human person is offered God's love and his or her existence is enveloped by this deepest call to relationship, to a sharing in the life of the Trinity. Our nature is graced from the beginning; there is no 'pure' nature that is self-sufficient in its own right and devoid of an eternal destiny. The only aspect of our lives in which God is not involved is sin. Yet even in our sin God is present, first, as the one who leaves us free to accept or reject God and second, present in drawing us out of and beyond sin, through healing grace, to a fully restored and growing relationship with God. God reaches us where we are; how else could those vocation stories have acquired life? Calling unrespectable people (Matthew, Zacchaeus, me, you!) and surprising them with an outpouring of divine love, God breaks through and we follow, never quite sure how we heard God's voice in the first place or deserved God's attention in the midst of our daily lives. But that is how it is with us human beings: we are 'God-tagged' from the start; we carry a divine 'chip'; our ordinary lives are suffused with the divine presence; we live in a divine milieu, whether we notice it or not (and in spite of the presence of sin); and, in the depths of our experiences, relationships and activities, God is there, God who never abandons us and can truly be found in all things. The holy and the human, the sacred and the secular, the supernatural and the natural interpenetrate.

All this talk of the interpenetration of the holy and the human, of grace and nature, may be a bit confusing, perhaps even somewhat irritating by now, because some of us have been taught to oppose the human to the holy, the secular to the sacred, and so on, and a vision that mixes them may seem a little confused. Yet it is not what is human but rather what is sinful that opposes the holy. And while it is true that when grace touches the human world it must heal and cleanse it in so far as it is sinful, it will nevertheless build on and perfect all that is human in so far as this retains the excellence that was conferred upon it when it was created. For any Christian minister, then, and hence for every Catholic priest, the ministry is principally about highlighting for people the 'always already there' (thus Rahner) presence of God and bringing them more fully to God and attempting to bring God more fully to them. The basic pattern is incarnational: the Word becomes flesh. Following this pattern of Jesus, the priest is the bridge, the 'open space', the mediator between God and the world and the world and God. Because the pattern is incarnational, it will, of course, also be paschal, because it will follow the steps of Jesus' own life, and his path leads through the Cross and not around it. In a world which, although good, also knows sin, the path of grace will also pass through the wounds of sin – for these are healed and forgiven only through suffering, redemptive love. Thus the Christian priest will know something about the Cross also both in personal life and in the life of ministry and service.

If the Cross and the Paschal Mystery are left out of the picture, the vision of the relationship between nature and grace becomes too smooth, too continuous, as if, between us and God, there was no 'unevennesses'. But of course there is, and there is genuine distance. However, if this distance is exaggerated in a way that opposes the human and the holy – when in fact it is only the sinful (a corruption of the human) and the holy that are opposed – then we separate what God, in undertaking Incarnation, wished to keep together: divinity and humanity. God sent his Son, Jesus, as a mediator, a bridge between Godself and ourselves. Now a bridge brings challenges: it allows the two sides to mix; it makes 'border-control' much more difficult; it deprives us of the neatness of being able to say 'precisely here is God, precisely here is humanity'. A famous rabbi once longed for a kind of neatness like this and said to God: 'Lord, I am so sick of your people; they ignore your law; they follow their own ways; from now on I will speak with you alone.' And God thundered back: 'I have sunk my presence in my people; if you want my company, you will find it in them; so go back!'[9] We might add: 'for nature and grace interpenetrate in a concrete world that, as created, needs perfecting and that, as sinful, needs healing; but God is distant from no aspect of it.' Thus the ministry of the priest in such a world is happiest and most fruitful when oriented, following the pattern of Jesus' own life, to bringing this world to God and God to this world rather than huddling in the questionable purity of the abstract sacred that would keep grace for the holy alone.

Notes

1. Italics mine, highlighting the papal motto. The words of Bede are quoted in 'The Coat of Arms of Pope Francis', available at www.vatican.va/holy_father/francesco/elezione/stemma-papa-francesco_en.html (accessed 2/4/2013).

2. Leonardo Boff, *Liberating Grace* (Maryknoll, New York: Orbis Books, 1979), 3.

3. This is a phrase of Thomas A. Marsh, used in his *The Triune God: A Biblical, Historical and Theological Study* (Dublin: Columba Press, 1994), 9.

4. See Boff, chapter 9, especially 88–105.

5. See Titus 2:11-14, also 3:4. And see the homily of Pope John Paul II at Midnight Mass on 25 December 1984, at www.vatican.va/holy_father/john_paul_ii/homilies/1984/documents/hf_jp-ii_hom_19841225_messa-natale_it.html (accessed 2/4/2013).

6. See Preface II of the Nativity of the Lord, available in the *Roman Missal* (Dublin: Veritas, 2011), 408.

7. See Elizabeth A. Johnson, *Quest for the Living God: Mapping Frontiers in the Theology of God* (London and New York: Continuum, 2007), 39–40, where Johnson, drawing on a prayer of Karl Rahner, speaks about how God, in Jesus Christ, speaks 'an abbreviated word in the language of our common humanity'.

8. Gerard Manley Hopkins, 'As Kingfishers Catch Fire', *Gerard Manley Hopkins: Poems and Prose* (London: Penguin Classics, 1985), 51.

9. I owe this story – trusting that I remember it correctly – to Scottish theologian John McDade, who told it once at a conference I attended.

Do We Really Know Christian Teaching About Jesus?

ENDA LYONS

The priest is called to act in a unique way in the person of Christ. It is therefore essential that he has as full an understanding as possible of the humanity and divinity of Christ. This is especially the case because so many popular misunderstandings exist, both among the faithful and among those who find belief in the Incarnation impossible to accept.[1]

'Do we really know Christian teaching about Jesus?' This must surely seem a rather strange question to ask of Christians. After all, Jesus is the very centre of Christianity: its very basic conviction has to do with him. To ask in a Christian context if we really understand what the Christian community teaches about this central figure must indeed appear strange. Yet it seems to me that this is a question that needs to be asked. After years of listening and talking to groups of committed Christians, I am convinced that many do not know, not to mention understand, what their community really teaches about Jesus. And this is so despite their obvious piety and devotion. What I am setting out to do in this essay is to point out some misunderstandings that, in my experience, are common even among Christians.

'Jesus is God'

The first has to do with the formula 'Jesus is God'. This phrase has a long and venerable history in Christian piety. The formula has the strength of emphasising the extraordinary and unique unity between God and Jesus. As such, when it is properly understood, it will always have a special place in Christian devotion.

Theology, however, is different from devotion, though good theology ought itself to be devotional and ought to foster devotion. But theology has its own special, and very important, function. Its function is to attempt *to explain, to make sense of* and *to understand* the Christian Mystery. Its classic definition is, 'faith seeking understanding'.

'Jesus is God' is often taken as a simple and accurate summary of the official Christian understanding of Jesus. Accordingly, it is commonly used as a simple test of the orthodoxy of a particular statement. In truth, however, it is not at all an accurate summary of Christian belief and it may not, therefore, be used as a test of orthodoxy. Indeed, it can mislead us in our effort to understand how the community sees Jesus, and it may give unbelievers, and those struggling to believe, a very wrong impression of Christian belief. In this way it can be a stumbling block to belief.

The Eternal word of God Incarnate

After giving it even a little thought, we can see that a much more accurate summary of Christian belief is: 'Jesus is *the Eternal Word of God Incarnate*' (that is, 'made flesh'). In any serious attempt to understand the Christian position, this formula needs to be taken seriously.

Jesus is the *Word* of God. 'Word', as we know, is that in which we express ourselves, for example, in speaking or writing. But, we need to note, before we write or utter a word, there is within us an inner word or idea that we want to express. When we do express it, we actually press out – ex-press – that inner word and give it existence outside ourselves. The existence we then give it is in a new form. Now for the very first time, the word that is within us exists also outside us, in the form, for example, of writing, sound, gesture and so on.

Incarnate tells us about the new form of existence the Word that was within God is given in Jesus. It is the form of 'flesh' (*caro*), human life. To say then that Jesus is the Eternal Word of God Incarnate is to say this much at least: that in him, God, who expresses Self eternally within the Divine Self, 'presses out' that Eternal Word and gives it a new way of existing, a created way of existing. It is to say what John, in the prologue to his gospel, says:

> In the beginning was the Word,
> and the Word was with God,
> and the Word was God ...
> The Word was made flesh,
> he lived among us ... (1:1ff.)

Christian teaching, then, does not see Jesus as simply God, as the phrase 'Jesus is God' suggests. In the Christian understanding, God did not become God in Jesus; God became 'flesh'. The whole point of the Incarnation is *incarnation*. A summary statement of Christian belief that makes no reference to this is obviously inaccurate and misleading.[2]

Jesus: a human 'person' or just a human 'nature'?

Another rather common misunderstanding concerns the new form in which God expressed self in Jesus. The catechism – and popular – formula is that in Jesus there are two natures, human and divine, united in one 'person', the Eternal Divine Word. What is important to note here is the impression that this way of speaking gives about the form in which the Eternal Word of God expressed Self in Jesus. Being presented here as one person, the Divine Person of the Word, Jesus would not seem to be a human 'person'. God, then, would seem to have expressed self, not in a human person but in a human 'nature', which would seem to be an inert 'block' of humanity devoid of its own freedom and spontaneity. So, Karl Rahner comments:

> The idea exists that God ... makes gestures by means of a human reality which is used in such a way that it is not a real man with independence and freedom, but a puppet on

strings which the player behind the scenes uses to make himself audible.[3]

Contrary to what is often thought, this is not at all the true Christian understanding of Jesus. So, Rahner adds:

> But this is mythology and not Church dogma, even though it may be a fair description of the catechism in many Christians' heads in contrast to the printed catechism ... And it may be that some non-Christians are thus led to rely on a cryptogamous heresy of Christians ... thinking that it is a dogma of Christianity.[4]

The most obvious truth about Jesus, the one that did not require any faith whatsoever in those who knew him in Palestine, was that he was a human being, not a human 'nature'. To them he was Jesus, the woodworker from Nazareth, obviously a real man. That he was a human being, not just of human 'nature', was something even his worst enemies could never have thought of denying. It was only in later centuries, when Jesus was thought of first and foremost as divine, that some did wonder how, then, he could be fully and really human. But, and this needs to be emphasised, the Christian community insistently taught that Jesus was truly human, a 'true man'. As such, he was not just 90 per cent human, or just 99 per cent human, or just even 99.999 per cent human, but 100 per cent human.[5]

So, for example, in the language of its time, the Council of Chalcedon (451) says Jesus was:

> ... complete in humanity ... true man ... consisting of a rational soul and a body ... of one substance with us in humanity .... The difference of natures will never be abolished by their being united, but rather the properties of each remain unimpaired.

Jesus: a human 'person'

As a genuine human being, Jesus was therefore, as all people are, a free human being – a point clarified by the Council of Constantinople (680–681).[6]

It is clear then, if only from that council, that the human 'nature' in Jesus

> ... does not lack anything that characterises the human 'person': presence to himself, freedom, a dialogical creaturely relationship with God through adoration and obedience ...[7]

Today, in common English usage, the word 'person' is used to describe a creature who is composed of body and spirit, and who is intelligent and free. In other words, it is used to describe 'a free human being'. Anytime we encounter such a human being, we can say: 'There is a human person'. It would be a serious misunderstanding of Christian teaching to think that Jesus was not a human person in this everyday sense of the English term. In fact, such a view of Jesus would be heretical.

That in which the Eternal Word became incarnate in Jesus, is a free, independent, human being – a human 'person' in the everyday sense of the word. What the early councils mean by 'person' (*hypostasis*) will arise again later.

Creation: a word of God Incarnate

Yet another mistake is to see, or present, the Incarnation of the Word of God as coming into the world like a bolt from the blue, or as a sort of *deus ex machina* to resolve the human predicament. The Incarnation has as its context the long history of God's dealings with the universe as a whole, a context that is wider than that of human sin. Its context is God's self-expression throughout history. For, in terms of time at least, Jesus was not the first word uttered by God. It was in creation itself that God first ex-pressed Self outside Self, and this Self-expression is the background against which the Incarnation ought to be seen. Creation, too, being a word uttered by God, can be seen as a word of God made 'flesh'.

As such, of course, it reveals something of God's inner life: 'The heavens declare the glory of God.'[8]

In the words of Dermot Lane:

> The Incarnation, therefore, is not some isolated divine intrusion that took place at one moment two thousand years ago but is rather the culmination and crystallisation of a divine cosmic process initiated at the dawn of time. The Incarnation was 'first' in God's intention – but not in time.[9]

The Christian conviction is that 'in the fullness of time', God expressed self outside self, in created terms, as fully as possible, as radically as possible, and – to borrow a phrase from Karl Rahner – 'with the utmost truth'. Since human beings are free, and able to think and love, they can mirror God in a way other created beings cannot. This fullest possible divine self-expression necessarily, therefore, took place in a free human life. It necessarily took place in the most perfect, most complete human life. It resulted, Christians believe, in Jesus of Nazareth, in his life and in his death, in his words and in his works, in his resurrection and exaltation. In him God had brought a human being and a human life to completion and fulfilment. In him God had, in principle at least, brought humankind – indeed creation itself – to completion.

As Pope John Paul II stated:

> The Incarnation of God the Son signifies the taking up into unity with God not only human nature, but in this human nature, in a sense, of everything that is flesh ... The Incarnation, then, also has a cosmic significance, a cosmic dimension.[10]

In the Christian view, Jesus is then the 'high-water mark' of God's involvement in creation. He is the Eternal Word of God translated as accurately and as perfectly as possible in created terms, in terms of a human life. He is God's 'last word' about self – not God's final word, but God's perfect word about self. God is invisible, incomprehensible – Mystery. *The* human question is the question about God: what is God like? What would God be like in our terms, in our situation? Philip expressed it in John's gospel: 'Lord, let us see the Father and then we shall be satisfied' (14:8). Jesus' reply to Philip was: 'To have seen me is to have seen the Father' (14:9). In the words of John A. Robinson, Jesus is 'a window into God at work'. The phrase 'at work' is important. We do not see God in the physical appearance of this man, of which of course we know nothing. We see God in Jesus' message and ministry, in his life and in his dying – a dying that led to his being raised and exalted. If theology literally means 'a word about God', then, as Karl Rahner says:

> Christology is the theology which God himself has taught by speaking out his Word, as our flesh, into the void of the non-divine and sinful.[11]

In the words of a Christmas Preface:

> In the wonder of the Incarnation
> your eternal Word has brought to the eyes of faith
> a new and radiant vision of your glory.
> In him we see our God made visible
> and so we are caught up in love of the God we cannot see.

A self-portrait and its artist

One of the most common mistakes about Jesus is the tendency, the great tendency, to simply equate Jesus with his Creator, as if there was no difference between them – despite the fact that the Council of Chalcedon definitively declared that there is a difference. It will help us to see the fault in this tendency, and also to understand better Christian belief, if we focus on the familiar image of an artist creating a self-portrait.

We might think, first, of a human artist choosing to express self through a medium other than self: we might think of the artist choosing to create a self-portrait in oils on canvas. And we might think of the artist creating a masterpiece. Of course when the artist sets out to do this, he or she deliberately chooses the self-expression to be limited by the limitations imposed by the chosen medium, in this case, oil on canvas. The masterpiece, then, will be two-dimensional and, when all is said, will be lifeless. It will not by any means match the level of being that the artist has.

Somewhat similarly, we might think of God as the Divine Artist who chooses to express self through a medium that is different from self: we might think of God setting out to create a self-portrait in 'flesh', that is, in a human life. And we might imagine God creating, through this medium, a masterpiece. Again we need to remember that in choosing this medium, God would also choose to work within the constraints the medium necessarily imposes. No sane person would expect Jesus as God's self-portrait to know everything that God knows and to be able to do everything that God can do. To expect this would be like expecting a Van Gogh self-portrait to be able to talk and walk and even to paint a masterpiece! Yet many seem to forget this: I find that when a preacher or teacher says, for example, that Jesus did not, and could not, have known everything, but had to grow in knowledge throughout his life, the objection is frequently put: 'But wasn't he God?' The portrait and the artist are here confused.

It is worth noting in passing that such a self-portrait would give us a unique insight into God. An artist's self-portrait is very different from, for example, a photograph. The photograph would only present the artist as seen from the outside. In a painting, however, the artist would start out, of set purpose, to express and reveal in as creative a way as possible how he sees himself. If we look on Jesus as God's self-portrait in flesh, we would then see him as one in whom we are given not an outsider's view of God, but rather – amazingly – an insight into how God sees and experiences God.

The implications of this are, of course, quite amazing. We might reflect, for example, on Jesus' emphasis on service rather than lordship, on his empathy with the poor, the downtrodden, the sinner, the weak and the wounded ones of the world, and reflect on what all this says about God's experience of being God. Jesus was known – and criticised – for being 'a friend of tax collectors and sinners' (Mt 11:19), and as one who 'welcomes sinners and eats with them' (Lk 15:1). Here a common saying comes to mind: 'Tell me your company and I will tell you who you are.' It might be said of Jesus: 'Tell me your company and I will tell you who *God* is.'

Portraits with a difference

In the Christian view, there is, of course, one particularly important difference between the self-portrait of a human artist and the self-portrait that Jesus is of God. The self-portrait by a human artist owes its existence to the artist in the first place, but there the relationship ends. Once finished, the self-portrait remains completely distinct from the artist. It has its own separate existence, it goes its own separate way, and its history in art galleries, auction rooms, on walls or wherever, is its own history alone and has nothing to do with the personal history of the artist. As Christian belief sees it, the relationship between Jesus and the Divine Artist is altogether different. In what follows, I will deal with this difference in two stages: first, I will state the Christian view of the difference, and then I will suggest how we might try to have some understanding of it.

Stating the belief

Stating the difference is something we need to do very calmly. This is so for the simple but profound reason that the difference is, indeed, an amazing one. Understandably, it can be experienced in the way one of Jesus' own statements was, as 'a hard saying and who can hear it' (Jn 6:60).

The amazing Christian conviction is that this divine self-portrait, and the artist, do not go their different ways. In fact, they are believed to be united inseparably, and to be united in an unprecedented and unparalleled way. In creating this self-portrait, the Divine Artist is believed to have created a *real* extension of self, a *created* extension. The artist is believed to have found in it a new way of being and living – again, a created way. The life and history of the portrait is believed to be the human life of the Divine Artist. Whatever happens to the portrait is believed to be happening also to the artist. So, in the pain of Jesus, Christians see God*self* suffering, *really* suffering in this created extension of the Divine Self. They believe that, in an ultimate sense, the life of Jesus is the human life of the Eternal Word. Whatever, therefore, can be said of the portrait, can be said of the Eternal Word of God *Incarnate*. To take what is perhaps the best-known example, it is Christian belief that Mary, the mother of Jesus of Nazareth, is, by that very fact, the mother of the Eternal Word of God in his created existence. They believe, in the language of the Council of Ephesus, that Mary is the Mother, or Bearer, of the Eternal Word of God Incarnate. The last word here, though absolutely essential, is one that is often omitted or ignored, not just in devotional language, but in theological discussion, thus giving the impression that Christians believe that Mary is *simply* 'the mother of her Creator'.

In the popular version of the catechism, the word 'person' was used to describe this unity: the 'human' and divine in Jesus were united in the one Divine Person of the Eternal Word of God. What is often forgotten, of course, is that the language of the early councils was Greek, not English, and that the councils did not use either the word 'nature' or 'person'. They used *physis* ('nature') and *hypostasis* ('person'). Accurately stated, their teaching is that in Jesus there is a human *physis* and a divine *physis*, united in the one *hypostasis* of the Eternal Word of God. From what I have said so far, it is clear (again, especially from the Council of Constantinople) that *hypostasis* does not have the meaning the word 'person' in everyday English has. It is a technical term referring to the ultimate centre of unity of the divine and human 'natures' in Jesus. Put more simply, it means that when Jesus said 'I', he, the woodworker from Nazareth, was speaking freely for himself and of himself. He was the owner of this 'I'. But this human being, Jesus, was so united to the Eternal Word of God, that the ultimate 'I' speaking here was that of the Eternal Word of God. In Karl Rahner's words:

The official statement of the Christological doctrine of the Church uses the term 'person', *hypostasis* (of the divine *Logos*) to speak of the *ultimate centre of unity uttering himself and the created utterance in which and through which the utterance takes place.*[12]

In other words, Jesus was the created self-expression of the Eternal Word of God, so much so that his life and history was, in an ultimate sense, the life and history of the Eternal Word of God. When Jesus, this woodworker from Nazareth, spoke or acted, he was acting and speaking freely of himself and for himself. But being the Eternal Word of God in a created existence, he was speaking and acting as such; he was the Eternal Word of God speaking and acting. To return to the image of the artist, it says that, again in an ultimate sense, the 'I' of this divine self-portrait, Jesus, was also the 'I' of the Divine Artist of whose being he is a real created extension.

Making sense of the difference?

As I have already mentioned, the task of theology is to try to understand belief and to express it in the clearest language available. Here, it must be said at the outset that in talking about the unity between Jesus and God, we are dealing with the high point of God's involvement in history and have reached the edges of Christian and human experience. We have moved here beyond the ordinary. This unity, as Karl Rahner puts it, is 'such as is not found elsewhere and remains profoundly mysterious'.[13]

Indeed, it is because the unity in question is, in the strict sense, unique, that Christian tradition has used a special word, *hypostatic*, to refer to it. It is a word to which we will return.

Being different from anything else in our experience, the Incarnation will always remain, to some extent at least, beyond our grasp. But this does not have to mean that we can make no sense at all of it – that this basic Christian belief must always appear to us as non-sense. Even though it is in the very strict sense unique, the Incarnation is still an event of divine creativity. And creativity itself is something of which we do have direct experience. It is this human experience of creativity, it seems to me, which offers us a key to understanding better the relationship between Jesus and God.

Expression

The word 'expression' provides us with a good starting point. As I have already pointed out, 'ex-press' literally means to press out. When we express ourselves we are pressing out the being that we are, giving it some form of existence outside ourselves. We are thus extending the being that we are. So, the artist or the author, in expressing themselves in their respective ways, press out something of their being into their creation and give it existence outside themselves. Here it is interesting to note that we often say of these that they 'put themselves into their work'. This reminds us that all our creations exist because they participate in our being, that is, because we have put something of ourselves into them. They are, then, an extension of ourselves. So, interestingly, we say of the work or creation into which we have poured our being: 'There is a lot of me in that'. If it is a creation in which we have been intensively involved, we might even say: 'I have put my all into that'.

Since the act of expressing ourselves is always an attempt to 'press' ourselves out, and extend ourselves, the perfect self-expression would occur if an artist were ever to succeed in really putting self into the creation. Then the creation would become a real extension of the artist. Christian faith, I have said, understands Jesus to be the high point of God's involvement in history. It believes that God was, and is, involved in this human life as much as it is possible for God to be involved in a single human life. We might say that, as Christians see it, God put God's 'all' into this creation.

Even we humans can succeed to some extent in putting our 'all' into our creation – as we note whenever we say, 'There is a lot of me in that'. Still our creative powers, though wonderful, are very limited. It is only in a very loose sense that we can say that a Van Gogh self-portrait is a real extension of himself: we would be very slow to say that he *really* lives on in his portrait.

God, however, is not a human artist, but is Creator. Our own experience of limited creativity might help us to think of God as 'pressing out' Divine Being, as putting self into this creation, Jesus; as to have succeeded in expressing self in a way that a human artist might wish to do, but cannot. And this is so even if the human artist had all the intensity and creativity and passion of a Michelangelo saying 'Speak!' to his completed statue of Moses. In the light of our own, sometimes considerable, creative achievements, might we not then think of God achieving the ultimate in creativity and self-expression? If we could think in this way would we not then be thinking of God as expressing self in Jesus in the way Christians believe? The fact that we cannot think of a creature, with its limited creative powers, achieving such perfect self-expression does not necessarily mean that we cannot think of the Creator, *creativity itself*, achieving it.

Human or divine — a dilemma?

Is Christian teaching not faced with a dilemma here? Jesus was a free human being, free even before God. If Jesus' human life belonged to God as God's own human life, how could Jesus be free before God? Surely the more he belonged to God, as God's very own, the less he belonged to himself?

When we consider this dilemma seriously, we find that it turns out to be a false one. Strange as it may seem, it arises out of a very inadequate notion of God – a notion common among Christians.

God, as we know, is different from created things. We think of God as being hugely different from creatures, even infinitely bigger and more powerful than they.

God, of course, is not a creature. God, and God alone, is not a creature at all. God is Creator. As Creator, God creates. God gives being, and upholds being. Everything else receives being – is created. If we really have any appreciation of what it means to say that God is Creator, that is, if we have any idea at all of transcendence, we can see that God's way of being active and present is radically different from a creature's way. God's presence is always a creative presence, always giving, never taking away. Of course, deep down we know this. When we talk about a room in which there is one person present, it never occurs to us to say that really there are two there, not even if we believe that God, being everywhere, is also there. Nor would it occur to us to say that God's presence means that there is less room for creatures: we would never think of having to reserve a seat for God! In a context like that, we know that God's presence is of such a radically different kind from that of creatures, that there can be no conflict between them, no either/or. We know that, in fact, the opposite is the case: without God's presence there is no creaturely presence. Strangely, in the context of the coming together of the divine and human in Jesus, we seem to forget this radical difference between God and creature. We seem to forget God's transcendence. When we think of the coming together of the divine and the human in Jesus we think, as Paul Tillich put it, of two blocks lying side by side. Far better if we focused on the coming together of two very different realities. An example that I find helpful is that of the coming together of light and glass in a stained glass window. The sunlight does not take anything away from the contribution of the coloured glass itself. On the contrary, it brings it into its full brilliance and glory. God's presence in Jesus, far from taking from his human reality, brings it into the fullness of human life. To see God's involvement in Jesus as taking away from the action or involvement of or freedom of Jesus himself is, then, to make a very serious mistake. It is to put God's action and that of creatures on the same level. Far from being the case of 'either God or creature', it is, rather, 'without God, nothing creaturely at all'.

Notes

1. Editor's note.
2. For a more detailed and somewhat different approach to this, see my *Jesus: Self-Portrait by God* (Dublin: Columba Press, 1994), chapter 8.
3. *Theological Investigations*, Vol. 4, 118.
4. Ibid.
5. For a fuller treatment of the early controversies concerning the 'humanity' of Jesus, see chapter one of *Jesus: Self-Portrait*.
6. The context of this clarification was the monothelite view, associated with Sergius I, Patriarch of Constantinople, that Jesus had no human

freedom. See *Jesus: Self-Portrait*, chapter one; see also Alan Richardson, *Creeds in the Making: A Short Introduction to the History of Christian Doctrine* (Norwich: SCM Press, 2012).

7. Karl Rahner and Herbert Vorgrimler, *Concise Theological Dictionary* (New York: Crossroad, 1985), 381.

8. Psalm 19.

9. Dermot Lane, *Christ at the Centre: Selected Issues in Christology* (Mahwah, NJ: Paulist Press, 1991), 154.

10. *Dominum et Vivificantem*, 50.

11. *Theological Investigations*, Vol. 4, 117.

12. *Sacramentum Mundi*, Vol. 3, 206; italics mine.

13. Ibid., 196.

'With Joy You Shall Draw Water From the Wells of Salvation': Scripture and the Contemporary Priest

FEIDHLIMIDH T. MAGENNIS

When I was asked to reflect on the place of scripture in the life and ministry of today's priests, I had just celebrated my silver jubilee of ordination. It seemed appropriate to approach the topic in terms of my personal experiences of reading and listening to the Word of God. I was equally aware of the milestone in the life of God's people that is the fiftieth anniversary of the opening of the Second Vatican Council. The Constitution on Divine Revelation opens with the words, 'Hearing the Word of God with reverence and proclaiming it with faith ...' (DV, 1). As the Council's new characterisation of the Church, *Dei Verbum* reshapes the life and ministry of those who serve the People of God. This reflection on scripture and priesthood will draw on both personal experience and ecclesial identity. I will seek to outline some of the key developments flowing from *Dei Verbum*, and their impact on the experience of priesthood in the intervening years.

Where have we come from? The impact of Dei Verbum

Dei Verbum marked a significant change in the Catholic Church's engagement with the Word of God. It was one of the last of the conciliar documents to be approved, in December 1965, so perhaps it stands as an expression of the Council's mature thoughts on the nature of Church, of revelation, of ministry and engagement with the world. The Council represented the moment when several developments in Catholic life – theological *ressourcement*, that is, a return to origins of Tradition, the liturgical reform, the biblical movement and ecumenical engagement – moved centre-stage.[1] Both the liturgical and the biblical movements were well under way when the Council convened, but its deliberations and decisions placed these movements at the centre of Catholic life. And these changes created a new context and form for priestly ministry at the heart of the Church. To what extent, and how successfully, has the initial formation of priests changed in response to these developments? And how has ongoing formation enabled priests to explore and grow in their new roles and in the new forms of ministry that have emerged? To answer these questions, we need to explore some of the key developments that *Dei Verbum* and other conciliar documents introduced.[2]

A key aim of the Council was to place the Word of God at the heart of Catholic parish life. This manifested itself in the major liturgical reforms which went hand-in-hand with this biblical renewal. The prominence given to the Table of the Word, alongside the Table of the Sacrament, placed new demands on the priest to share the Word of God with the people. For example, every celebration was to include the reading of scripture, with the attendant opportunity for preaching. Not only was the priest the dispenser of sacraments, he becomes the proclaimer of the Word of God. For the celebration of the Eucharist, a new lectionary provided a greater range of readings over a cycle of three years (in the case of the Sunday lectionary). The wealth and riches of the new lectionary have enabled the Catholic community to encounter scripture in a new way. But while these reforms have greatly improved the opportunities for a growing knowledge and engagement with scripture, one could add that the wealth of readings has also had drawbacks. The provision of three readings for Sunday Masses has led to confusion about the focus or theme of the day, with perfunctory attention to or even disengagement from one or more of the texts (particularly the second reading, often taken from the letters of Paul). Have we moved from a previous state of too little exposure to scripture to a point where we are sated and dulled? Undoubtedly, as priests we need ongoing formation in how best to interpret and present the scriptures today.

Another interesting area of development after the Council lay in the use of scripture in catechetics.[3] The older form of catechesis based on the question-and-answer format of the Catechism quickly gave way to a new kerygmatic form of catechesis which placed an encounter with the scriptures, especially the gospels, at the heart of the learning experience. Yet that model of catechesis gave way to an experientially-based form of catechesis which began, not with the biblical text, but with the experiences and questions of the contemporary child or adult in their search for meaning in life. One wonders whether the replacement of the kerygmatic model of catechesis was in some way linked to the quality of formation of priests and people in their engagement with scripture.

Where are we now? Some personal reflections

In both areas, we see that the training of priests (and laypeople) to dialogue with the Word of God may have been an important factor in the success or otherwise of the conciliar reforms. Following the Council, there was an explosion of interest in biblical study, and Catholic scholars quickly engaged with that interest. Those scholars had been given a 'green light' by *Dei Verbum* to make use of modern scientific methods to study the Bible, particularly to make use of the historical-critical methods. From the 1960s, Catholic exegetes engaged increasingly with wider scholarship. And they also contributed to the popularisation of the results of that scholarly work for the Catholic community. The results of historical criticism found their way into seminary programmes of formation so that priests could use contemporary scholarship to inform and shape their preaching and pastoral care.

Dei Verbum explicitly states that:

> ... all the clergy must hold fast to the sacred scriptures through diligent sacred reading and careful study, especially the priests of Christ and others, such as deacons and catechists who are legitimately active in the ministry of the word. This is to be done so that none of them will become 'an empty preacher of the word of God outwardly, who is not a listener to it inwardly'. (25)

My experience of seminary formation, two decades after the Council, supports the commonly held view that training in biblical studies had advanced significantly in those intervening years. Our teachers had benefited from advanced training in the historical-critical method not only in Catholic universities but also in Protestant and secular institutes. The fruits of historical-critical studies were being shared with seminary students in a curriculum with greater space given to the study of the Bible. But the results were patchy. Developments in biblical studies did not always impact on other aspects of the seminary curriculum. There was certainly a stronger emphasis on the need for homiletic preparation that was biblically based: priests were expected to deliver 'homilies', rather than sermons, that explained the scriptures within the context of the Church's faith (SC, 51 and 52), as *Dei Verbum* stressed that the scriptures should nourish preaching (DV, 21). But it was rare for those two strands of seminary education – biblical studies and homiletics – to integrate and deliver a coherent curriculum. The academic study of scripture and its spiritual and pastoral application often remained separate entities.

While attending the Pontifical Biblical Institute in Rome, the observations of one professor, Fr Luis Alonso Schökel, gave me an insight into this separation that finds its roots in the text of *Dei Verbum* itself.[4] At the time of the Council, the prevailing focus of scientific biblical study was to reconstruct what the original author intended to say in the biblical text. When the Council gave its approval to such studies, it was seen to support historical critical work. However, the text of *Dei Verbum*, 12, is much more subtle:

> So that the interpreter of Sacred Scripture may understand what God wanted to communicate to us, he must conscientiously investigate what the hagiographers really wanted to express <u>and</u> God pleased to manifest by their words.[5]

That little 'et' has often been overlooked in the translations. For example, in the Flannery edition of Vatican documents[6] it is ignored, so that the latter phrase is presented as an explanation or further elaboration of the former. In other words, interpretation was limited to 'what the author intended' by equating this with the divine intention. As Alonso Schökel pointed out, the conciliar text opened the door to a wider sense of Catholic hermeneutics – not only to author-hermeneutics but also to text-hermeneutics; not only to academic study but also to spiritual reading of scripture.

I was therefore not surprised to see the debates within Catholic biblical scholarship that were beginning during my studies in Rome. There was an increasing desire to widen the scope of exegesis to include literary methods and other contextual approaches. There were well-publicised challenges to the monopoly of the historical-critical method.[7] There was a growing debate about what is truly Catholic about biblical studies.[8] Often portrayed as a rejection of historical studies, the staple diet of seminary education at that time, it was nothing of the sort. Rather, as the Pontifical Biblical Commission (PBC) demonstrated in its 1996 survey, 'The Interpretation of the Bible in the Church', the historical critical method holds a primacy among a range of methods and approaches. This document goes further to locate Catholic biblical studies at the service of the appropriation of the Word of God by the believing community. Citing principles from *Dei Verbum*, the PBC document highlights the process of 'actualisation' of scripture, by which new circumstances and contexts can lead to new interpretations of familiar biblical passages (4.a.1). The document indicates that examples of such 're-readings' can be found within the biblical tradition itself, and goes on to locate contemporary re-reading within the living Tradition of the Church.

What is emerging within Catholic biblical scholarship is a new appreciation of the richness of the hermeneutical principles outlined in *Dei Verbum*. Rightly, following the Council, the Church had to come to terms with the inclusion of modern scientific biblical study – and for some time, it focused strongly on that aspect in its formation and teaching programmes. Having established such biblical study, it is time for the Church to retrieve the other half of the hermeneutical principle – what God pleased to make manifest in the authors' words – and once again to integrate academic and faith orientations in our study of scripture. In practical terms, this means that in the ongoing education of priests, there needs to be a catholic openness to the wide range of scholarly methods (historical-critical, literary and contextual), to the notion of reading within living faith traditions, and a willingness to retrieve ancient insights for earlier times. And this study must be orientated towards the actualisation of the biblical text, allowing it to speak to us in our current locations.

Where are we going? Some suggestions for priestly formation in scripture

Clearly, initial and ongoing formation of clergy needs to take account of this renewed balance between academic and spiritual readings of scripture. How is this to be achieved? I would like to end this essay with some reflections drawn from my own experiences.

Catholics, and in particular priests, operate in a cultural context that is shaped by the Bible – even if we are not always conscious of that fact. At one level, those of us who are priests are very conscious of the role of scripture in our lives as we pray the Divine Office and celebrate the Eucharist and other sacraments. We are constantly reading the biblical texts and are called to help others understand and pray them. But at another level, we are unconscious of the extent to which the Bible shapes our existence. This, I suggest, in part explains the resistance to the new translation of the Missal and attempts to make more explicit the scriptural texture of its prayers. Have we really grasped the biblical warp and weave of our ecclesial language and imagery? Are we more comfortable with our own words than with the Word of God as the source of our speech and imaginations? If we are to be truly ministers of the Word, we need to accept that Word into our inner being. We need to be able to voice the Word, not merely repeat the formularies, with confidence that they are the very ground of our imaginings. Whether it is in a homily or in the quiet word of comfort at the sickbed, God's people seek to hear God's word – not just our own.

The reforms of Vatican II sought to ensure that as we celebrate today, we listen to a biblical text. We are agreed, at some level, that we should attend to what it says. We look to this Word, in partnership with the celebration of sacrament, to communicate 'life in abundance' (cf. Jn 20:31). But how will this 'life' flow from scripture and reach into the lives of those listening to it, if it does not flow through someone who has already received it? For St Paul, this was the real credential of the preacher (cf. Rm 10:14-15). The homilist is someone who has received life and is trying to give it away. In a perceptive article about the relationship between scripture and pastoral care, John Shea argues that Christian pastoral care 'begins from an interior space where we gratefully receive abundant life and flows from that space with creativity, freedom and perseverance into the lives of others'.[9] He goes on to describe pastoral care as an interpersonal activity in which one person holds onto a biblically inspired consciousness and invites the other to enter into that space. For this to happen, the priest must allow the text to structure his consciousness so that action flows from that inner wisdom.

Shea offers the story from Chapter 13 of John's gospel as a model. This story of the Last Supper opens with a description of Jesus' self-awareness, of his centred existence in relation to the Father; 'knowing that the Father had given all things into his hands, and that he had come from God and was going to God' (Jn 13:3). All the action of Jesus washing the feet of his disciples flows from that knowledge, that inner wisdom. Jesus expresses himself in these focused acts of care and service. In that moment, incarnation takes on a particular form: the Word becomes flesh. The Truth is no longer a concept but a form of activity. Pastoral care is likewise an incarnational activity in which the wisdom of the biblical text becomes the wisdom of the person:

> Be doers of the word, and not merely hearers who deceive themselves. For if any are hearers of the word and not doers, they are like those who look at themselves in a mirror; for they look at themselves and, on going away, immediately forget what they are like. For those who look into the perfect law, the law of liberty, and persevere, being not hearers who forget but doers who act – they will be blessed in their doing. (Jas 1:22-25)

The challenge here is to allow texts of the Bible to 'massage our minds'. When meditating on scripture, I make use of a version of *lectio divina*, the classic formulation of prayerful reading of scriptures within the Church. There are many guides and discussions of this technique: evidence of both its enduring effectiveness and its adaptability to individual circumstances. At heart, *lectio divina* combines prayer and study, attention to the text and to one's life situation. I am often asked which texts are most suitable – and I have no answer for that question. In principle, each and every passage of scripture, as God's word to his people, is potentially a source of inspiration and guidance. But I would gravitate towards the gospels as an entry point into the reading of scripture. In doing so I am conscious of two guiding matters: first, the prominence of gospel passages in our daily lives as priests, and second, the injunction of Church tradition since the time of Irenaeus of Lyons, that, for his followers, Christ is the key to unlocking all of scripture.

I try always to bring together study and prayer. Study without prayer can lead to a theology that is dry and stale, the sort of engagement with scripture that has frankly turned many people, lay and clergy, away from the Word of God. Prayer without study can lead to a biblical fundamentalism, a piety in which my personal preferences are unchallenged by the text. I am a biblical scholar so one can complain that it is easy for me to delight in scholarly commentaries. That is true, but often my study starts with a slow and careful reading of the text to detect its nuances and textures – for that, a careful eye and ear, a comfortable pencil and wide margins in one's Bible are sufficient.

Careful study with the help of guides will not take me all the way. Ultimately, the text is speaking to me, challenging my resistance to change and coaxing me to journey further with Christ. I cannot surrender this personal dimension to a higher authority or greater knowledge. I must engage myself, in prayer, with the text I am reading.

I could address at this point the objection that my reading becomes something of importance for me alone. Does it help me break open the Word for the congregation? The answer to that question is both yes and no. The negative answer is that I am not reading for a functional or ministerial goal – I am reading for my personal engagement with the Lord. But it is also correct that my engagement hopefully makes me a channel of grace for those who listen to me. This can happen at two levels: while they are my own circumstances, I share similar questions and needs with those of the congregation; but more importantly (and I would say, more often), I am placing myself at the disposal of the Lord who will speak through my openness to the Word to those willing to hear his voice.

Ultimately, the text is both a mirror in which I see my image maturing and developing. It is also a window through which I see the image of Jesus Christ. With continuous attention and reflection, I hope that those two images come to coalesce as one, as I put on Christ, the One who loved me and gave his life for me (cf. Gal 3:27, 2:20). This takes grace and perseverance. But is that not the message of the parable of the seed sown secretly? There is much work on our part, but ultimately the Word grows in a way we know not. Our priestly role is to be both the fruitful ground and the sower of the seed, open to the gift and ready to labour in the fields of the Lord.

Notes

1. A useful survey of these developments can be found in John W. O'Malley, *What Happened at Vatican II* (Cambridge MA: Belknap Press, 2008).
2. A useful survey of *Dei Verbum* and its impact has been provided by Ronald D. Witherup, *Scripture: Dei Verbum (Rediscovering Vatican II)*, (Mahwah, NJ: Paulist Press, 2006).
3. The following paragraph quickly summarises the Irish experience since the 1960s.
4. For a more detailed discussion of the following points, see the published version of Alonso Schökel's lectures in L. Alonso Schökel, *A Manual of Hermeneutics*, Biblical Seminar, 54 (Sheffield: Sheffield Academic Press, 1998), 37–8.
5. 'Interpretes Sacrae Scripturae, ut perscipiat, quid Ipse nobiscum communicare voluerit, attende investigare debet quid hagiographi reapse significare intenderint et eorum verbis manifestare Deo placuerit' (DV, 12).
6. A. Flannery (ed.), *Vatican II: The Conciliar and Post-Conciliar Documents* (Northport, NY: Costello Publishing Co., 1984), 757.
7. A famous event was the well-publicised lecture of Cardinal Joseph Ratzinger delivered in New York in January 1988, entitled 'Biblical Interpretation in Crisis', in which he criticised some of the practice of historical critical studies. However, in interviews at the same time, he gave a much-nuanced clarification. And he would later write the preface to the PBC's 'Interpretation of the Bible in the Church' (1996).
8. Among American Catholic biblical scholars, the address of Luke Timothy Johnson at the 1997 AGM of the Catholic Biblical Association, entitled 'What's Catholic about Catholic Biblical Scholarship', precipitated a debate that rumbles on to the present.
9. John Shea, 'Persevering in the Perfect Law of Liberty: Scriptural Resources for Pastoral Care', *Scripture as the Soul of Theology*, E. J. Mahoney, ed. (Collegeville, MN: Liturgical Press, 2005), 68.

181

Communicating the Church's Moral Teaching

JOHN SHERRINGTON

Jesus the Good Shepherd offers the gift of life and love in abundance to those who listen to his voice: 'I came that they may have life, and have it abundantly' (Jn 10:10b). Jesus' proclamation offers an invitation to follow a path that leads to human flourishing, growth in holiness, friendship with God and neighbour and ultimately the promise of eternal life. In response to the invitation of Christ, 'Come follow me', the Christian moral life is an invitation to live in conformity with the Will of God and to be transformed to walk in newness of life:

> I appeal to you therefore, brethren, by the mercies of God, to present your bodies as a living sacrifice, holy and acceptable to God, which is your spiritual worship. Do not be conformed to this world, but be transformed by the renewing of your minds, so that you may discern what is the will of God – what is good and acceptable and perfect. (Rm 12:1-2)

The priest shepherds people towards human flourishing through his witness to the Christian life, his preaching and teaching, and through his sacramental ministry. It is a joyful and fulfilling task, but one made somewhat difficult and challenging today because of the complex and conflicting visions of the moral life in contemporary society.

The difficulty of communicating the truth

At the outset, it has to be acknowledged that the task of presenting the Church's moral teaching has been damaged by the revelation of sexual abuse of children by a minority of clergy and religious, and by the reality that cases were sometimes mishandled by bishops and superiors. This has seriously damaged the credibility of the Church and impaired its ability to speak on matters of personal morality.

However, the task of presenting the Church's moral teaching and facilitating its reception is also difficult because of the contemporary emphasis on the authority of personal experience. Very often the focus today is on personal moral values based solely on life experience and feelings about what is right, rather than upon principled positions. The TV soaps, for instance, show just how dominant differing and subjective moral value systems are in contemporary society.

In contrast to these subjective and emotivist approaches, the Church's teaching can help people to rediscover a foundation for life and relationships, characterised by stability and justice, and built upon an understanding of the goodness of human sexuality, the meaning of the body, and of respect and love.

The recent intense debate about the meaning of marriage in the context of the British government's intention to legislate for same-sex marriage is an interesting case in point. In this debate, the Catholic Church in Great Britain faced the challenge of presenting to the wider society the meaning of marriage as a permanent commitment of a man and a woman for the good of the spouses and for the procreation and education of children within marriage.

In particular, we were concerned to emphasise the role of the family in promoting the common good as well as the complementarity of the sexes. There is a real danger that the recognition of same-sex unions as marriages will transform, and diminish, the meaning of marriage for everyone over time.

In general terms, the debate has shown how it is difficult to be heard in the media and how critical voices can be instantly dismissed. In this case, it was very hard to put forward the Church's nuanced position on marriage without being branded homophobic. The Catholic Church in England and Wales worked hard not to focus the discussion on homosexuality and constantly to affirm the dignity of persons who are homosexual while at the same time arguing for the vital distinction between marriage and other forms of legal contract such as civil partnerships.

Fundamentally, underpinning the debate are two different understandings of human nature and of the basis for human flourishing and the common good. The Church's teaching is rooted in the natural law, which reveals what it is to be human. In contrast, many of those in the debate who have been proposing legislation for same-sex marriage begin with a more existentialist understanding of freedom, which is also essentially relativist.

These different starting points and presuppositions dominate much of the moral debate, whether concerning abortion, euthanasia or marriage. Some approaches deny that there is an objective moral law which is accessible to reason and which provides some absolute principles that cannot be changed. These different approaches are highlighted in Pope John Paul II's encyclical *Veritatis Splendor* (1993), which helps illuminate the differences at the heart of moral debates because of moral theories that separate truth and freedom from one another.[1]

Overcoming hesitancy to communicate truth

In this complex moral context, the priest may be hesitant to present the Church's teaching and fearful of the consequences. However, he is called to lead his people along the path of truth by helping them deepen their moral response through prayer, conversion and following Christ the Teacher, while listening to the promptings of the Holy Spirit.

The natural law enables us to know the good that we are to do and the evil we are to avoid. It leads us to understand that human life is to be protected, that there is a natural tendency to marriage and the education of children and towards living together in a just society.

The gospel builds upon these foundations: the capacity to act for the good with reason and freedom is a gift given to us by God. Human reasoning about what is good is fallible because of the effects of original sin. However, revelation is God's gift to help perfect our understanding of the natural law. The Church in its teaching gives further clarity in terms of norms and principles about how the natural law and revelation provide the foundations for doing the truth in love. To do the will of God requires doing the truth in love and growing in freedom to live this truth. There are various dimensions to growth in the moral life: developing the life of the virtues, growing in the capacity to love, putting on the beatitudes as fundamental attitudes to life and internalising the teaching of the Church through educating conscience.

Through our choices we become particular people, i.e. we develop our character. People recognise this when they say, 'she is a very loving person' or 'he is just'. One's character reveals an ethical identity that is shaped and formed by a narrative identity. The implication is that in order to understand why someone acts in a particular way, we need to examine the stories that shape their moral imagination. A starting point for growth in the moral life is to examine the various narratives that shape identity: the narratives of family, school, church, and the world of social media – being a human person, a Christian, and a Catholic. People receive many messages from different sources today, some of which complement one another, others that compete. The priest in his ministry can help people examine these stories (through teaching and adult formation) and to discern in the light of the gospel where the Holy Spirit is leading them to deepen their vocation to holiness and the perfection of charity (cf. VS, 19).

The importance of witness

The priest's personal life, if it witnesses to the gospel, is an important communication about the moral life in and of itself. Therefore, integrity needs to be at the core of faithful priestly ministry. People recognise and are inspired by a priest who prays, who is available for service, and whose life is rooted and shaped by the Gospel of Christ and his Church. In Vatican II's Decree on the Life and Ministry of Priests (*Presbyterorum Ordinis*), there is the call for priests and bishops to live a simple lifestyle characterised by voluntary poverty, which will witness to their calling to service and love:

> Led by the Spirit of the Lord, who anointed the Saviour and sent him to evangelise the poor, priests, therefore, and also bishops, should avoid everything which in any way could turn the poor away. Before the other followers of Christ, let priests set aside every appearance of vanity in their possessions. Let them arrange their homes so that they might not appear unapproachable to anyone, lest anyone, even the most humble, fear to visit them. (17)

The priest's prayer life, moral living, detachment from material goods, focus on community and the common good, are all important forms of teaching with regard to the moral life. Priests are also encouraged to pray for the courage to speak the truth in love and for the virtues of temperance and prudence, witnessed effectively through a life characterised by simplicity and freedom in the service of the gospel. In time, the power of this witness may restore trust in the Church and her ministers where this has been lost by the misdeeds of a few.

Growth in the virtuous life

The priest is encouraged to foster the life of the virtues as part of the communication of moral teaching. The virtues are those ethical dispositions that help shape the moral life and enable people to act well and easily for the good in complex moral situations. It is therefore worth considering how the priest himself measures up in terms of the cardinal virtues of prudence, justice, temperance and fortitude, as well as the theological virtues of charity or love.

The virtues help us to develop as persons and build character. Some examples illustrate the role of the virtues in the ethical life. Prudence enables people to choose what is right and good based on reason and will. People exercise the virtue of prudence when, for example, they consider the various options of care that an elderly relative needs: what does the person want? Is it safe to stay at home? How is the best care to be provided? What are the other duties that must be considered in making the choice? The virtue of temperance tempers desires, whether for the new gadget, excessive consumption or immoral pleasure. Chastity is part of the virtue of temperance and assists right and appropriate choices about sexual desires as part of one's life-commitments. Temperance moderates the use of the limited goods of the earth for oneself and leads to good stewardship.

Justice renders what is due to others and ensures that trading transactions are just and respectful of persons. There are many implications for purchase and sales, land and property, and to ensure that the common good is fostered and care provided for the poor and vulnerable. This latter virtue reminds us that we are not created simply as a set of individuals but persons called to live in community with one another and to cultivate relationships of solidarity and love because we are created in the image of God who is a Trinity of Persons. While private property is good and useful for efficient use of resources, the Church teaches that God has given the goods of the earth to all people. In a society where many people tend to be individualists and perhaps pay insufficient attention to the needs of the poor, an important aspect of moral teaching of the Church concerns the Church's social teaching and its implications for the virtue of solidarity, justice and outreach towards refugees and migrants as well as solicitude for those on the margins of society. Courage enables people to act for the good in difficult circumstances.

Putting on the mind of Christ

The priest is called to help his people put on the mind of disciples in light of the teaching of Jesus. For most people, their opportunity to see or hear the priest will be at Mass. Through the homily the priest breaks open the word of God to help people understand the call of discipleship, for example, the meaning of the Beatitudes, the implications of the commandment of love, and the call to forgiveness not seven times but seventy-seven times. By linking the pastoral situations of the people with the word of God, the priest can communicate important moral truths which offer a critique of different situations and which deepen faith in action. He will relate the commandment of love and the call to forgiveness, justice and taking up the cross, to everyday life. For some people, the Christian moral life will demand martyrdom for the sake of the truth (e.g. protecting human life and the impossibility of working in some areas where this is threatened). The Mass itself teaches that we gather to be nourished by the Word of God and the Body and Blood of Christ in order to be sent out as the Body of Christ in service in the world. The words of dismissal call for the imitation of Jesus who washed his disciples' feet and gave an example to be followed.

The law of the gospel is taught by Christ and it is also the grace of the Holy Spirit. Through the commandment to love and the Sermon on the Mount it teaches what must be done (cf. CCC, 1966). The New Law can be summed up in terms of 'love one another as he has loved us' (Jn 15:12, 13:34). The Holy Spirit and the life of prayer inspire the decision about what is to be done in the here-and-now, building upon the moral foundations of the natural law, revelation and the teaching of the Church. The priest has a particular ministry in guiding people to educate their conscience in order to make before God their prudential judgements in particular situations.

The priest has a duty to present the Church's teaching faithfully and accurately. The *Catechism of the Catholic Church* presents a summary of the Church's teaching and is a valuable starting point to help people understand this teaching. When people struggle with a particular teaching, the priest has the task of helping them to understand it more fully so that they may give assent and follow it in their lives. The priest will help them with making prudential judgements about what is right to do in a particular situation when there are a variety of options to be considered. It will be through prayer that the final judgment of conscience becomes known deeply within the heart.

Celebrating God's forgiveness

Celebration of the sacrament of penance and reconciliation is important in the life of the priest and helps him acknowledge more deeply that he is weak and in need of mercy. It can also help him to grow in compassion towards his people. The one who recognises weakness, sin and forgiveness can minister more effectively to others and help them experience the freedom that comes from the healing ministry of Christ. The priest provides pastoral support and encouragement to the believer who is trying to grow in virtue and live a life which is more truthful and loving. To answer the question of the rich young man about the way that leads to eternal life, Blessed Pope John Paul II writes, 'Jesus, as a patient and sensitive teacher, answers the young man by taking him, as it were, by the hand, and leading him step by step to the full truth' (*Veritatis Splendor*, 8). This provides a model for priests. It urges them to help people with patience and sensitivity and so lead them step by step to the full truth. Such a method requires time and careful communication so that what is heard can be understood and assimilated. The pope gives us a profound insight into this approach and the tension, which the priest, following the example of Jesus the Good Shepherd, will need to hold, in being faithful to the truth and sensitive to the disciple:

> Still, a clear and forceful presentation of moral truth can never be separated from a profound and heartfelt respect, born of that patient and trusting love which man always needs along his moral journey, a journey frequently wearisome on account of difficulties, weakness and painful situations. The Church can never renounce 'the principle of truth and consistency, whereby she does not agree to call good evil and evil good'; she must always be careful not to break the bruised reed or to quench the dimly burning wick (cf. Is 42:3). (VS, 95)

People struggle with many burdens in the moral life because of complex situations. Their faith is often fragile and may be likened to the dimly burning wick of a candle. It is important that the approach of the priest does not snuff it out. Others may be like bruised reeds that may be broken by a harsh or ill-timed word. While the priest is always called to proclaim faithfully the teaching of the Church, the method and timing with which he does this is a subject for discernment and prudential judgement. The authentic teacher will be able to teach appropriately on all matters of morality with keen awareness of the needs of his people. The priest is called always to speak the truth and never to compromise it but at the same time to encourage, support and show mercy where there is weakness and frailty.

By witness, word and sacrament, the priest communicates the Church's teaching about the moral life. As a disciple, he is a pilgrim on a personal spiritual journey. An awareness in his own life of the necessity of God's grace and the need of God's mercy will enable the priest to identify with his people and help them on their path to holiness. The verse printed at the head of the invitatory psalm in the breviary can inspire priests on a daily basis: 'Every day, as long as this "today" lasts, keep encouraging one another' (Heb 3:13).

Note

1. Pope John Paul II, *Veritatis Splendor* (1993), 32.

The Ecumenical Imperative

PATRICK FINTAN LYONS

The movement promoting the unity of all Christians is part of the programme of renewal of the Catholic Church set in motion by the Second Vatican Council. In fact, the first document issued by the Council, the Constitution on the Liturgy mandating liturgical renewal, stated in its opening paragraph that the intentions of the Council included encouraging 'whatever can promote the union of all who believe in Christ' (*Sacrosanctum Concilium* [SC], 1).

The Vatican Council's principles of Catholic ecumenism

Re-reading the Council's Decree on Ecumenism over fifty years later, it becomes clear how tentative and yet courageous the Council Fathers were in setting out principles for the practice of ecumenism. In the light of theological perceptions then emerging on the one hand, and received wisdom and established norms on the other, it became obvious that there was going to be a clash of principles, and this fact was honestly faced. The eventual decree noted:

> [P]rayers in common are certainly a very effective means of petitioning for the grace of unity, and they are a genuine expression of the ties which still bind Catholics to their separated brethren ... Yet worship in common (*communicatio in sacris*) is not to be considered as a means to be used indiscriminately for the restoration of unity among Christians.

Because unity should be a distinctive mark of the worshipping community and, equally importantly, worship is a means of grace, the dilemma could be further sharpened thus: 'The expression of unity very generally forbids common worship. Grace to be obtained sometimes commends it' (*Unitatis Redintegratio* [UR], 8). In this approach, experience and principle were being set in tension with one another and the Council Fathers seem to have thought that principle should 'generally' win rather than the grace 'sometimes' received.

In the years since the Council, the approach of the Catholic Church has retained a certain tension between principle and practice. This has been the case especially at the highest level, while practice at the local, pastoral level has been reasonably extensive but usually without raising questions of theological principle.

Ecumenism and the Holy See

There have been interactions between the Holy See and other Christian bodies both by engagement in a large-scale programme of bilateral dialogues (dialogues unfortunately little known to the faithful at large) and in meetings between the pope and various dignitaries. It was a significant gesture that Pope Benedict XVI invited Archbishop Rowan Williams to address the Synod of Bishops on the New Evangelisation in October 2012, despite previous interventions on his part, on Anglican Orders for example, and the ecclesial status of other denominations, which had caused disquiet in ecumenical circles, when he was Prefect of the Congregation for the Doctrine of the Faith.[1] The relationship with the Anglican Communion has had difficult phases, principally because of the ordination of women and more recently the acceptance in some areas of homosexual unions among the clergy. This represents a change from the immediate post-Council period as at that time Pope Paul was willing to have the question of Anglican Orders re-opened 'in a broader context than the historical'. In a remarkable gesture, he placed his episcopal ring (from his days in Milan) on the hand of Archbishop Michael Ramsey of Canterbury at St Paul's Basilica, Rome, on 24 March 1966, in effect recognising his episcopal status.[2]

Since that time there have been some reverses, but the encyclical of Pope John Paul II in 1995, *Ut Unum Sint* [UUS], reasserted official commitment to the ecumenical movement, describing it as an imperative. The prayer of Christ, which gave the document its title, becomes, the pope said, 'an imperative to leave behind our divisions in order to seek and re-establish unity' (UUS, 65). Further on he said:

> A Christian community which believes in Christ and desires, with gospel fervour, the salvation of mankind can hardly be closed to the promptings of the Holy Spirit, who leads all Christians towards full and visible unity. Here an imperative of charity is in question, an imperative which admits of no exception. (UUS, 99)

Ecumenism at local level

Within a short time after the end of the Vatican Council in 1965, Catholics in general had taken to heart the teaching set out in the decree on ecumenism. People in the parishes in Ireland seemed to grasp readily that its time had come. This in itself might be regarded as surprising, because only a short time before that the denominations seemed closed off from one another.

There seems to have been an instinct for ecumenical initiatives at grassroots level; a commentator at the time remarked that the walls of separation did not seem to reach to the ground. Initial moves were easy enough; neighbourliness provided motivation where theological principles had not yet been absorbed. But as in a gardening project where clearing the ground is relatively easy but the going becomes harder as digging goes deeper, so too the initial comings together for prayer on special occasions, such as the Week of Prayer for Christian Unity, gave way to hesitation about moves towards what would be in effect some recognition of the churchly reality of 'the other'.

Here, theological principles and practical norms for implementing them were important. The principles had been set out in the Decree on Ecumenism but also in the Constitution on the Church, both of which had been published on the same day in

1964.[3] A provisional Directory on Ecumenism appeared in 1967, giving necessary guidelines to bishops and clergy enabling them to respond to what had become a real pastoral need in parish life. A more comprehensive Directory for the Application of Principles and Norms on Ecumenism (hereafter Directory) came in 1993, much of its practical guidance having already been set out in the new *Code of Canon Law* in 1983. In 1970, *Matrimonia Mixta*, on the regulations governing marriages between Catholics and non-Catholics, was published and was noteworthy in giving recognition to the rights of conscience of the non-Catholic party.

The demography of the various non-Roman Catholic populations in Ireland obviously affects the ecumenical opportunities and challenges for the Catholic Church. So too do attitudes towards ecumenical relations. Quite a number of evangelical and non-denominational communities have appeared in recent years, concentrating on their own growth and inclined to be dismissive of the traditional denominations.[4] In the major populations centres where other Christian communities are more in evidence, officials and commissions charged with the task of promoting ecumenical relations in the various dioceses obviously have well-defined responsibilities and parish clergy can call on these resources to plan for events such as the Week of Prayer for Christian Unity in January. In recent years the observance of this week of prayer has tended to be concentrated into one celebration involving Church leaders, with little attention being paid to it in individual parishes. This is the inevitable outcome of the lack of shared prayer services at various times through the year at parish level, and this in turn comes from the fact that at central level, that of the diocese, there are no regular events of this kind. This lack of ecumenical activity points in fact to a problem relating to the Church's own internal renewal, in the sphere of liturgy.

Liturgical renewal and ecumenism

It is now nearly fifty years since the Constitution on the Liturgy decreed that: 'Pastors should see to it that the principal hours, especially Vespers, are celebrated in common in Church on

Sundays and on the more solemn feasts' (SC, 100). That such celebrations are extremely rare is due to various factors but the most important one is surely a lack of conviction of the importance of so doing, this in turn being due to a defective understanding of the nature and full scope of liturgy and unfamiliarity with liturgical history. It would certainly come as a surprise to many to learn that in the early centuries of the Church, when Mass was not celebrated daily, many of the most noted of the Church Fathers laid great stress on the obligation of the faithful to attend the daily Liturgy of the Hours.[5]

Both liturgical renewal in the Catholic Church and the ecumenical cause could be advanced by the introduction of shared celebration of the Liturgy of the Hours. But it must be remembered that in the pattern of public prayer in the early centuries, the bishop had a crucial role. The bishop was not only the celebrant of the Eucharist but the leader also around whom the praying community gathered, morning and evening. If public prayer is to return to its central role in the life of the community, that same leadership will be needed and it is for the bishop to provide it, both personally in his cathedral and through his delegates in the parishes. If this is a major challenge in the Catholic context, it is hardly less demanding for the other traditions.

If, for example, the cathedrals of the Catholic and Church of Ireland dioceses are in the same town and if the two bishops were to preside regularly at one of the Hours, each in his own cathedral, the anomaly of disunity would be more evident than it is now. Both the attractiveness and the urgency of praying together would become more compelling.

Admittedly, there is much that is hypothetical in such considerations and they leave out of account the need to involve the non-episcopal traditions in any plans for shared worship. Nonetheless, in present circumstances, where there are adjoining communities showing ecumenical awareness, it should be possible to have a combined celebration of Sunday Vespers regularly.

Sacramental sharing — the Eucharist

People in parishes, even those with strong ecumenical aspirations, tend to think of sharing only in terms of Eucharist. However, this could change if people were more familiar with the communal celebration of the Liturgy of the Hours. Sound theological principles and official regulations in the 1993 Directory, echoed in the British and Irish Episcopal Conferences' document of 1998, *One Bread, One Body* (OBOB), make it clear that eucharistic sharing – in effect eucharistic hospitality to non-Catholics – 'can only be by way of exception' (OBOB, 101), to take account of the fact that in theological tradition the Eucharist is the 'sign of unity and the bond of charity'. The ecumenical problem is that of the lack of unity, the as yet unachieved reconciliation between the various communities.

The regulations for eucharistic hospitality, that is, admission of non-Catholics to Holy Communion, set out in the various documents, can be briefly summarised: 'Except when there is a danger of death, it is for the diocesan bishop or those delegated by him to judge whether there is a grave and pressing need' (OBOB, 113) on the part of a non-Catholic Christian requesting sacraments (Eucharist, Penance, Sacrament of the Sick). Four conditions must always be fulfilled: that the person be unable to approach a minister of his or her own community for the sacrament desired; that the person greatly desire to receive the sacrament and ask to receive it of his or her own initiative; that the person manifest Catholic faith in the sacrament desired; that the person be properly disposed (cf. *Code of Canon Law*, 844.4).

These regulations reflect the official view of current relationships between the Catholic Church and the other Christian denominations. However, there are groups within the churches who would hold that their relationship is at a greater level of reconciliation, a more advanced stage on the way to unity. The case for eucharistic sharing in order to recognise an advanced stage of reconciliation between ecclesial communities at least on occasion was argued by Michael Hurley SJ in a 1969 article and repeated in a book in 1998, 'on the basis of the traditional Catholic doctrine of reconciliation, penance, conversion.'[6] His case was built on an earlier chapter of his book which showed the priority of forgiveness, of generosity, in the whole process of reconciliation. What he had in mind would seem to be the situation of ecumenical groups within the institutional Churches rather than the institutions themselves. His approach was similar in many respects to that of Enda McDonagh, though the latter went further when in 1999 he appealed to the Churches as such to invite and encourage each other to celebrate the eucharist together as a sign of their continuing conversion to one another.[7] For both authors, taking the conversion or reconciliation dimension of the Eucharist seriously has the effect of relativising though not eliminating the 'continuing differences between the Churches concerning the complete understanding and sharing of the Eucharist.'[8]

However, the importance of shared non-sacramental liturgy should not be underestimated in regard to the conversion and reconciliation process. The spiritual, one might say the ecclesiological, effect of such shared celebration over an extended period could be expected to be profound as members of the different Churches gradually became accustomed to a shared liturgical ethos, one which would call for theological articulation and therefore prepare the way for theological agreement between the Churches. Such theology would be concerned first of all with defining liturgy itself – what the worshipping community is actually doing – and this would provide a way to approach together the hitherto controverted issues concerning the sacramental rites. And it is at the level of the various congregations that agreement in these matters is finally of critical importance and a necessary concomitant to the already existing agreements between commissions of experts. What is at issue here in fact is the process of reception of these agreements, something on which little progress has been reported so far in that mechanisms for the process are generally lacking. To engage in 'official' but non-sacramental worship together would seem one of the most useful mechanisms as well as being an attractive and accessible ecumenical strategy.

The ecumenical significance of Baptism and Marriage

The sacrament of Baptism offers special ecumenical possibilities.[9] It is the rite by which people become united with one another in Christ and at the same time divided by denominational affiliation. Everything to do with its celebration and its influence on the day-to-day living of the Christian life is of ecumenical importance.

While there is often reference to the fact that Baptism creates a certain degree of unity between Christians of the different communities and is the foundation on which all ecumenical efforts are built, little attention is paid to the ecumenical possibilities afforded by the liturgy of Baptism itself. One must be realistic about possibilities, however. In many Catholic parishes, there is still much to be done to make the celebration of Baptism (especially that of infants) a truly community event; very often, the celebration is seen very much as a family and private affair. Consequently the pastoral challenge is generally that of bringing it to the level of a truly parish celebration. But if Baptism were a truly community celebration and if the community itself were conscious of ecumenical ties, then the question of its ecumenical import and possibilities would arise much more naturally. Anglican and Protestant congregations are often more successful in bringing out the community dimension, with the rite in most cases including an explicit liturgical role for the community itself.

Where Baptism had been rescued from the tendency towards private celebration, ecumenically minded congregations could show a real interest in each other's baptismal celebrations, arranging even for participation of representatives having a witnessing role at each other's celebrations. Clearly, the special case of Baptism of the child of an interchurch couple offers special opportunities and these are in fact often availed of, though it is hardly fair to expect interchurch couples always to be in the forefront of the ecumenical movement.

There was a period in the 1970s when people involved in the Interchurch Families Associations in Britain and in Ireland promoted the idea of joint membership of two Churches for their newly baptised children. There has never been any corresponding formal registration and the Catholic Church's regulations hold that the rite (with appropriate minister) used in the Baptism decides the Church to which the child belongs. However, the website of the Association in Britain gives information on possible double registration of a Baptism where a Catholic priest administers the baptism in an Anglican church. But not all Catholic dioceses in Britain allow such an arrangement.[10]

The Directory does permit a baptised person who belongs to another Christian community to be admitted as a witness to the Baptism, but only together with a Catholic godparent. A Catholic may do the same for a person being baptised in another ecclesial community.[11]

Ecumenism and the other sacraments

The Directory also refers to situations in which non-Catholics might receive the sacraments of penance or anointing. The ecumenical issues here are interesting and complex. Anecdotal evidence is that the case of penance arises more frequently than anointing, and will be considered here briefly. The same conditions apply as in the case of the Eucharist and a question arises at once in relation to the reconciliation aspect of the sacrament, as distinct from the forgiveness of an individual's sins. The Directory considers the penitent as an individual Christian, without reference to denominational belonging, and allows that the person receives forgiveness of sins and so is reconciled to God. But what of the significance of reconciliation in relation to the Church? The most reasonable interpretation is that the person is reconciled to the Church as Mystical Body of Christ, the community of the baptised, through restoration of baptismal status. This does not imply reconciliation to the Catholic Church, in which the Church of Christ subsists, but it would seem reasonable to assert that reconciliation is achieved with the institutional expression of the baptismal life to which the person belongs.

Conclusion

The Catholic Church has been 'endowed with all the means of grace' (UR, 4) and has therefore greater responsibility than other Christian communities not to be 'closed to the promptings of the Holy Spirit, who leads all Christians towards full and visible unity' (UUS, 99). The movement promoting the unity of all Christians is part of the programme of renewal of the Catholic Church set in motion by the Second Vatican Council, which, from its first decree, encouraged 'whatever can promote the union of all who believe in Christ'.[12] The extension of the sacramental life to those who are not members of the Catholic Church focuses attention on what John Paul II described as 'the imperative of charity'. This situation calls for symbolic acts, patient ecumenical dialogue and pastoral action at all levels of responsibility in the Church.

Notes

1. In a document from the Congregation for the Doctrine of the Faith in 1998, it was stated that the bull *Apostolicae Curae* issued by Leo XIII in 1896 declaring Anglican Orders invalid was a definitively proposed Church teaching, one of 'the truths connected to revelation by historical necessity and which are to be held definitively, but are not able to be declared as divinely revealed' (*Doctrinal Commentary on the Concluding Formula of the* Professio Fidei, 11). The Declaration *Dominus Jesus* of 2000, also from the Congregation of the Doctrine of the Faith, stated that 'the ecclesial communities which have not preserved the valid Episcopate and the genuine and integral substance of the Eucharistic mystery, are not Churches in the proper sense' (DJ, 17).

2. See Peter Hebblethwaite, *Paul VI: The First Modern Pope* (London: Harper Collins Religious, 1993), 463–5.

3. The teaching on ecumenism in the latter document was to be interpreted, according to Pope Paul VI, in light of the former. Cf. Francis A. Sullivan SJ, *The Church We Believe In: One, Holy, Catholic and Apostolic* (Dublin: Gill & Macmillan, 1988), 25.

4. '[Evangelicalism] must present its own message and show that what it is offering is a genuine third way that is radically different from both traditional religion and from liberal, postmodern and largely secular thinking.' Seán Mullan, 'The Way Ahead', *Evangelicals in Ireland: An*

Introduction, Robert Dunlop, ed. (Dublin: Columba Press, 2004), 231.

5. Robert Taft SJ, *The Liturgy of the Hours in East and West* (Collegeville, MN: Liturgical Press, 1986), *passim*.

6. Michael Hurley SJ, 'The Sacrament of Unity. Intercommunion and Some Forgotten Truths', *The Way* 9 (1969), 107–17; *Christian Unity. An Ecumenical Second Spring?* (Dublin: Veritas, 1998), 139.

7. Enda McDonagh, 'Invite and Encourage – a millennial proposal for sharing the Eucharist', *The Furrow* (January 1999), 18–25.

8. Ibid., 23.

9. Cf. 'Baptism in Ecumenical Perspective', Chapter 7 of M. Hurley, *Christian Unity*, 115–31.

10. 'Some couples are also very keen for the Baptism to be registered in both their Churches. This is usually more difficult for the Roman Catholic priest, if he does not perform the actual Baptism, i.e. the pouring of the water and the saying of the baptismal formula. If the service takes place in the Anglican church building, he may be permitted to do this under Anglican ecumenical canons (if it is a Local Ecumenical Partnership under canon B44.4 (1) (e); if not, under canon B43 clause 9). He can then register the Baptism as the celebrant, and the Anglican priest who shares the service with him can register the Baptism because of the place. This will not be allowed in all Roman Catholic dioceses. What will be allowed is for the Anglican priest to take part in the Baptism in the Catholic church. Some Anglican priests have been willing to register the Baptism in this situation.' http://www.interchurchfamilies.org.uk/baptism.htm (accessed 19/2/2013).

11. Directory 98 (a).

12. *Sacrosanctum Concilium*, 1.

The Priesthood of All the Faithful

DONAL MURRAY

Most of us priests have lived through an extraordinary renewal of the Church. Like all renewals, we get used to it, we take it for granted and we become dissatisfied or frustrated because not all of our hopes have been fulfilled.

Those of us who remember the celebration of Mass in the 1950s and 1960s find it hard to think ourselves back into that era. At that time the parish priest of Greystones in County Wicklow was seen as avant garde; he celebrated what was called a Dialogue Mass, where the congregation actually spoke some of the Latin responses out loud. We now take for granted not just participation in responses, but the involvement of members of the congregation in readings and processions and prayers and singing; the use of vernacular languages has brought a whole new experience of liturgy.

At the same time, we have seen a declining participation in the liturgy, in the actual attendance at Mass, and in the reception of the sacraments of Reconciliation, Marriage and even Baptism.

It is important to face the reality of this decline. We need to ask why the hopes raised by the Council for a new, vigorous and evangelising Church are largely unfulfilled. Would a deeper and more wholehearted response to the vision of Vatican II have made a difference? Perhaps it is not too late.

Pope Benedict XVI stated the situation bluntly and pointed to the need to see things in greater depth:

> The Second Vatican Council rightly emphasised the active, full and fruitful participation of the entire People of God in the Eucharistic celebration. Certainly, the renewal carried out in these past decades has made considerable progress towards fulfilling the wishes of the Council Fathers. Yet ... it should be made clear that the word 'participation' does not refer to mere external activity during the celebration. In fact, the active participation called for by the Council must be understood in more substantial terms, on the basis of a greater awareness of the mystery being celebrated and its relationship to daily life.[1]

Greater awareness of the mystery

That mystery is the core and purpose of our existence. We learn about it, and about ourselves, through 'self-abandonment, in a continuous crescendo, into the hands of a love that seems to grow constantly because it has its origin in God'.[2]

The challenge of living, of preaching, of celebrating the mystery of faith today is to awaken and deepen in ourselves and in others an awareness of the love that has its origin in God. The heart of Christianity is found in meeting that love which is made visible in Jesus:

> Being Christian is not the result of an ethical choice or a lofty idea, but the encounter with an event, a person, which gives life a new horizon and a decisive direction. Saint John's Gospel describes that event in these words: 'God so loved the world that he gave his only Son, that whoever believes in him should ... have eternal life'.[3]

Our culture relentlessly pressurises us to manage the complexity of life today by putting things in slots. There is the family slot, the financial slot, the political slot, the recreational and sporting slot, the work slot, perhaps the slot for personal reflection and growth, and so on.

The secularised culture of today may be willing to accept that some people may also have a slot for faith, a God slot. But there can be no such thing as a 'God slot'. Anything that can be put into a slot cannot be God! God is all-knowing, all-powerful, in every time and place, in every atom of the universe. Faith is about another dimension, immeasurably deeper than all the rest, the meaning, origin and destiny of all the rest.

The great weakness of our culture is that it has no all-embracing vision. It therefore regards any claim that faith is about the meaning of the whole of existence as arrogant, if not absurd. It feels that faith should know its place and should not intrude into 'real life'.

The task of priests is to try to foster in others and in ourselves the awareness that, when we celebrate Mass, we are not just taking care of one of the many priorities of our lives. We are entering into the mystery of life itself and of the whole of creation.

Vatican II's Constitution on the Liturgy says:

> Although the sacred liturgy is above all things the worship of the divine Majesty, it likewise contains much instruction for the faithful. For in the liturgy God speaks to his people and Christ is still proclaiming his Gospel. And the people reply to God both by song and prayer.[4]

'Above all things', the liturgy is the worship of the divine Majesty. In other words, it is about the dimension which surpasses and gives meaning to everything else. Liturgy has to touch the real lives of people; it has to touch the deepest questions and longings of their hearts; it listens to the gospel. But it has to do something more. 'Above all', it has to awaken us to the presence of God and to worship of the divine Majesty.

On the one hand, what is said and done must touch the experiences and the hearts of the people who take part; on the other, what is said and done must point to a dimension which is present in all of those experiences but which opens them up to the dimension which breaks through the 'normality' of our daily lives. We must speak of God and to God in a language that makes sense to us; but we must also recognise that speaking to God is different from our daily conversations, however profound we think they are.

The people who come to Mass on Sunday, including priests, come with minds full of all the other spheres and dimensions of their lives. We come with minds racing about something that worries us, some problem that is unresolved, our irritation with someone we just met, our anger or fascination with something we read in the paper, our anticipation of a match or of some family event that will take place later. In other words we do not arrive 'tuned in' to the worship of the divine Majesty.

That is not to suggest that we have to drive all of these concerns out of our minds. It is rather a question, as Pope Benedict says, of seeing the relationship of the mystery we are celebrating to these realities of daily life.

Blessed John Paul describes what he calls 'a contemplative outlook' in which we see the relationship between the mystery of God's love and our lives:

> It is the outlook of those who see life in its deeper meaning, who grasp its utter gratuitousness, its beauty and its invitation to freedom and responsibility. It is the outlook of those who do not presume to take possession of reality but instead accept it as a gift, discovering in all things the reflection of the Creator and seeing in every person [the Creator's] living image. This outlook does not give in to discouragement when confronted by those who are sick, suffering, outcast or at death's door. Instead, in all these situations it feels challenged to find meaning, and precisely in these circumstances it is open to perceiving in the face of every person a call to encounter, dialogue and solidarity.[5]

205

Such an atmosphere of prayer and of seeing the deeper meaning should characterise every Church gathering, from Sunday Mass to the parish pastoral council, to the council of priests and to the school board of management. These meetings are not meant to be a zone of negotiation, with each of us seeking to get our own way; they are a searching together for God's way. We should not, as Pope John Paul suggested, 'become so immersed in the work of the Lord that [we] neglect the Lord of the work'.[6]

Universal priesthood

What, then, is the relationship between the mystery being celebrated and daily life? When the *Catechism of the Catholic Church* begins to speak about faith or belief, it starts with the human quest for God and God's quest for us.

God never ceases to call and seek each human being. That call is responded to not only in religious terms but also in loving relationships, in the honest search for truth and meaning, in art and music and culture, in the seeking of justice and solidarity, and in a life which is loving and grateful. That is the unique role of humanity in the world:

> Although one might think that all created life should be a hymn of praise to the Creator, it is more correct to maintain that the human creature has the primary role in this chorus of praise. Through the human person, spokesperson for all creation, all living things praise the Lord. Our breath of life that also presupposes self-knowledge, awareness and freedom becomes the song and prayer of the whole of life that vibrates in the universe.[7]

Through the centuries of human existence, people sought the truth and even sometimes came to understand something of God's care for us. In the Hebrew tradition there was a further step: God spoke to the children of Abraham, formed covenants with them and guided them. God was most fully revealed in the life, death and resurrection of the One who is our Brother and who is also the eternal Word through whom all things were made.

In the Church, we are baptised into him. He is with us always, but especially in the liturgy:

> He is present in the sacrifice of the Mass both in the person of his minister ... and most of all in the eucharistic species. By his power, he is present in the sacraments so that when anybody baptises it is really Christ himself who baptises. He is present in his word ... he is present when the church prays and sings since he has promised 'where two or three are gathered in my name, there am I in the midst of them'.[8]

What is offered to God the Father in the Mass is the sacrifice of Christ on Calvary, made present for us. The sacrifice of Christ is more than the sacrifice of his own individual life, it is the sacrifice of all those who, as St Paul put it, share in his sufferings so as to become like him in his death (Phil 3:10). It is the offering of the Body of Christ – and we are his Body: 'Now I rejoice in my sufferings for your sake, and in my flesh I complete what is lacking in Christ's afflictions for the sake of his body that is the church' (Col 1:24).

What we suffer is united to what he suffered, because it is a suffering of the Body of Christ. The role of everyone who is present at Mass is to offer him or herself along with the offering Jesus made of himself. Everyone in the Church is offering the sacrifice of Christ and at the same time and inseparably each one is offering his or her own life. We are all sharers in what is called the priesthood of all the baptised. Ordained priests need to remember that we, together with all the baptised, are offering ourselves and every aspect of our lives:

> To [the laity] whom he intimately joins to his life and mission, [Christ] also gives a share in his priestly office of offering spiritual worship for the glory of the Father and the salvation

of humanity ... For all their works, if accomplished in the Spirit, become 'spiritual sacrifices acceptable to God through Jesus Christ': their prayers and apostolic undertakings, family and married life, their daily work, relaxation of mind and body, even the hardships of life, if patiently born (cf. Pt 2:5) ... And so, worshipping everywhere by their holy actions, the laity consecrate the world itself to God.[9]

What that passage says is true not only of the laity, but of all the baptised. This is the fundamental meaning of all that we do and are. The way to the new creation is through the Paschal Mystery. Christ's human nature has already entered the glory that is our hope. Humanity is called into that glory with him.

So we, priests and people, unite everything in our lives and in our world to that passage which Jesus Christ has already made. We all come to make the offering of our own lives – the lives of our families, the lives of our neighbours, the political and economic issues, the sport and recreation, the hopes and fears, the achievements and failures, all the things that are buzzing around in our minds and hearts, and we say: This is where all of these things and events find their meaning; this is where everybody, those close to us and the whole human family, find hope.

Faith is intensely personal, but it is also about the entire cosmos and the whole of history. With and in Christ we offer the fruit of the earth and the work of human hands, the human achievement, solidarity and freedom which we will find again, 'illuminated and transfigured, when Christ presents to his Father an eternal and universal kingdom'.[10] All of that is part of the Passover, which the whole Body of Christ is making, through, with and in the One who died and rose for us.

In the liturgy it is the whole Church that acts, the whole Body of Christ, Head and members. The Eucharist strengthens and deepens the call all of us received in Baptism to be members of his body. 'Because there is one bread,' St Paul reminds us, 'we who are many are one body' (1 Cor 10:17). The *Catechism of the Catholic Church* remind us of St Augustine's words:

> If you are the body and members of Christ, then it is your sacrament that is placed on the table of the Lord; it is your sacrament that you receive. To that which you are you respond 'Amen' ('yes, it is true!') and by responding to it you assent to it. For you hear the words, 'the Body of Christ' and respond 'Amen'. Be then a member of the Body of Christ that your Amen may be true.[11]

Vatican II called on the faithful to participate in the liturgy and not to be present 'as strangers or as silent spectators'.[12] They should not simply speak the responses, do readings and so on. More fundamentally, 'offering the immaculate Victim, not only through the hands of the priest, but also together with him, they should learn to make an offering of themselves'.[13]

A deeper understanding of the truth that we are all priests, offering our lives as part of the offering of Christ, would bring a great enrichment of our liturgical celebrations and of our lives. Lay members of the Body of Christ do not come simply to watch a priest carrying out the liturgy. They come as members of the Body of Christ to offer themselves and the whole of creation to God.

A misplaced fear

Perhaps one reason why this fundamental truth is not emphasised as it should have been has been a fear that it might undermine the importance of the ministerial priesthood. That fear is misplaced.

'The liturgy is the summit toward which the activity of the Church is directed; at the same time it is the font from which all her power flows.'[14] The uniting of our whole selves with the offering of Christ is both the goal of human life and the source of our strength. It is the highest expression of humanity's longings and of praise and thanks to the Creator.

In that summit and source of Christian life the priest is irreplaceable. He acts in the person of Christ, the Head of the

Body. His presence, so to speak, authenticates this congregation as being not simply as a gathering of Christians who happen to have come together, but as *the Church* in this particular place. It is the whole Church, not just this particular congregation, that celebrates in the name of Christ.

The priest presides over that assembly and solemnly recalls the Last Supper and the Cross. He speaks the words in which Jesus left us his Body given up for us and his Blood poured out for us. He leads the congregation in uniting themselves to that offering. The assembly, the *ecclesia*, is called together by God and is linked through the priest and the bishop to the universal Church. People are called to belong through faith, through responding to God's word. That is why Vatican II says that priests have as 'their first duty', the preaching of the word.[15]

> Through the ministry of the priests, the spiritual sacrifice of the faithful is made perfect in union with the sacrifice of Christ. The ministry of priests is directed to this goal and is perfected in it. Their ministry, which begins with the evangelical proclamation, derives its power and force from the sacrifice of Christ.[16]

How could the ordained priesthood be diminished by leading the faithful in the most fundamental Christian task? The more one understands the greatness of the Eucharist the more one understands the importance of the ordained priesthood.

The priest is called to lead the People of God in bringing their 'spiritual sacrifice' to its peak and its source. In offering his own life with its pain and joy, its failures and its sadness, he is doing what the whole congregation, the whole Church, is seeking to do. But as the one who is called to lead others in that offering, his responsibility to do so wholeheartedly and honestly is especially demanding. He is playing a central and essential role in the Church's basic task and privilege of consecrating the world itself to God and of being 'a sign and instrument of communion with God[17] and the unity of the entire human race'.[18]

The ministerial and universal priesthood belong together:

> While the common priesthood of the faithful is exercised by the unfolding of baptismal grace – a life of faith, hope, and charity, a life according to the Spirit – the ministerial priesthood is at the service of the common priesthood. It is directed at the unfolding of the baptismal grace of all Christians. The ministerial priesthood is a means by which Christ unceasingly builds up and leads his Church.[19]

The liturgy takes the fruits of creation, it takes the deepest longings and hopes of humanity and, through them, it meets and worships the Creator of all who is unlimited love and who speaks and acts in us through these signs. For all our busyness and disillusionment, that is what our world, our parishioners and ourselves need to understand and live more deeply.

Notes

1. Benedict XVI, *Sacramentum Caritatis* [Sac Car], 52.
2. Benedict XVI, *Porta Fidei*, 7.
3. Benedict XVI, *Deus Caritas Est*, 1.
4. Vatican II, *Sacrosanctum Concilium* [SC], 33.
5. John Paul II, *Evangelium Vitae*, 83.
6. John Paul II, Address to priests, missionaries and religious, Maynooth 1 October 1979.
7. John Paul II, *General Audience*, 9 January 2002.
8. SC, 7.
9. Vatican II, *Lumen Gentium* [LG], 34.
10. Vatican II, *Gaudium et Spes*, 39.
11. CCC, 1396, quoting from Augustine, *Sermo* 272.
12. SC, 48.
13. Sac Car, 52.
14. SC, 10.

15. Cf. Vatican II, *Presbyterorum Ordinis* (On the Ministry and Life of Priests), 4.
16. Ibid., 2.
17. Cf. LG, 34.
18. LG, 1.
19. CCC, 1547.

Mary's Hymn of Praise

EAMONN CONWAY

The instinct to praise God

It is a central theme in the Judaeo-Christian tradition that we humans are most fully ourselves, most true *to* ourselves, when we are praising God. It is by placing praise of God at the heart of our lives that we become fully human beings. It is also how we fulfil our human destiny of knowing and loving God. What does praising God mean? It means giving God the recognition God deserves, and the place in our lives due to God as our Creator.

For St Augustine, it is not just that our hearts are restless without God, but that they are restless if we are not *praising* God. His *Confessions* begins:

> 'Can any praise be worthy of the Lord's majesty? How magnificent his strength! How inscrutable his wisdom!' (Psalm 144). Man is one of your creatures, Lord, and his instinct is to praise you. He bears about him the mark of death, the sign of his own sin, to remind him that you 'thwart the proud' (Psalm 146). But still, since he is part of your creation, he wishes to praise you. The thought of you stirs him so deeply that he cannot be content unless he praises you, because you made us for yourself and our hearts find no peace until they rest in you.[1]

Similarly, in his *Spiritual Exercises*, St Ignatius of Loyola says:

213

> Human beings are created to praise, reverence, and serve God our Lord, and by means of this to save their souls. The other things on the face of the earth are created for the human beings, to help them in working toward the end for which they were created.[2]

Despite our sinfulness, which weakens and threatens our friendship with God, and despite the terrifying knowledge that we are finite creatures and therefore subject to biological death, the instinct to praise God persists. And it is this instinct that eventually saves us from death, for by putting praise of God at the heart of our lives we affiliate ourselves with Christ; we become his brothers and sisters. We 'put on Christ'[3] and, with him, our share in his divine nature, through which sin and death are overcome. In this way we also become participants and sharers in Christ's prayer of praise to God on behalf of all humanity.

In our ability to praise God we are unique among creatures. While the whole of creation reflects God's power, wisdom and goodness (see St Bonaventure, *Itinerarium mentis in Deum*, I, 10) only humans have been made in God's image and likeness. We are the only creatures who can consciously praise God on behalf of all creation. It is a gift to be able to do so; it is also a responsibility.

Praise is not something we do in addition, as a kind of add-on, to everything else in our lives; it is more the disposition and spirit that informs, underpins and directs all that we do as we go about our daily lives. By appreciating life, even when faced with disappointment, frustration and suffering, we praise God. By being grateful for and delighting in every gesture of kindness and love we are able to give and receive, we praise God. This is because in doing so we are accepting our lives as gift, and this, in itself, is a fundamental act of praise and thanksgiving.

Furthermore, we nurture our instinct to praise when we pray and celebrate the sacraments. In prayer we are gathering up, recollecting and explicitly formulating in word and song the praise of God that constitutes our daily lives. Such explicit praise is not an optional extra. It is an imperative for those who have come to know and love God. As one of the prefaces at Mass says, God has no need of our praise and it adds nothing to God's greatness, but it makes us grow in God's grace.[4]

By offering praise we accept God's plan of salvation for us, and the responsibility that our unique place in God's creation bestows upon us.

There are times when praise of God can be difficult. During times of joy and fulfilment, when we are flush with life's triumphs, we can easily forget to praise God. On the other hand, there can be moments of anguish when we are close to despair and when praising God can seem foolish or impossible or the words just will not come. It is at such times that we can appreciate the value of belonging to a praying and praising community.

At such times we can take comfort from these lines of a hymn in the Divine Office:

> As o'er each continent and island
> The dawn leads on another day,
> The voice of prayer is never silent,
> Nor dies the strain of praise away.[5]

The prayer of praise is bigger than us and yet we are an essential part of it. When we turn to God in praise, even if praying alone, we are still contributing to that voice of constant prayer united with our fellow Christians and with Christ.[6] Perhaps we can imagine the prayer of the Church to be like a storehouse of praise to which (hopefully) mostly we contribute, but upon which we can also draw when times are personally difficult.

Mary: model of praise

Very often when we strive for perfection in some aspect of our life, it can be hard to find anyone with whom we can identify in a meaningful way. Our role models and heroes can seem distant and their achievements beyond our reach. In terms of becoming the perfect disciple of Jesus Christ, however, this is not the case.

We have a concrete example in salvation history of the perfect disciple: Mary.[7] It is extraordinary how consistently throughout the history of the Church people have identified with her and found her a source of consolation and encouragement. For the most part, Christians have seen Mary as someone to intercede for them with her Son, but she is a model not just of prayer of petition but of praise as well.

The Australian Jesuit, Richard Leonard, tells the deeply moving story of eight mothers reclaiming the bodies of their tortured and murdered sons – victims of Pinochet's terror campaign in Chile – from a Santiago morgue, and during the long drive back to their village cradling the bodies of their dead loved ones in their arms while reciting the rosary over and over. He quotes one of them as explaining, 'We pray with Mary at times like this because she knows what it's like to bring a child into the world and claim his dead body in her arms.'[8]

The ability to pray with Mary at such times of profound human tragedy, or indeed also at times of great joy, has deep theological roots and intuitions. Earlier, we spoke of praise of God as the disposition that underpins everything we do, and as giving God due recognition in our daily lives. We find in Mary someone who models this perfectly for us, from the first moment when she made her young life available to God in perfect openness even in the midst of what scripture testifies as terrifying anxiety, confusion and doubt, to the dreadful moment when she accepted back into her arms the abused, bruised and beaten body of her murdered son.

We need to understand how, on the one hand, Mary is special and unique among creatures, and, on the other, how she is at the same time enough like us that we can identify with her. As we shall see, there is no tension here: it is because Mary is special that she is the model of perfect discipleship for us. We don't have time to explore it here but each of the Marian dogmas, properly understood, reveals something of Mary's uniqueness and at the same time the redemption to which each Christian is called through Christ.

So how and why is Mary special and unique? Karl Rahner's exploration of the dogma of the Immaculate Conception can be a help to us here. Clearly, Mary is unique in being conceived without original sin.[9] At the same time, this same grace is given to each Christian at Baptism. So there must be more, Rahner argues, to the dogma than the fact that Mary 'was graced a little earlier, temporally speaking, than we were' (through Baptism).[10]

The 'more' is that it was God's plan that from the moment of her conception, Mary would play a constitutive part, an indispensable role, in salvation history. Through Mary, God's promise of redemption is put into effect; the promise of redemption is rendered possible for the whole of humanity; through her, it literally takes flesh. Thus, Mary belongs to the very fabric, the structure of salvation history.

The Gospel of John (Jn 1:1) tells us that in the very beginning the Word was with God, the Word that would at the appointed time in history become flesh. God's plan to give God's self to creation is coterminous with creation itself. This also means that from the very beginning, Mary's unique role in enabling God's self-giving was also determined.

We can only speculate as to what might have happened if Mary had said 'No' instead of 'Be it done unto me according to thy word' (Lk 1:38). However, we need to ask if Mary was free to say no to God's special role for her in the plan of salvation because if she was not free, if she was, in effect, a 'conscript', then it weakens the case in terms of her being a role model for us in our struggle to surrender in our own lives to God's will.

It helps if we clarify what is meant by freedom. The popular (mis-)understanding of freedom is that it is merely liberation from constraints, the freedom to do whatever we want. This is very far from the Christian understanding. In the Christian understanding, we only really become free when we, who after all are limited creatures, cooperate in our Creator's plan for us; that is, when we discern God's plan correctly, and accept it willingly. At the end of the day, the gift of freedom is given to us precisely so we can surrender our lives lovingly to God, and freedom only achieves its purpose in such surrender.

This does not mean that we cannot say no to God. We can act against God's plan for us, but this ties us up in all kinds of knots in ourselves; effectively, it renders us un-free. Because we are made for relationship with God, a decision against God is also a decision against our deepest selves.

Genuine freedom only comes from saying to God, in whatever situation we find ourselves, 'Be it done unto me according to thy will'. Ultimately, there is no contradiction between doing God's will and the proper exercise of our freedom, because the only way freedom can be properly exercised is in fulfilment of our deepest end, which is God's plan for us.

Mary is a model of discipleship for us because she cooperated freely in God's plan for her, as we also must do. However, in her case God's plan saw her, a creature, being woven into the very fabric of salvation history. It is in this way that she is different from us, but not in having to struggle to accept and follow God's will.

If we cooperate with God's will, then we too participate in salvation history, but our participation is only possible because Mary played her part.

In reflecting on Mary as the perfect disciple we can imagine that she had to 'dig deeply' to find in herself the freedom to accept God's will for her in the confused circumstances of her life. We can imagine her having had to 'dig more deeply still' if this was not her original plan for her own life. And, as the full implications of her 'yes' became clear in the precarious path her Son's life took, we can only begin to imagine the struggles, the doubts, the fears that must have made it so difficult to remain faithful and trusting in God's plan. Was Mary still saying 'Let it be done unto me according to thy word' at the foot of the cross? We can believe that she was. And this was praise of God, understood as putting God's plan at the heart of one's life, at its very toughest.

The tradition of the Church notes that Mary was the first to bring forth Christ but that all Christians are called to do the same by finding in themselves the perfect openness, unswaying commitment and self-surrender that she had. A serious challenge for individual sinful Christians, it is nonetheless the reality for the Church as a body, and this is why Mary is considered to represent the true nature of the Church. Given the distinctive ministry of the priest in enabling fellow Christians to 'bring forth Christ', Karl Rahner notes that:

> Devotion to Mary, built into and included within the wholeness of the Christian life, is something essential for the Christian and particularly for the priest: something for which we can and should seek God's grace, in order really to possess, cherish and maintain this living personal relationship to Mary the mother of the Lord and thus our mother also.[11]

The Magnificat: Mary's Hymn of Praise

Prayer gathers up and expresses explicitly the praise of God that is going on in our daily struggles to surrender to God. In the Liturgy of the Hours we are invited to recite Mary's Hymn of Praise, the Magnificat, at that key moment in our day when, in the words of John Henry Newman, 'the fever of life is over and our work is done'.[12] Like each of the canticles in the Divine Office, the Magnificat expresses praise and thanksgiving for our redemption, and the General Instruction tells us that it should be accorded the same dignity as the hearing of the gospel.[13]

Sometimes, my praying of the Magnificat cannot get past thinking of a few people I have encountered during the day that I would not mind seeing among the mighty cast from their thrones. It is sobering to consider that at that same hour others are probably listing my name in that same category! So how can we best pray the Magnificat?

Biblical scholars tell us that the Magnificat is modelled on the Hymn of Hannah, mother of Samuel (1 Sm 2:1-10), and that it is likely that it was a common prayer among very early Christians who would have seen themselves as the faithful remnant of Israel.[14] They would have understood the salvation brought about in Jesus of Nazareth as 'the definitive act by which God has kept his covenant with Israel, the ultimate manifestation of his mercy to his servant people.'[15]

This means that by praying the Magnificat we are placing ourselves in historical continuity with some of the earliest disciples. It also explains why it is such a powerful canticle of joy, and should always be recited joyfully.

The basis for praise in the first part of the hymn is the events in Mary's own life; the remainder of the hymn recounts the impact of salvation history on the whole of humankind, but in particular its benefits for the faithful remnant, that is, the powerless, the hungry and the lowly.[16] As we pray the first part, with Mary we can give praise for the ways God's grace has triumphed in our lives. At the same time, we are reminded that this is God's doing, not ours. It is because God has had regard for our lowly state (Lk 1:48).

In the second part we are invited to praise God for the gift of salvation, and by so doing we are committing ourselves to the transformation in our own lives that embracing salvation entails. In particular, to pray the Magnificat is to invite divine power into our lives, the power that overshadowed Mary (Lk 1:35). It is an enabling, life-giving power rather than a power of domination; it is the power of self-giving, that comes through suffering and sacrifice, not violence and terror.

Conclusion

The emphasis here has been upon understanding the constitutive and indispensable role played by Mary in salvation history, and the honour due to her in the Christian faith because of this. We have also explored how she can teach us to give praise to God both in our daily lives and in our prayer.

Of the Gospels, it is Luke's that gives Mary the most attention. Scripture scholars would suggest that the passage we have cited above, 'Let it be done to me according to thy word' (Lk 1:38), needs to be considered alongside two other Lucan passages in which

Jesus, surprisingly, and rather sharply, seems to distance himself from Mary.[17] The first is 'My mother and my brothers are those who hear the word of God and do it' (Lk 8:21). And, as if this wasn't clear enough, when a woman in the crowd exclaims, 'Fortunate is the womb that bore you and the breasts that you sucked', Luke has Jesus respond, 'Fortunate rather are those who hear the word of God and keep it' (Lk 11:27-28). As Sandra Schneiders points out, for Jesus, physical kinship is less important than the kinship generated through discipleship, that is, through hearing the Word of God and acting upon it.[18]

A test of authentic Marian devotion, therefore, is that it brings us, as Mary herself did, to Christ, and that he takes flesh in our own lives. If this happens, then our lives will, like Mary's, be lives of praise, and our hearts will find the contentment and peace of which Augustine spoke.

Notes

1. St Augustine, *Confessions*, Book 1, 1 (London: Penguin Classics, 1961), 21.
2. St Ignatius of Loyola, *Spiritual Exercises*, 23, in George E. Ganss SJ (ed.), *Ignatius of Loyola, The Spiritual Exercises and Selected Works. The Classics of Western Spirituality* (New York: Paulist Press, 1991), 130.
3. See Rm 13:14.
4. See Common Preface IV, *Roman Missal* (Dublin: Veritas, 2011), 484. The new translation is worded 'our praises ... profit us for salvation'.
5. 'The day thou gavest', J. Ellerton (1826–93). From Hymns for Night Prayer, from *The Divine Office*.
6. 'Christian prayer is primarily the prayer of the entire community of mankind joined to Christ himself. Each individual has his part in this prayer which is common to the one Body, and it thus becomes the voice of the beloved Spouse of Christ ...' Paul VI, Apostolic Constitution *Canticle of Praise*, 8. See also Vatican II, *Constitution on the Sacred Liturgy*, 83. As we are reminded at the very beginning of the *General Instruction on the Liturgy of the Hours* (1), properly speaking the Divine Office is the prayer of the entire people of God and its celebration should be public and communal. When priests and religious celebrate the Liturgy of the Hours alone, they are fulfilling in a representative way 'the duty of the whole community'. Much more can and should be

done to make this a tangible reality. Although the General Instruction (28) says that, 'the Liturgy of the Hours is entrusted to sacred ministers in a special way', it makes clear that the absence of the people should be the exception.

7. Philip Endean points out that the emphasis upon Mary as 'perfect disciple', developed among others by Raymond Brown, was adopted by Paul VI in the post-synodal exhortation *Marialis Cultus* (1974) because of its ecumenical acceptability. However, he would consider it as limited and insufficient, and in what follows his concerns will be taken into account. See Philip Endean, 'How to think about Mary's privileges', *Priests and People*, 7/5 (May 2003), 190–5.

8. Richard Leonard, *Why Bother Praying?* (New York: Paulist Press, 2013), 118.

9. Speaking at the Angelus in St Peter's Square on 8 December 2013, Pope Francis said: 'In view of [her] maternity Mary was preserved from original sin, that is, from that fracture in communion with God, with others and with creation that wounds every human being deep down. But this fracture was healed beforehand in the Mother of him who has come to free us from the slavery of sin. Mary the Immaculate is inscribed in God's plan; she is the fruit of the love of God that saves the world.'

10. Karl Rahner, 'The Immaculate Conception', *Theological Investigations*, Vol. 1 (London: Darton, Longman and Todd, 1961), 201–12.

11. Karl Rahner, *The Priesthood* (New York: Herder and Herder, 1973), 264.

12. From the online *Book of Common Prayer*, http://www.bcponline.org/Misc/Prayers.htm (accessed 2/12/2013).

13. General Instruction, 50 and 138.

14. Raymond E. Brown, *An Introduction to the New Testament* (New York: Doubleday, 1997), 232.

15. Raymond E. Brown, *The Birth of the Messiah* (London: Geoffrey Chapman, 1977), 364.

16. See Robert J. Karris, 'The Gospel according to Luke', in Raymond Brown et al., *The New Jerome Biblical Commentary* (London: Geoffrey Chapman, 1991), 681. See also Brown, *The Birth of the Messiah*, 356.

17. *The Birth of the Messiah*, 343.

18. Sandra Schneiders, *Written That You May Believe: Encountering Jesus in the Fourth Gospel* (New York: Herder and Herder, 1999), 98.

Section Three

Person and Role

'Is the Priest at Home?': The Personal Maturity and Mental Health of the Priest

BRENDAN S. O'ROURKE

From false to true self

Underpinning these thoughts on the mental health and personal maturity of the priest is the conviction (psychology) that at the very centre of the human being is the desire for and thrust towards relationship, and the belief (theological) that this desire and thrust is a reflection of the relational core of the mystery of God, which we call Trinity.

The more our surroundings facilitate and promote connection and relationship, the greater our potential for growing into maturity. When circumstances frustrate our connecting and undermine our trust, the journey towards maturity and emotional balance is made more difficult, and sometimes impossible.

The mature priest is not necessarily a well-rounded personality. He's far from perfect. But he is able to love, to befriend, to be befriended, and minister effectively. In developing a solid sense of self which allows him to be available for friendship and closeness to people, the priest is establishing a firm foundation for all he does.

Many priests were warned of the dangers of closeness. Many recount stories of formation which praised independence and caution. At best the intent may have been to alert the priest to the power he possessed, and the responsibility to use that in the service of the needs of the other, especially people who were vulnerable. The negative side of this training, even apart from its delaying the human development of many priests, was that it did not recognise the damage that is caused by relating to people in an impersonal, disconnected manner. Super-independence is not a virtue. It damages the self and others. It is not human. It is immature. It weakens all aspects of priestly ministry.

One of the lies of super-independence is that the priest doesn't need others. This is a dangerous denial of his deepest self. It violates 'the human condition of interrelatedness.'[1] It impedes the priest from a healthy awareness of his own feelings, his need for friendship, for support, and contexts of mutual, honest sharing. Super-independence leads to isolation, and priests who live isolated lives tend to have their needs met in unhealthy, manipulative ways.

To achieve closeness, a priest needs some level of trust in self and others. He needs some positive sense of who he is. If deep down, sometimes beyond consciousness, he suspects that he is faulty, bad or seriously defective, or if, for example, he deeply doubts his capacity to be really human, or if he is unsure or afraid of himself sexually, or if his needs and feelings are foreign territory, or even judged as shameful or sinful, then in his encounters and ministry he is likely to put up a shield, a mask, a false self. He will do this to avoid being rejected, disliked or disapproved of by others.

The journey from the false self to the real self may be part of the journey towards maturity for many priests, moving from a service of (rather impersonal) duty to one of genuine care, compassion and justice.

Unless priests work at being in relationship with themselves and others, their ministry will suffer. The Word of God needs to resonate in their whole selves. They need to preach with their whole selves. They don't need to be perfect but they do need to be real.

Being real and mature will mean that the priest does not have all the answers. This is a struggle for men who have been trained to be problem solvers. It is a journey into humility, into an awareness of the complexity of life, into vulnerability and weakness, and into letting go of black and white thinking. It is a journey into awareness of and gradual acceptance of one's sexual orientation. This maturity calls priests into equal relations with men and women. It usually requires a deep listening to the reality of the experiences of men and women, starting from the freedom of realising that his job is to learn and not know in advance.

Claudia Black summarises rules for unhealthy relationships as 'don't talk, don't trust, don't feel'.[2] The journey to maturity for priests often involves a growing awareness that these are the rules by which they have lived.

In the journey towards maturity, which is a lifelong path, priests often discover that there are patterns in their lives which block relatedness. A common one is that of operating mostly on an intellectual level. The priest who does this will function on the level of ideas and facts, but will not be available for the give and take of relationship. He will not be vulnerable. He will not share his hopes or fears. He will hide. Some priests can hide by keeping at a distance from others. They may feel uncomfortable not being in charge and having the cover of 'father'. Other priests can use humour as a way of avoiding facing reality. Some priests use the topic of Rome or Church authorities generally as a way of not engaging personally; others use the past or 'talk Church' all the time, while others still talk politics. Clearly these issues are worthy of conversation but may be focused on in a way that blocks the priest from a real engagement with others.

Boundaries

'The purpose of establishing boundaries is to promote the well-being of the priest and that of the people to whom he ministers, in the hope of creating a safe and predictable environment. Boundaries help to establish clear roles and expectations; they also serve to protect and preserve the integrity of relationships.'[3]

If someone asks to speak with the priest, in order to give them his full attention he needs to choose a time when he is not distracted, rushed or too tired. He needs to meet with them in a place that is conducive to listening. Boundary setting is important both for him and for the other person. In the way he puts aside time to be available for the other, he increases the likelihood of prioritising the needs of the other while also attending to his own needs.

It is important that the priest does not do for the other person what they can do for themselves. That would be to take on too much responsibility. If he finds himself doing this he needs to wonder why and to talk to someone about it. On the other hand, he needs also not to be under-involved. There is always the requirement to be attentive, to communicate understanding and empathy, even if he determines early on that this situation is beyond him and requires referral. Boundaries are respected when he recognises that someone needs expertise he doesn't have. The priest also respects boundaries by having ready a list of trustworthy professionals to whom he can refer people. However, some priests fall into the trap of using referrals as a way of avoiding even listening to people initially. This is not good ministry (and is an abuse of boundaries).

There is sensitivity needed when it comes to physical expressions of support or affection. The question that needs to be uppermost for the priest is: whose need is being met? The priest is entitled to, and needs, to have a variety of ways of experiencing support and affection in healthy ways. If he is not attending to this, he is likely to seek to meet those needs inappropriately.

A weakness in the training of many priests, and in their current ministry, is not having a supervisor with whom they can talk about their ministry. Most people in the caring professions would not dare to function solo. They know how complex relationships can be and how helpful and necessary it is to have a safe, confidential context in which to process experiences.

Father John Heagle gives a fine rule of thumb for good boundaries in our work with people. He writes: 'In our day to day pastoral contacts with people, approach each encounter as if we want our closest associates and friends – those who respect and trust us most – to know exactly how we are conducting ourselves.'[4]

In ministry the priest is saying: 'I am here for you.' In order for that to be true, the priest needs to attend to his own needs – not in a selfish way. A simple and crucial prerequisite is adequate sleep and rest. Workaholism is an addiction that is often seen as a virtue. However, it is destructive for the life of the priest and his ministry. Priests need to be very aware of this and take responsibility for achieving a healthy balance in their lives. Luisa M. Saffiotti speaks of the fact that 'increasingly priests are faced with more and more work demands. For many a seventy-hour week is not so exceptional. This leaves them fatigued and often lacking in the energy or enthusiasm for creative responses to the world's pain.'[5] Part of good boundary setting is learning the skill of saying no! The priest needs to say no to whatever will result in his not really being able to say 'I am here for you.' Many bishops and priests (together with the faithful) are struggling with declining numbers and are questioning some of the emerging coping strategies, such as the clustering of parishes. This concern is crucial for establishing solid boundaries in ministry. The fewer the priests, the less personal contact with people. And so, priests run the risk of becoming depersonalised functionaries rather than servants of the faith community.

Balance

An ongoing struggle for many priests is to maintain a sense of balance in how they live their lives. While some may under-work, many struggle with becoming overly busy and living unhealthy lives, with the inevitable weakening of their ministry. Maturity asks of us to give energy and attention to balance in our lives. Balance is achieved when I give enough time to the important aspects of life. The following questions can help to assess life balance:

› Do I eat regularly and healthily?
› Do I make time for exercise?
› Do I attend to my medical and dental care?
› Do I get enough sleep?
› Do I take time away from phones and computers?

> › Do I make time for entertainment, sport, film or theatre?
> › Do I regularly make a list of things I'm grateful for in life?
> › Do I try at times not to be in charge or the expert?
> › Am I vulnerable with myself, others, God?
> › Do I pray daily?
> › Do I spend time in nature?
> › Do I spend time with good books and music?
> › Am I open to not knowing?
> › Do I stay in touch with friends and family regularly?
> › Do I cherish people who give me honest feedback?
> › Do I take time to chat with others?
> › Do I accept that on any given day things will remain undone?
> › Do I get regular supervision or peer support?
> › Do I have realistic expectations for myself and others, e.g. being human, vulnerable, imperfect?
> › Am I learning to be mutual in my friendships (self-disclosing, empathic, able to give and receive challenge or feedback)?
> › Do I invest time and energy in updating myself professionally, emotionally, spiritually?
> › Am I learning to be more intimate with others – to have my human needs for appreciation, intimacy, touch, affection and caring – met with a variety of people in healthy and appropriate ways?
> › Do I take holidays each year (an average of four weeks)?
> › Do I make an annual retreat?
> › Do I attend professional development training regularly?
> › Do I take a sabbatical (of at least three months) every ten years?[6]

For balance in life we need to develop an awareness of our feelings and skills in reading them. We can be like an airport control tower whose radar is down. For many priests, skill in befriending their feelings and learning from them was not part of seminary formation, nor was it part of their development as men. For healthy balance in life and ministry it is a crucial skill to develop. Otherwise, a lot of unnecessary 'crashes' can take place.

For balance in ministry it is also important that we not get caught in the trap of 'only seeking confirmatory experiences'[7] and avoiding whatever is unfamiliar or different. So, crucial to the maturing of the priest is openness to experiencing newness in ministry.

Grief

A missionary priest got that dreaded phonecall telling him that his sister had days to live. He made arrangements and travelled home, with fear in his heart. One might expect that he was anxious he wouldn't make it in time. However, his fear was he would make it in time. He was afraid that his sister would be still alive when he arrived and he knew that he would not be able to deal with loss. He knew that he was frozen around loss. He was unable to feel or show love or grief. So he hoped, for his sister's sake so as not to hurt her, that she would be dead.

Numbness, inability to access our feelings and difficulty in acknowledging or communicating them are struggles many men experience. The returning missionary was at least aware that there was something frozen, a way of relating he could not access or demonstrate. Maturity in priesthood necessitates grief work, otherwise our ability to relate, to connect, to be present is greatly diminished.

The priest needs to grieve over his last parish in order to be ready to engage fully in his next one. It is important to ritualise this ending in some way, to express it, to find a way to express gratitude to parishioners, and to receive their gratitude in return. It is important to say goodbye, and to feel our goodbye. If there is just numbness, stoicism or a heady response to goodbyes, the people being left are damaged. They are left with a sense that they did not really count in the life of the priest. If the reality of leaving is not felt by the priest – and leave-taking can often be a mixture of sadness, relief, excitement and anticipation of new possibilities – then the engagement in the new community can be weakened.

We need to have said goodbye to be capable of saying hello to new relationships.

Maturity requires the priest to deal with his grief in the course of his ministry, which may so often place him in positions of witnessing – and in some ways, of being a part of – the loss and tragedies of others. Often the priest has to face the trauma of being an early witness to sudden death through accidents, suicide or violence. The priest is often present with families torn by grief. The priest may have journeyed with people, old and young, and their partners, their children, or their parents, and witnessed the heartbreak of sickness and death. Many priests demonstrate great heart and sensitivity in helping people cope with the sorrows of their lives. What is not always attended to so well by priests is their own grief and the price they pay for so often dealing with trauma, pain and loss. It is important for the priest to deal with the sometimes strong feelings he experiences in journeying with people. He needs to be able to talk through his own experience, his own pain, his own numbness, his own anger and frustration. These are best shared with a trusted other. Professionals debrief because it helps them to stay available in healthy ways. The priest needs to bring his own feelings and experiences into prayer but also into conversation with trusted others. Otherwise he risks numbing himself with alcohol, over-eating, compulsive television or computer use, by over-working, or becoming short-tempered.

An area of grief that many men, and priests, need to deal with is what Steve Biddulph calls the 'hidden grief of "father-hunger"'.[8] Many men suffer from an alienation or distancing from their fathers, whether they are living or dead. Some call this 'the father-wound'. It is important for the maturing of a man to come to terms with his relationship with his father. Biddulph's book, *Manhood*, outlines a process of discovering the energy of the father–son relationship and blessing. Dealing with unresolved issues around the father–son relationship is particularly important for priests who are in leadership roles. Coming to terms with this relationship is a process of coming to terms with masculinity and authority.

Conclusion

As the priest works at relating well, with balance and solid boundaries, together with the ongoing grief work that life requires, he will be found to be at home. At home in himself, and grounded in God and in God's people.

Notes

1. Sheila Murphy, 'Spirituality, Sexuality, Intimacy, and Ministry', *Handbook of Spirituality for Ministers*, Vol. 1, Robert J. Wicks, ed. (New York: Paulist Press, 1995).
2. Claudia Black, *Don't Talk, Don't Trust, Don't Feel*, audio recording, 5779g.
3. 'The Priest as Servant Leader: Developing Values for Priestly Ministry', The Canadian National Federation of Presbyteral Councils, 2008.
4. Father John Heagle, 'Priestly Ministry and Healthy Boundaries', *Priestly Relationships: Freedom Through Boundaries*, The National Organisation for Continuing Education of Roman Catholic Clergy, USA, 1997.
5. Luisa M. Saffiotti, 'Forming Ministers for the 21st Century', *Human Development*, Summer 2005.
6. Some of these questions are from the unpublished notes of Sr Lynn Levo, CSJ, PhD.
7. Raymond F. Dlugos, OSA, Atlanta NOCERCC Conference address.
8. Steve Biddulph, *Manhood: An Action Plan for Changing Men's Lives* (Stroud: Hawthorn Press, 1999).

Celibacy and Intimacy

BRENDAN GEARY

> One of the untold stories of priesthood is the large number
> of life-giving, joyful, loving friendships between celibate
> priests and their committed friends.[1]

This chapter will explore the relationship between celibacy and
intimacy, reflecting upon what we have learned about how to live
celibately and manage the human need for intimacy in our lives.
It will also explore attitudes and behaviours that can undermine
celibate commitment, and understand better the ways that men
who are priests can live this commitment in a healthy way.

Intimacy

At its simplest, intimacy involves revealing innermost parts of the
self to another. As such it involves taking the risk of allowing oneself
to be known, and of trusting another person with information
that is considered private. Donald B. Cozzens writes that we
experience intimacy when we can be present to another person
without the defences that we normally use.[2] It requires honesty
and transparency, with the ability to let another see parts of the
self that we might otherwise find embarrassing or shameful. It
also involves sharing hopes, dreams, feelings, achievements and
moments of satisfaction, as well as hurts and disappointments.
Seán Sammon, former Superior General of the Marist Brothers
and a clinical psychologist, adds that celibate intimacy means
'pursuing and developing ways of loving that are non-genital'.[3] Our
culture often equates 'intimacy' with sexual contact. However, it

is possible to be intimate without being sexual, and it is evidently not uncommon for people to have sexual experiences that do not involve a sharing of intimacy. Erik Erikson, a psychologist of human development, noted that a capacity for intimacy requires the ability to be committed to a relationship, and that ethical strength is required so that the boundaries and commitments of the relationship are supported and respected.[4] Leaving aside inappropriate sexual behaviour, there are people who can best be described as 'emotionally promiscuous', who are ready to share freely aspects of their personal lives that preferably should be shared with a small number of confidants. What is becoming clear is that it is not possible to develop fully as a human being without the care and affection of intimate friends.

The current situation in the Church where the human need for intimacy is both recognised and valued is a recent phenomenon. A seminary rector was asked in the late 1950s, as part of an interview for a television programme, 'What do you do about feelings?' He replied without hesitation, 'We crush them.'[5] Research shows that the lack of human and spiritual formation in the pre-Vatican II Church was a contributory factor to the abuse crisis.[6] Thomas F. Nestor, an American priest who undertook research on priests and intimacy, noted the change of values and emphasis that occurred after Vatican II:

In more recent times the programme of spiritual formation not only views interpersonal relationships more kindly, but also sees them as critical factors in the development of ministerial skills and interiority. Those who successfully enter close interpersonal relationships will be better able to establish ministerial relationships and develop a relationship with God.[7]

Over the last forty years a capacity for interpersonal relationships has come to be seen as a key personality characteristic in priests, foundational for human development, spiritual growth and ministerial effectiveness.

Celibacy

At the same time as the Church was rediscovering the value of intimacy, celibacy as a value was being questioned and rejected by the wider society. The ordination of married Anglican priests and the ordained from the other Catholic rites who may be married has shown that celibacy is not a requirement for priestly ministry. The change in the attitude to sexuality and the prominence given to sexual activity and fulfilment, as well as the damage done to celibate commitment by the various crises in recent years, have created a different climate for those making this choice. Andrew Brown, a columnist with the *Guardian*, wrote:

> The traditional model of Catholic priesthood in the West – where men lived together in large groups, admired by their parishioners but existentially remote from them, and in any case brought up in a seminary throughout their adolescence – provided an interior world where celibacy seemed normal and attainable. That model collapsed in the latter half of the twentieth century.[8]

Marie Keenan has suggested that whereas clerical masculinity was formerly highly valued, it is now marginalised in society. This change of culture makes it more difficult to live celibately.[9] Sammon outlines four motivations for choosing celibacy:[10]

1. It is a law of the Church.
2. It is a discipline that is accepted as part of spiritual commitment to priesthood.
3. It has functional value enabling the priest to be free for ministry.
4. It is a gift (charism) that priests freely embrace as their way of living the gospel.

Sammon quotes a young priest who said, 'You can pray and pray, but you will never pray a law into a charism!'[11] Nestor noted that thirty-two out of thirty-four priests he surveyed said that they were celibate because the law required it.[12] For these men, and many like them, it may not be possible to provide a rationale that can convince them that their sacrifice and the denial of the basic human desire for companionship and sexual intimacy have value. It is, however, possible to show that a priest can live a healthy life without sexual intimacy.

Healthy celibacy

Regarding the personal qualities and characteristics necessary for ordination, Pope John Paul II wrote:

> The priest should be able to know the depths of the human heart, to perceive difficulties and problems, to make meeting and dialogue easy, to create trust and cooperation, to express serene and objective judgments.[13]

Pope John Paul II also highlighted the importance of prayer (29), interior freedom (36 and 44), a capacity to relate to others (34) and a 'properly understood sexual education' (44).

Those who have feelings of shame, guilt or anxiety about sexual issues should be given help before ordination – or advised that this is not the appropriate way of life for them, as they may lack the resources to live it in a healthy way. Seminarians without problems have no difficulty being transparent throughout the formation process. However, those with anxieties often attempt to conceal them, or at least not explore them, out of fear of being rejected for ordination. It has been said repeatedly that the priesthood is not a place for immature men who wish to avoid the challenges of the world of adult relationships, or who are confused about their sexual identity or are unable to accept and come to terms with being homosexual or bisexual.

Healthy intimacy (whether or not one is sexually active) requires interpersonal and intrapersonal skills.[14] Self-awareness is a key skill, followed closely by a capacity for self-disclosure. A significant moment of adult development occurs when a person takes the risk to share something that is meaningful or painful with a trusted friend, and to find not only that he/she is accepted and loved, but that he/she becomes more valued by the other person. Those who cannot do this, out of fear or lack of skills, have missed a key developmental threshold and may be less effective in pastoral ministry.

In order to live a life of celibacy and establish and nurture intimate relationships, the priest has to have a good sense of self, and to have clear but flexible boundaries. All adults have to learn how to self-regulate, both their behaviour and emotional states. Fortunately, it is possible to learn skills in this area, in order to strengthen one's ability to manage emotions and needs.[15] Failure, if it occurs, does not mean that one's celibate commitment has no value, but that lessons need to be learned in order to live it with integrity and fidelity. This can be done through personal reflection and dialogue with one's values and primary commitments, but will be more effective and honest if done with a trusted friend or professional counsellor or spiritual director. It will probably involve a change of behaviours and priorities, and some difficult conversations.

Self-awareness and spirituality

Those who write about celibacy, fidelity and intimacy all emphasise the importance of cultivating a healthy spiritual life, which must be at the core of a priest's celibate commitment. Sadly, many priests either have never learned the skills necessary for personal prayer, or have abandoned this practice because of the demands of ministry, and possibly because of feelings of inadequacy or failure in this area of their spiritual lives. When people take time to meditate they often find that they will grow in self-awareness, by becoming aware of their desires, hopes, dreams, fears, preoccupations and needs. They will learn what makes them angry or sad, what they desire (including sexual desires), and what makes them anxious. With a skilled spiritual director they can learn how to hear God's voice when they pray, and the invitation to growth *within* the distractions, and not only *despite* them.[16] The experience of meditation provides opportunities for contact with Jesus that can reinforce the sense of call that lies at the heart of ordination and celibate commitment.

A capacity to listen to critique and feedback increases our capacity for self-awareness, as does humility and a sense of humour. Arrogance and pomposity are not good friends of self-awareness. Priests who avoid means of growth and awareness are limiting their capacity to manage their celibate and priestly commitments, as well as their personal growth as adult men.

Barriers to healthy celibate intimacy

It is undoubtedly true that a life of chastity (partnered or single) is not possible without discipline. Ronald Rolheiser, a spiritual writer and retreat giver, reminds us that we are all unfinished, and that part of the ache of being human is an acceptance of our unfinished state.[17] None of us can have everything in life, and we all need to live with the tension of yearning for more while accepting that each choice means saying no to another attractive and good option.[18] William Kraft described the commitment to celibacy as a 'no' in the service of a 'yes'. The 'yes' to ministerial priesthood requires a 'no' to marriage and sexual relationships.[19]

Role-playing, understood as living a kind of double life, is clearly a barrier to intimacy, as honesty is a primary requirement of intimacy.[20] Similarly, priests who are overly invested in their priestly identity will form intimate relationships only with difficulty. Allied to role-playing is narcissism, reinforced by clericalism, which tells the priest he is special and entitled to special treatment. Narcissists can be enchanting and exciting, and often bring a certain electricity and energy to social situations,[21] however their needs and sense of entitlement interfere with meaningful reciprocal relationships, and their sexual needs can lead to what Sperry calls 'pseudo intimacy', where intense sexual feelings are interpreted as real intimacy.[22] They can be superficial, and, at worst, exploitative.

Many writers advise priests to find a hobby or an interest that enlarges their lives, possibly leading to involvement and sharing leisure time with others (often other priests), and providing an alternative (healthy) source of enjoyment. Unfortunately, there are some priests who develop obsessions that can be a barrier to intimacy. Their free time may be given over to the pursuit of a single activity, or they can be driven by a particular religious conviction or devotional interest.

Addictive behaviours are often a signal of problems with intimacy. Spiritual writers suggest that promiscuous relationships indicate a yearning for intimacy, as does compulsive use of internet pornography sites.[23] These sites give the illusion of intimacy because of the visual stimulation they offer and the feelings of excitement and arousal that the viewer experiences.[24] However, they often lead to intense feelings of guilt, abandonment of the priest's spiritual life, and hours of time spent surfing the limitless supply of online material (often late at night, when the capacity to self-regulate is already diminished).[25] Whereas a capacity for solitude is a healthy indicator of a capacity for intimacy, viewing pornography often leads to isolation and shame.

Loneliness is related to difficulties with celibacy and intimacy. Dean Hoge, in his study of the priests who left ministry in the first five years after ordination, noted that all the priests who left felt lonely and unappreciated.[26] Loss of commitment to mission, a loss of spiritual vigour and abandonment of spiritual practices, 'settling for less' through unavailability or a style of life that is not compatible with gospel simplicity, and seeking compensation through drink, medications, an ideal job, sexual gratification, power or academic ambition, can all interfere with the human need to develop intimate relationships and live celibacy in a healthy way.

Life stages

Bernard Bonnot wrote a helpful article outlining stages in a celibate's life. He suggests that in the first years of ministry, 'young adults pursuing celibate life generally do not face the deep challenge of ministry'.[27] Others have said that the combination of idealism and satisfaction in ministry often carry the young priest through these early years. The young priest will be aware of sexual desires and temptations, but may have the support, and possibly the fear of breaking his promise, to help him to remain committed.

For young homosexual priests, the desire to avoid revealing their orientation or face up to it properly themselves, along with the genuine attractions of ministry and service of God, can lead them to avoid issues related to sexual identity and needs.

Male development in the twenties and early thirties is concerned with the desire to prove oneself and be successful; this is normal. The real challenge comes in mid-life where the celibate may have lost some of his idealism, or experienced failure, hurt and disappointment. There is often a desire at this stage to enter into an intimate relationship. Being single is seen as a loss of important human needs and experiences. Successful resolution of this stage is shown in an ability to be compassionate and generative in relationships, with a capacity for close friendships and an ability to form community with and for others. This is done without compromising commitments 'physically or psychologically'.[28]

If a priest comes to see his celibacy as a deprivation, it will be difficult to find meaning in this commitment. At this point he will need to make choices that may lead to finding the means to rekindle a sense of priestly vocation that requires celibacy, grieving the loss of sexual intimacy, having his own children, home, career and other freedoms, and facing his mortality. This process can take a number of years, and often requires a spiritual experience, like an awakening, 'consolation' or conversion, where he can recommit himself meaningfully to what he has freely undertaken. Clearly many priests manage this successfully.

Male and female differences in intimacy

Roy Baumeister, a social psychologist, has written about the differences in male and female intimacy.[29] In his view, women prefer intimate, close relationships (dyads), whereas men tend to form and be comfortable in groups. If this is the case, it is perhaps one of the reasons that priests' groups are so effective in supporting priests in their ministry and vocation. Both men and women can enjoy the consequences of being expressive with feelings and sharing with another, but women appear to be more inclined to this form of closeness than men.

Baumeister notes that there is a trade-off in our culture. Intimate relationships are wonderful for providing support and the deeply satisfying sense of being special. Groups are effective for social development and achieving social needs and progress, for example, the police, army, religious orders, diocesan organisations, political parties, sports teams and industries. The downside for men is that members of groups are expendable.

Some authors write about men as if they suffer from some kind of intimacy deficit because they do not share personal feelings and form intimate bonds as easily as women. Criticising priests in this way is like criticising apples for not being oranges. In fact, priests score higher for intimacy than men generally.[30] This is hardly surprising. As has already been noted, priests are expected to have a capacity to create relationships as part of their pastoral ministry: it is often a priest's well-developed capacity for intimacy that can lead to challenges with celibacy, rather than any deficits. Thomas Nestor also noted that the priests who were most satisfied in their ministry were most capable of intimacy and happiest with their celibate commitment. Generally, those who are faithful to their spiritual lives, and who have healthy interests outside of the world of Church and ministry, often manage to live celibacy successfully.

Conclusion

There are many priests who live their celibacy faithfully (even with struggles and lapses), and who have developed mature, appropriately intimate friendships with men and/or women. Successful living of celibacy requires self-awareness and the ability to self-regulate (and not self-medicate with drink, or internet sex). It cannot be done without discipline and a spiritual life. The conviction of being rooted in the love of God, and a capacity to accept the consequences of this life choice – in the way that others have to live with the consequences of their choices – reflect a mature ability to be faithful to one's commitments and to live in public what one has professed in one's heart. Intimacy is a requirement of healthy living. Celibate intimacy is challenging, but possible.

Sadly we hear the stories of failure more than the stories of success. Careful nurturing of friendships with fellow priests, and with single, vowed and married companions, with whom one can be honest and vulnerable, is undoubtedly a support that helps a priest to hold together the celibate commitment and the human need for warmth and closeness. There are many priests who are mature individuals who nurture and support others. Their witness assures us that priesthood can be a way of living that facilitates the growth of the individual, and that intimacy can be achieved by celibates, as long as it is supported by healthy boundaries,[31] self-awareness, spirituality, humour and honesty.

Notes

1. Donald B. Cozzens, *The Changing Face of the Priesthood* (Collegeville, MN: Liturgical Press, 2000), 43.
2. Ibid., 24.
3. Seán D. Sammon, *An Undivided Heart* (New York: Alba House, 1993), 20.
4. Kevin P. McClone, 'Male intimacy', *Touchstone* 4 (2001), 5–11.
5. Private conversation, Ushaw College.
6. John Jay College Research Team, 'The causes and context of sexual abuse of minors by Catholic priests in the United States, 1950–2010' (2011), Report presented to the United States Conference of Catholic Bishops, http://www.usccb.org/issues-and-action/child-and-youth-protection/upload/The-Causes-and-Context-of-Sexual-Abuse-of-Minors-by-Catholic-Priests-in-the-United-States-1950-2010.pdf (accessed 11/3/2013); and Marie Keenan, *Child Sexual Abuse and the Catholic Church: Gender, Power and Organizational Culture* (Oxford: Oxford University Press, 2012), 47–51 and 227.
7. Thomas F. Nestor, *Intimacy and Adjustment Among Catholic Priests*, unpublished doctoral dissertation, Loyola University of Chicago, 1993, 52.
8. Andrew Brown, 'Cardinal O'Brien has exposed Vatican dishonesty on celibacy', *The Guardian* (5 March 2013); http://www.guardian.co.uk/commentisfree/andrewbrown/2013/mar/04/cardinal-obrien-vatican-dishonesty-celibacy (accessed 6/3/2013).
9. *Child Sexual Abuse and the Catholic Church*, 243.
10. *An Undivided Heart*, 114–16.
11. Ibid., 115.

12. *Intimacy and Adjustment Among Catholic Priests*, 16.

13. John Paul II, *Pastores Dabo Vobis*, 43; http://www.vatican.va/ holy_father/ john_paul_ii/apost_exhortations/documents/hf_jp-ii_exh_25031992_ pastores-dabo-vobis_en.html (accessed 11/3/2013).

14. Martin Pable, 'Skills Needed for Celibacy', *Review for Religious* 3 (May/ June 1998), 275–85.

15. Roy Baumeister and John Tierney, *Willpower: Discovering Our Greatest Strengths* (London: Penguin, 2012).

16. Robert J. Wicks, *Prayerfulness: Awakening to the Fullness of Life* (Indiana: Sorin Books, 2009).

17. Ronald Rolheiser, *The Holy Longing* (New York: Doubleday, 1999).

18. *An Undivided Heart*, 21.

19. William Kraft, quoted in Pable, *Review for Religious*, 1998.

20. Robert J. Silva, 'Role Playing vs Honest Living', *Touchstone* (Winter 2001), 16.

21. Sandy Hotchkiss, *Why Is It Always About You?: The Seven Deadly Sins of Narcissism* (New York: Free Press, 2002), 9.

22. Len Sperry, *Sex, Priestly Ministry and the Church* (Collegeville, MN: Liturgical Press, 2003).

23. *The Changing Face of the Priesthood*, 21.

24. Brendan Geary and Edward Hone, 'Sex and the Internet', *Sexual Issues: A Christian Handbook,* J. M. Greer and B. Geary, eds (Suffolk: Kevin Mayhew, 2010).

25. Roy F. Baumeister and Todd F. Heatherton, 'Self-regulation Failure: An Overview', *Psychological Inquiry* 7.1 (1996), 1–15.

26. Dean R. Hoge, 'Priests in the First Five Years: Satisfactions and Dissatisfactions', *Touchstone* (Winter 2001), 27–30.

27. Bernard R. Bonnot, 'Stages in a Celibate's Life', *Human Development* 16.3 (1995), 1–22.

28. Ibid., 21.

29. Roy F. Baumeister, *Is There Anything Good About Men?: How Cultures Flourish by Exploiting Men* (New York: Oxford University Press, 2012), 93–5, 177–8.

30. *Intimacy and Adjustment Among Catholic Priests*, 133.

31. Brendan Geary and Alison Moore, *Sexual Dynamics in Ministry* (Suffolk: Kevin Mayhew Ltd., 2011).

Realising Leadership Potential

SEÁN RUTH

Leadership today operates in a very challenging and difficult environment. Over the past number of years, trust in leaders has been severely shaken by a series of scandals in the religious, political and financial spheres in particular. The credibility of people in leadership roles has taken a beating and there is a greater air of suspicion, low expectations and pessimism surrounding leaders at all levels. In certain contexts, the Roman Catholic Church being one, this has added to an already existing unease about the nature of traditional leadership and a reluctance on the part of some people to see themselves, or be seen by others, as leaders. For many, leadership has connotations of authoritarianism and hierarchy that they would wish to disavow.

To talk about realising leadership potential in the context of these difficulties then requires us, first of all, to clarify what exactly we mean by leadership and to contrast this with other roles of authority or management. From this starting point, we can then examine the barriers to being an effective leader and outline elements involved in realising leadership potential.

The essence of leading
There is a prevalent image in the literature of the leader as a kind of superhero, a person with exceptional talents and skills. This is a distorted image. Leaders are ordinary people who, for one reason or another, decide to make a difference, often in the face of

self-doubt, confusion, fear or a myriad of other feelings that they struggle with. They are leaders because of what they do and how they behave, not because they are inherently exceptional.

So, what is it that leaders do? Asking the question in this way highlights that leading is something we do, a process, not a position that we occupy. Being a priest, for example, puts someone in a position of leadership, but whether or not they actually lead depends on what they do in that position.

It turns out that the most important thing that leaders do is to think.[1] Before anything else, the fundamental role of a leader is to think about people and the situation facing them. One thing that distinguishes a more effective leader from a less effective leader is their ability to think well or think clearly about what is going on around them. One of the difficulties with the recent scandals was the sense that leaders were not able to think clearly about what was happening. When people cannot tell that a leader's mind is working well, they become anxious, stressed, angry, scared or hopeless. On the other hand, in the face of a crisis, when it is clear that someone's mind is working well, people relax and their own minds are able to keep working flexibly.

Doing this well means that people have to be thought about on different levels. They have to be thought about individually and they have to be thought about collectively. We have to ask how this individual is doing but also how this whole group is doing. We also have to think about the wider situation surrounding people, what is happening out there that affects us and that we need to take into account. Finally, we have to think about all of this over time, understanding the background and history, the current situation and what might happen in the future. Effective leaders are able to think well on all these different levels.

As they do this thinking, leaders pay attention to people's strengths and potential. For each individual they deal with and for the group as a whole, they are interested in and pay attention to the particular strengths, abilities, talents and achievements that are manifested.

They also focus on the potential that exists for each individual and for the group, and on what might be possible if they got things right.

At the same time, leaders pay attention to where people struggle, both individually and collectively. Where does it get hard for people? 'Struggle' is a useful term because it encourages us to think about things from the perspective of the person or the group rather than approaching them critically from the outside. It encourages us to put ourselves in their shoes and to understand the struggle as they experience it and as it interferes with their hopes, their dreams or their potential. As leaders, part of our role is to support people to address their struggles. Unless we can *think* about the struggle, we are unlikely to be a useful resource for them.

The difficulty with this picture is that no one person can do all of this on their own. No one person has enough information or is smart enough to figure out all the intricacies of very complex situations. If we are to do this effectively, we have to draw other people into the process. By its nature, effective leadership is a collaborative process. And central to the collaborative process is listening. The only way we get our thinking clear and are effective is by listening to one another.

Listening

Listening is not a simple process. In practice, the important information that we need in order to understand what is going on is communicated in a variety of ways. Sometimes, when we ask what people think, what we get is how bad they are feeling. Some of the most important information of all is communicated at the level of feelings, and if we are to make sense of any situation, we need to be comfortable paying attention to these and even finding ways to draw out the feelings that people are struggling with.

At times, we also pick up important insights by listening to the stories or anecdotes that people tell. If we ask them what they think, they may simply tell us what they have experienced over the last while. However, if we listen well to these stories and if we listen to different people's stories, we may begin to see a pattern in what they are saying. Part of the role of a leader is to listen long enough and widely enough to detect the common elements that make up a picture of where people are struggling.

This kind of listening often occurs outside of formal meetings. For example, it commonly happens informally or spontaneously in the course of short interactions with people. We may find that important information is communicated over a break or over lunch. Sometimes, we may learn important things from asides or throwaway remarks that people make. In general, unless we specifically and carefully structure formal meetings to get at feelings or experiences, we are likely to miss significant contributions to our understanding of any situation.

Relationships

An important principle is that all effective leadership rests on building solid, one-to-one relationships with people. Other activities, such as organising meetings, setting up committees, establishing task forces, making speeches, writing, and so on, may be very important but they are no substitute for the building of relationships. Without these close, one-to-one relationships, it is unlikely that leaders will manage to stay on track. It is within these relationships that we listen and put our finger on the pulse of situations.

We can take each of the elements highlighted so far, reverse the order and characterise leading as a process of building close relationships, within which we listen to people, so that we can think about them. These are not the only important aspects of the leadership process but they are fundamental to it and they highlight key functions we have to perform in order to realise our leadership potential.

Confusion between leadership and authority

As a step towards realising our potential, it helps also to focus on some of the barriers that get in the way of being effective as a leader. For many people, there is confusion between the roles of leadership and authority, and this confusion has had an impact on the approach to leadership taken by many priests and religious. There are many people with no authority who regularly take leadership and, by the same token, there are many people with authority who, for a number of reasons, rarely take leadership. In practice, these two processes sometimes overlap and are sometimes separate.

In theory, where authority is exercised in an authentic way, it should coincide with true leadership. In practice, however, authority often operates without leadership. As Richard A. McCormick points out, the more people rely on mere authority to get things done (for example, by ordering people, emphasising rules and regulations, insisting on recognition of their status), the less they do those things that are central to true leadership.[2] Under these conditions, actual authority is reduced, and as this happens, authority figures rely more and more on the trappings of authority. They become authoritarians rather than leaders.

On the other hand, the more true leadership and authority actually do coincide, the less appeal there is to formal authority to get things done. Because the people in authority are genuine leaders, they have a relaxed and flexible approach to getting things done. People follow them out of belief in and commitment to them, rather than out of fear or obligation. Their power comes from their expertise and credibility rather than their position.

In many cases, the difficulties that people have around leadership arise as a result of their bad experiences with abusive authority. Their feelings about such authority can then become attached to all leadership. The confusion between these processes has led, in some cases, to a suspicion or distrust of leaders and reluctance on the part of some people to play leadership roles or to be seen to be leading. An important challenge in realising our leadership potential is recognising that leadership, in its true sense, is both a necessary and a very positive resource in any setting. Confusion with authoritarianism should not deter us from welcoming opportunities to lead.

Absence of vision

Many people in leadership positions adopt a fire-fighting approach that settles for addressing immediate, short-term problems that disturb the status quo while neglecting the longer-term, bigger-picture vision of what needs to happen to realise potential. Some have lost sight of their own personal vision, have quite low expectations about what it is possible to achieve, or have lost hope in the ability of the institution to adapt to the challenges facing it.

Isolation and lack of intimacy

One barrier to being effective has particular relevance in the context of a male, celibate priesthood. In working with priests over many years, I have been struck by the depth of isolation that has often surrounded them. Both in the case of diocesan priests and of members of religious congregations, I have seen many examples of individual priests who felt alone and unsupported by their fellow priests, who had difficulty trusting their fellow priests, who rarely talked openly or deeply about themselves to their fellow priests, or who had divisive or destructive relationships with their fellow priests. In many cases, they had no one else in their lives that they could or would easily turn to, and often no one with whom they could be intimate in a close, loving way. Sometimes, the contrast between the Christian message of love and the reality of their own relationships was quite striking. The quality of the day-to-day lives of these men, in simple human terms, made it hard to see how they could be effective leaders over any extended period of time.

Failure to include diversity

We saw earlier that central to leading is an understanding of how people struggle. In practice, many of the struggles are not just individual, they are collective. They are connected to people's social identity, for example, as men, as women, as middle class, as working class, as young people, as elders, as Travellers, as people of colour, as gay or lesbian, as Roman Catholics, as Protestants, as priests, and so on (the list of possible identities is a long one). In most complex situations, people's social identity is a key factor but one that is often unrecognised and unacknowledged. As leaders and people who collaborate in leading, we bring our social identities and their particular struggles into our relationships and the work we do. These affect how visible we allow ourselves to be (or are allowed to be), how much we contribute to discussions, the roles we take on, who we feel comfortable with, how confident we feel, how we handle conflict and many other aspects of how we participate and lead. Our social identities also give us unique perspectives in any situation and make for much more creative and thoughtful responses to any problem. The failure to nurture diversity and include diverse social groups in the leadership process is a common failing in leadership.

Destructive reactions
There is a particular barrier to effective leadership that is quite pervasive but rarely addressed. This is the widespread tendency for people to react in destructive ways to those who take on visible leadership roles.[3] One type of destructive reaction, *isolation*, involves allowing people in leadership roles to become isolated. Leaders in this situation cannot tell if they have any support. No one seems to show any understanding of, or interest in, what it is like for the leader. Few people reach out or try to be there for the leader. This is not done maliciously. Mostly it is subconscious and seems to be connected to an expectation or assumption that leaders do not need support, help or understanding.

A second type of destructive reaction, *attack*, seems to be much more deliberate and direct. In particular, this involves abusive criticism of the leader, criticism of the leader behind their back, deliberate exclusion or ostracism of the leader and various forms of undermining the leader.

The combination of isolation and attack interferes with the ability of people to lead effectively and often has consequences for their psychological well-being and health. While they are often legitimised as necessary to ensure good leadership, their effects are almost always counter-productive. No leader ever improves as a result of attack and no one functions well in isolation.

Realising our potential
A central part of realising potential is addressing each of these barriers – deciding to play a leadership role, connecting to a vision,

building close relationships, nurturing diversity and building a support structure to combat isolation and attacks.

Deciding to be a leader

Given the distrust and low expectations that can become attached to leadership, it makes a difference, to begin with, if we consciously make an actual decision to lead. We are not leaders because of the position we occupy. It requires a decision on our part to play this role and behave like a leader. Implicit in this decision is an acceptance that we can make a difference, a belief in ourselves as having something significant to offer and an active decision to be influential.[4] Without this decision, without an intention to be a leader, we limit what we can possibly achieve.

Connecting to a vision

We become more effective leaders as we connect to, and operate from, a vision of what is possible. It helps to stop and ask ourselves what matters to us, why we do what we do, what is close to our heart about this work. Instead of reacting to events or fire-fighting, we are guided by an inner sense of what is important. Much of this vision is informed by listening to people's struggles. In many of the critical situations facing us in Church and society, people are desperate for encouragement and hope. Offering this is a key role of a leader. Being able to do it depends on being connected to our vision.

Building close and diverse relationships

For any person taking on a new leadership role and wondering where to start, the answer is with building relationships. We realise our potential through other people. It is not the role of a leader to have all the answers. No one person can. Expecting to be able to, however, is both an unnecessary burden and an obstacle to being effective.

We become even more effective as leaders when we build relationships across diversity, when we include in our circle of collaborators people from a wide range of different social identities. So we can ask ourselves who we are not connected to, both in terms of key individuals and key social groups. Who are the people who have the potential to be influential or to make a difference? To whom do we need to get closer and listen? What are the particular social groups to whom we need to get closer, the groups that deserve to be part of the leadership process and whose contribution will enhance the quality of the thinking we do? Which groups fail to be represented in leadership and decision-making processes because of prejudice, exclusion, social invisibility, fear or thoughtlessness?

Building support

Support can take various forms such as peer support groups, counselling, spiritual direction and supervision. It also builds closeness, intimacy and fun into our lives and helps us to pay attention to our health and well-being. Such support breaks through isolation and makes it more difficult for attacks to damage us. Just as listening is central to leadership, so is the question of who will listen to the leader. Setting this up requires initiative on our part, as well as a clear understanding that looking after our physical and emotional well-being is essential for good leadership and not a selfish luxury.

Conclusion

Priests today cannot lead effectively in isolation. Effectiveness requires diverse relationships with people from a wide range of social backgrounds as well as close, personal relationships that nurture and support. These relationships along with a positive, hopeful vision and a conscious intention to offer leadership are a solid basis for realising leadership potential.

Notes

1. Seán Ruth, *Leadership and Liberation: A Psychological Approach* (London: Routledge, 2006); *High-Quality Leadership: A Self-Assessment Guide for Individuals and Teams* (Dublin: Veritas, 2006); 'Leadership Development: Time For a Rethink', *HRD Ireland* (Spring 2006), 10–13; 'Leadership and Liberation', *Doctrine and Life* 57.2 (2007), 15–24.

2. Richard A. McCormick, 'Authority and Leadership: The Moral Challenge', *America* 175.2 (1996), 12–17.
3. Ruth, 2006.
4. J. Kouzes and B. Posner, *The Truth About Leadership: The No-Fads, Heart-of-the-Matter Facts You Need to Know* (San Francisco: Jossey-Bass, 2010).

Authority and Power

TOM DALZELL

Power derived from vitality

The famous Italian-German theologian and priest Romano Guardini experienced his conversion when he was confronted with the words of Jesus in the gospel that whoever finds his soul will lose it and whoever loses his soul will find it (cf. Mt 10:39).[1] Losing oneself is not usually the hallmark of authority and power as they are exercised in our world, but it is a feature of Christian authority and power. Authority and power in the priesthood, as in any other ecclesial role, can only ever take their lead from the self-emptying authority and power of Jesus himself. There was something different about Jesus. His authority was clear from his teaching and his mighty deeds (cf. Mk 1:22). Unlike the scribes and the Pharisees, he taught with authority. The scribes and Pharisees worked hard, as priests do today, but their words left people cold. The words of Jesus, however, were warm and full of power, not a power that lorded it over people but a power to change people's lives. As Guardini put it, that power derived from the vitality sounding through his speech. Everything about him was genuine, strong, straight from the mind and heart. It was candid and rang true.[2] Jesus could speak with authority because he was not just a prophet who spoke for God, even the last prophet. The prophets spoke God's word, but for the Christian community Jesus is God's Word, God's own Word, a saving Word, a Word of mercy for all, a Word he confirmed with his mighty deeds.

Authority is always something that has been conferred on a person. It doesn't originate in the person but is something given to him or her. This means that authority is always a delegated authority, a given authority. This was even the case for Jesus himself. As the Letter to the Hebrews states: 'It was not Christ who gave himself the glory of becoming high priest, but the one who said to him: You are my son, today I have become your father' (Heb 5:5). If this is so for the Risen Lord, it is certainly the case for the priest today. This is what helps the priest to achieve what Hans Urs von Balthasar called an 'un-selfing', so that God's glory can shine through.[3] If the priest has authority in the community, if he has power to exercise, he doesn't have them of himself. Rather, they have been given to him by God in Christ. It was after Jesus had said that all authority on heaven and earth had been given to him that he sent the apostles out to make disciples of all the nations, baptising them in the name of the Father, the Son and the Holy Spirit (cf. Mk 28:18-20). Their authority to preach and to cast out demons (cf. Mk 3:14-15) was only a participation in his authority. They didn't have it of themselves. So it is today for the priest. In fact, there is a curious paradox here. The priest has authority and power, and yet he is subject to authority and power, namely that of the Church, and, ultimately, that of God. But this too can be traced back to Jesus himself. If he could represent God – 'who can forgive sins but God?' (Mk 2:7) – he was also obedient to God. And, again, as Hebrews says: 'Though he was Son, he learned to obey through suffering' (Heb 5:8). As for power, the only power he was interested in was the power of love. He showed his power in the weakness of the cross. Hence, if God gave him glory as high priest, it is a glory that only ever shines through him as the crucified one. So it is with the priest. As he continues the mission of the incarnate Word in a specific way, as he too speaks with authority and forgives sins, so is he also obedient in the sense that he is also a listener to God's Word and that, like the crucified, he comes not to be served, but to serve and to give up his life as a ransom for many (Mt 20:28). Priesthood, therefore, is about service. The authority and power of the priest have nothing to do with lording it over people – they are about service. As Jesus said to the disciples who were indignant at the sons of Zebedee who wanted special positions in the Kingdom:

> You know that the rulers of the gentiles lord it over them, and their great men exercise authority over them. It shall not be so among you. Whoever would be great among you must be your servant, and whoever would be first among you must be your slave. (Mt 20:25-27)

Against careerism

The authority and power of the priest are not about his being 'greater' than others. In fact, it wasn't long after Jesus had spoken of his self-emptying death that his disciples were arguing about who was the greatest among them. While Matthew and Mark recount this after the third 'prediction' of the Passion (Mk 10:22, 24; Mt 20:25-27), Luke places it immediately after Jesus' eucharistic self-gift at the Last Supper. All three are probably telling the same story, but Christoph Schönborn, Archbishop of Vienna, amusingly suspects, given his experience of discussions among priests, that the argument wasn't a once-off occurrence.[4] He even sees the different accounts as proof of the historical authenticity of the gospels! Schönborn finds it shocking that what he calls a 'clerical row' about who was the greatest could take place in the 'sacristy', as it were, of the Last Supper's upper room. Over and against the desire for greatness, the response of Luke's Jesus is that the greatest must become the least and the leader must be the servant. 'Which is the greater', he asks, 'the one who sits at the table or the one who serves? The one at the table, surely. But here am I among you as one who serves' (Lk 22:27). Likewise, the 'greatness' of the priest is not about rank, position in the community, or about being looked up to, but his self-emptying service of others. That is the way authority and power are exercised in the Kingdom of God. In the view of Donald J. Goergen, status, prestige, privilege, power, greed and arrogance have no place in the lives of God's servants and no place in the vocation of the ordained or the baptised.[5]

This Christian approach to authority and power saves the priest today from the temptation of 'careerism', from the wish to advance in his career, to be promoted and, perhaps, gain more power. One can only be a priest by sharing in the self-emptying authority and power of the crucified Christ. In John's gospel, he designates himself as 'the gate of the sheepfold'. Anyone who 'climbs in' some other way is a thief and a bandit, he says (Jn 10:1, 7). Benedict XVI sees in this an image of careerism, the attempt to 'get ahead', to gain a position in the Church, to make use of and not to serve. It is the image, he thinks, of a man who wants to make himself important, to become a person of note through the priesthood, someone who intends his own exaltation, rather than the humble service of Jesus Christ.[6] From what we have seen, the only way to legitimately 'climb into' the priesthood is through the cross. In other words, it is only when the priest empties himself of self-interest that God's own authority and power can be felt by other people. If others place the priest on a pedestal, if they 'lift him up', the only lifting up which will actually touch hearts in the community and not leave them cold is the priest's sharing in Jesus' being 'lifted up' on the cross, his emptying himself of glory so that the glory of God might shine through him. Being a priest therefore is not a job. It is a vocation, a vocation to share in the authority and power of the crucified Christ. This too is the message of John's gospel when it contrasts the hired man and the shepherd of the sheep. The hired man, since he is not the shepherd and the sheep do not belong to him, abandons the sheep as soon as he sees a wolf coming. He runs away because he is only a hired man – we might say that he is only doing a job – and has no concern for the sheep. Jesus, however, is not only a shepherd, but the Good Shepherd, the one who lays down his life for his sheep (cf. Jn 10:12-14). This is where we see what the priest's power and authority are really about: the powerlessness of love where his 'laying down his life', in the sense of his being configured to the Good Shepherd's disinterested love and service, is a command he has received from God (cf. Jn 10:18). If the priest is to be a good shepherd, he won't pasture himself. He won't seek his own advantage. Rather, as Walter Kasper has put it, he won't spare himself, but will commit his life and sacrifice it for the other. His service as a good shepherd won't be limited to office hours, but will demand his whole life.[7]

Authority in the service of communion

Nor are the priest's authority and power exercised in isolation. Indeed a priest is not a priest on his own, but always in communion with other priests and the bishop. And he serves the communion of all the members the Church. For *Pastores Dabo Vobis*, priestly obedience has a community dimension or, better, a communion dimension. It is, as the text states,

> not the obedience of an individual who alone relates to authority, but rather an obedience which is deeply a part of the unity of the presbyterate, which as such is called to cooperate harmoniously with the bishop and, through him, with Peter's successor. (28)

Vatican II already promoted this communion dimension when *Presbyterorum Ordinis* taught that priests, according to their share of Christ's authority and in the name of the bishop, gather the family of God together (PO, 6). Bishops, according to *Christus Dominus*, are to love the priests under their authority and listen to them (CD, 16). In *Pastores Dabo Vobis*, the priest is the servant of communion because, in union with the bishop and closely related to the presbyterate, he builds up the unity of the Church community in a harmony of diverse vocations, charisms and services (PDV, 16). But *communio* ecclesiology can often be understood in an exclusively horizontal way. When *Lumen Gentium* understands the Church as communion, the communion in question is primarily the one Church's sharing in the communion in the Trinitarian God. Hence the view of *Presbyterorum Ordinis* that priests are to lead God's people through Christ in the Holy Spirit to God the

Father (PO, 6). In relation to this vertical axis of communion, the priest only ever shares in the authority of the incarnate Son who received it from the Father through the Holy Spirit. Horizontally, he exercises his faculties in union with his fellow priests and the bishop. Both of these axes of communion, vertical and horizontal, help to save the priest from making his authority and power felt in an autocratic way.

When *Lumen Gentium* teaches that there is an essential difference between the ministerial priesthood and the priesthood of all the baptised, it does not mean that the priests have authority and power and the laity do not (LG, 10). Lay Catholics ought not to be understood in terms of exclusion from authority and power but as exercising them in their own way in virtue of their participation in the prophetic, priestly and kingly mission of the whole Church. It's not that the priest has authority and power and the layperson does not. The way Gerhard Ludwig Müller, currently Prefect of the Congregation for the Doctrine of the Faith, has expressed it is this: the layperson is not a passive member of the Church and, unlike the priest, is not characterised by what he or she cannot do. Nor does the ministry of priests as shepherds and teachers imply a privileged position for a 'caste' separate from the community of believers. For Müller, what ultimately prevents the priest's authority from degenerating into a means of wielding power over others and promoting self-interest is its being grounded in his self-giving love after the example of Christ.[8]

Nevertheless, the authority of the priest doesn't come from the community but from the Good Shepherd, and his power derives from the episcopate. But it is obvious that the priest can really only exercise these if he has the good will of the community. A priest has to gain the respect of others if his authority is to carry any weight. And to be allowed to exercise his power in the community, he has to gain the trust of those he is called to serve. The priest is meant to be a leader, not a manager. A manager relies on his or her natural talent and organisational training. The priest as leader needs more than these. And yet, as Avery Dulles has recognised, it would be a mistake for the priest to rely only on his authority of office. For his shepherding role in the community he needs to be humanly gifted in the area of relationships. He needs to be able to work with other people, to consult them, respect their competencies and welcome their cooperation. He must be capable of recognising the talents of others and evoking their initiatives.[9] In other words, although he maintains overall responsibility as pastor, he has to be able to delegate authority and share his power, to include others in the decision-making process, just as his authority and power have been delegated to him.

Formation for the exercise of authority

Of course, the authority of priests has been called into question by the worldwide sexual abuse scandals, which can be understood, at least partly, in terms of an abuse of power in relation to children and vulnerable adults. Concerning the abuse of minors, the empirical evidence suggests that something other than true paedophilia, which can be understood in terms of a fixation at a childhood stage of psycho-sexual development, has driven clerical offenders to their crimes. It has been claimed that one factor is the institutional power-structure of the Church itself and a requirement of blind obedience on the part of its priests.[10] This is not the kind of obedience we are advocating here. If the priest promises obedience on the day of his ordination, it does not follow that he thereby abdicates his own authority. He exercises the authority given to him and he is expected to do so with maturity and freedom. Hence the importance of a good formation programme. As Karl Rahner urged long ago, the priest's formation must go beyond the study of philosophy and theology; it must be a formation not just of the intellect, but of the whole human being, including his emotional life. Only then will people have the impression that the priest is a loving, selfless and kind human being.[11] The priest's submission to those invested with ecclesial authority is in no way a kind of humiliation. In *Pastores Dabo Vobis*, it flows rather from the responsible freedom of the priest. Authentic Christian obedience, according to the text, when it is properly motivated and lived without servility, helps the priest to exercise the authority entrusted to him and his authority then, in its turn, is free from authoritarianism or demagoguery (PDV, 28). So the obedience of the priest to those who have authority over him, therefore, is not meant to be blind obedience. It is not the obedience of a child, but the obedience of an adult who exercises his own authority and power responsibly and for the good of others. And his power is not for subjugating other people for his own enjoyment, but for empowering them to flourish and to have the fullness of life that God wants for them. The priest, therefore, like St Paul, puts no obstacle in anyone's way, so that no fault may be found with his ministry (2 Cor 6:3).

Notes

1. Romano Guardini, *Stationen und Rückblicke. Berichte über mein Leben* (Mainz: Matthias Grünewald, 1995), 69–70.
2. Romano Guardini, *Jesus Christus: Meditations*, Peter White, trans. (London: Burns & Oates, 1960), 29.
3. Hans Urs von Balthasar, *The Glory of the Lord: A Theological Aesthetics I: Seeing the Form* (San Francisco: Ignatius Press, 1982), 216.
4. Christoph Schönborn, *Die Freude, Priester zu sein* (Freiburg: Herder, 2011), 109–11, 113.
5. Donald J. Goergen, 'Priest, Prophet, King: The Ministry of Jesus Christ', *The Theology of the Priesthood*, Donald J. Goergan and Ann Garrido, eds (Collegeville, MN: Liturgical Press, 2000), 206.
6. Benedict XVI, Homily for the Ordination to the Priesthood of fifteen Deacons of the Diocese of Rome, 7 May 2006 (Rome: Libreria Editrice Vaticana, 2006), 8–10.
7. Walter Kasper, *A Celebration of Priestly Ministry: Challenge, Renewal and Joy in the Catholic Priesthood*, Brian McNeil, trans. (New York: Crossroad, 2007), 106.
8. Gerhard Ludwig Müller, *Priesthood and Diaconate: The Recipient of the Sacrament of Holy Orders from the Perspective of Creation Theology and Christiology*, Michael J. Miller, trans. (San Francisco: Ignatius Press, 2002), 128–9.
9. Avery Robert Dulles, *The Priestly Office: A Theological Reflection* (New York: Paulist Press, 1997), 51–2.

10. See Marie Keenan, *Child Sexual Abuse and the Catholic Church: Gender, Power and Organizational Culture* (Oxford: Oxford University Press, 2012), 14, 34, 46.

11. Karl Rahner, *Der Priester von heute*, Andreas Batlogg and Albert Raffelt, eds (Freiburg: Herder, 2009), 24, 33.

Ordained Ministry – A View 'From Below'

ÉAMONN FITZGIBBON

The Bishop of Rome

The months of February and March of 2013 may well be remembered as heralding a new springtime in the life of the Church. The courageous decision of Pope Benedict XVI to break with the practice of six hundred years and resign from the papacy will no doubt impact on ecclesiology and on the theology of ministry for decades to come. The text of Benedict's statement makes it clear that he felt that he was no longer able to fulfil the requirements of his ministry as pope. My personal view is that what was also at play was his strong sense of a crisis of faith, especially in the Western world, and that it would require new blood to take up the challenge of the Year of Faith and the Synod on the New Evangelisation. What we can say for certain is that Benedict's decision has done something very significant to our perception of the papacy. The papacy has been somehow demythologised; it can now be seen more in terms of a ministry and function within the Church. The papacy has previously been identified with larger than life, charismatic personalities and this generated its own mystique and cultic dimension.

On a larger scale, Benedict's resignation may have done more for the reception of Vatican II's teaching on the papacy than all the words written and spoken since. There was a desire during the Council to counterbalance the centuries-long movement of the papacy towards a consolidation and centralisation of power whereby it came to resemble an absolute monarchy. Through the centuries the pope became identified as the Vicar of Christ rather than the Successor of Peter. Subsequently, a centralist, ultramontanist movement reached its peak during Vatican I with the definition of the conditions for infallible papal teaching:

> This teaching focused the attention of believers almost exclusively on the pope's role as supreme pontiff and pastor of the universal church, eclipsing his role as the pastor of the local church at Rome.[1]

The development of the office of the papacy is well described by John O'Malley in what he terms 'the long nineteenth century'.[2] There was certainly an attempt at Vatican II to correct and balance this movement, but within a few weeks Pope Benedict and his successor Pope Francis profoundly influenced our theology of papacy and episcopacy and indeed our wider ecclesiology.

When Pope Francis appeared on the central balcony of St Peter's Basilica on the evening of his election, he referred to himself as the Bishop of Rome (and indeed, he referred to Benedict as the emeritus Bishop), and spoke of the local diocesan community having its new bishop. This is a significant shift in emphasis and suggests that Francis sees himself as a bishop among bishops, and that it is because he is Bishop of Rome that he is pope, not vice-versa.

You may wonder what, if anything, all of this has to do with the ministry of the bishop. Yet within a tightly interrelated understanding of Church ministry and leadership, such as we have and such as was proposed by Vatican II, a change in one ministry will affect all the other key ministries, and the recent changes in the perception of the papacy is bound to have a 'ripple effect'.[3] Is it not the case that some of the autonomy, mystique and monarchical style which characterised the papacy through the ages were similarly reflected at local level? Daniel L. Migliore identifies the key challenge in understanding the role and ministry of today's bishop when he says:

> In summary, theology must avoid both a sacralising of ministry that separates ordained leaders from the rest of the people of God and a demeaning of ministry that trivialises the importance of this office in the life of the Church.[4]

The practice in Ireland has been to elevate the role of the bishop to the point that he is greatly distanced not only from the faithful but too often from his fellow priests as well.

Ministry 'from below'

The editing from the initial drafts to the final document of *Lumen Gentium* is most revealing. The preparatory draft (or schema) was significantly reworked, and the chapter 'On the People of God and Especially the Laity' was split, with the material on 'The People of God' being placed before the chapter on the hierarchy. This pointed to a significant ecclesiological development.[5] The various ministries and orders are situated within the context of the baptised People of God; it is from this starting point of equality and unity that we must proceed to understand any of the ministries, be they ordained (bishop, priest or deacon) or lay:

> For everyone's sake it will be important for bishops and priests to internalise clearly that they are not a second 'People' apart from the People of God. They could not be ordained if they had not been previously baptised. The most fundamental ecclesiological reality is the unity of the baptised in the one Body of Christ.[6]

John O'Malley tells us that, on 16 October 1963, during a meeting on the schema for *Lumen Gentium*, the bishops took up discussion on the chapter entitled 'On the People of God and Especially the Laity':

Insistent that in the final analysis the bishops are in charge, the chapter struck an unaccustomed note in ecclesiastical documents by being almost as insistent on initiative 'from below'.[7]

The phrase 'from below' is interesting here in that it is suggestive of Christian anthropology. Indeed this approach, which has been used to such great effect in other areas of theology such as Christology, has much to offer to the study of ministry:

> The point is that we are now in an era when the trickle-down thesis theology of the experts is giving way to dialoguing with the 'percolating-up theology' of the People of God.[8]

Margaret Lavin has made a very cogent argument for the anthropological approach to ministry:

> What, in our Christian theological tradition, can help us to name our new reality and to broaden our understanding of ministry in order to meet the current needs of the Church? In many respects, the answer is staring us in the face. In our tradition, we see the human person as created in the image and likeness of God. We are related to the humanity of God in Jesus Christ. In theological terms, this view of the human person is 'theological anthropology'.[9]

In this approach, Baptism is the starting point; any discussion of an ontological change at ordination must first give account of the ontological change at Baptism. Baptism is the fundamental sacrament through which ministers are called; all who are baptised share in the ministry of Christ and all the baptised, regardless of subsequent ordination as priest or bishop, continue to be members of the priesthood of the faithful.

However we interpret a subsequent ordained ministry, we should not lose sight of the once-for-all, life-long ordination of Baptism, which provides our primary identification.[10]

If we are to approach the ministry of the bishop 'from below', it will be necessary to truly engage with the meaning of the priesthood of the faithful as recovered in Vatican II:

If we call believers 'Christians' by virtue of their baptismal anointing by the Holy Spirit, so we also call the baptised 'priests' because, by virtue of that same anointing, they are all members of the only priesthood there is – the priesthood of Jesus Christ.[11]

The Council restored the rich theology of the priesthood of the faithful, insisting that any subsequent ordination is at the service of this. Indeed one major change introduced by the bishops at Vatican II was that they clearly and magisterially established the episcopacy as part of the sacrament of orders:

The sacred Synod teaches that by Episcopal consecration is conferred the fullness of the sacrament of orders, that fullness which in the Church's liturgical practice and in the language of the holy Fathers of the Church is undoubtedly called the high priesthood, the apex of the sacred ministry.[12]

It must be said first of all that the bishop is not receiving a new and different sacrament; he is ordained sacramentally as part of the sacrament of orders. In this, he is a bishop in his own right; he is not a delegate or vicar of the pope but is in fact called and commissioned by God.[13] This independent authority of the local ordinary is not always clearly evident in practice; it sometimes appears as if Rome acts as the centralised CEO, micro-managing its sub-offices throughout the world. It can sometimes appear that bishops are constantly looking over their shoulder, caught in the unenviable position of the middle-ground between the local opinion and the Vatican directive.

The phrase 'fullness of priesthood' cited above from *Lumen Gentium* is also something new introduced by the Council Fathers. Unfortunately its meaning was not clearly explained and it has been left to subsequent theology to work this out. The phrase has raised some difficulty for priests as they are left to wonder, 'If the bishop has the fullness of priesthood, what have I – a portion, a share?' The phrase has consequently left some clergy feeling diminished. However, the anthropological approach which I have been advocating, an approach to the theology of ministry from below, might prove to be very helpful here. Within the priesthood of the faithful some are ordained to ministerial priesthood (continuing to be part of the priesthood of the faithful) and within the ministerial priesthood some are ordained as bishops (continuing to be part of the priesthood of the faithful and the ordained priesthood); we are left with an image of concentric circles of ministry rather than pyramidical tiers of ministry. I do not wish to collapse the distinctions between ministries but I believe it is equally unhelpful to draw sharp lines between the various ministries of the Church, which can set them in opposition to each other. The phrase 'fullness of priesthood' is thus understood as enhancing the presbyterate in the same way that a positive understanding of the role of the ordained enhances the role of the laity. The *Catechism* says:

> The ministerial or hierarchical priesthood of bishops and priests, and the common priesthood of all the faithful participate, each in its own proper way, in the one priesthood of Christ. While being ordered one to another, they differ essentially. In what sense? While the common priesthood of the faithful is exercised by the unfolding of baptismal grace – a life of faith, hope, and charity, a life according to the Spirit – the ministerial priesthood is at the service of the common priesthood. It is directed at the unfolding of the baptismal grace of all Christians.[14]

'Fullness of priesthood' is not meant to say that the bishop is holier or more a priest than the ordained priest any more than the ordained priest is holier or more important than the laity.

> Ordination is not simply an intensification of the common priesthood: were that so the clergy would be better or more complete Christians, and this is obviously untrue. The common and the ordained priesthoods are not different on the level of being Christian. Rather, within the communion of all Christians, the distinction has to do with ministries.[15]

The ministry of unity

I believe that an aspect of the ministry of the bishop which urgently needs to find greater expression in today's Irish context is the ministry of unity. Each of the Council documents pertaining to the role of the hierarchy gives prominence to this dimension. *Sacrosanctum Concilium* and *Christus Dominus* offer us the image of a local church being like a eucharistic assembly united in communion around its bishop, expressing itself as the Body of Christ. The emphasis on collegiality among bishops was to be expressed in unity with the pope but also in local conferences of bishops. Similarly, the bishop is to be united with his priests and the people of his diocese working to form it into one community. It is also made clear that no bishop exists without a community. The Council spoke of the '*presbyterium*', intending that collegiality would also be replicated at local level.[16] In recent times, the pastoral life of bishops and indeed the personal life of bishops have become too individualised. The crisis around clerical sexual abuse has resulted in a great deal of anger being directed at the hierarchy; bishops are becoming increasingly isolated within the Church:

> Reflecting a long ecclesial tradition, the Second Vatican Council spoke of the bond between bishop and priest as that of father, brother and friend, envisaging a relationship of mutual trust and dialogue. As the domino effect of the

crisis continues, such an understanding of the relationship between bishop and priest would seem no longer practicable or even tenable.[17]

It seems the abuse crisis has left the call to unity and communion in disarray as bishops try to balance handling allegations and concerns to the satisfaction of complainants, the accused, families involved, the media, the public and other priests. Incidentally, I have often wondered about the title 'father', 'friend' or 'brother' for a bishop among the priests of his diocese. Theologically these terms may be helpful but they can lead to unreal expectations or even psychological baggage, as personal experiences of authority or family can cloud the relationship for what it really is. A bishop is often expected to be all things to all people. 'The mannerisms of an apostolic brother are different from the mannerisms of a patriarchal father.'[18] Perhaps Pope Francis, by identifying himself as a bishop among bishops, has given an example to be followed at local level – the bishop is first and foremost a priest among priests.

Finally, concerning the relationship between the bishop and the faithful of the diocese, Pope John Paul II gave us a wonderful image of *perichoresis* – an interplay which affirms the equal dignity of both bishop and people.[19] The 'from below' approach that I have been advocating is also helpful here:

> Before boundaries, then, there is an area of no boundaries. Before distinction there is interrelationality. Pastorally, all of this needs to be sorted out in a clearer way. Otherwise there remains a quibbling about pastoral boundaries that causes serious pastoral problems.[20]

Such unity is not only, or even primarily, about responding to a crisis, it is also necessary for true renewal in the Church. A number of years ago, Seán Mac Réamoinn said of the Irish context:

As we face a new century, a new millennium, a new world, and hence a new agenda for the Church, we must work and pray to be rid of all divisions which serve only to inhibit and frustrate our discipleship.[21]

The prophetic and kingly ministry

The Council documents remind us that all Christians share in the ministry of Christ and, as such, all ministers have a priestly, prophetic and kingly role. There is a great need for our bishops to give expression to their prophetic and kingly role at this time. The Church in Ireland needs strong, decisive leadership if it is to be sufficiently prepared for the challenges that lie ahead. A vision and pastoral plan to implement this vision is required throughout the Church. Allied to this governance role is the teaching ministry which is at the core of the bishop's responsibility. Dermot Lane reminds us that the Church of the future will require a 'mature, critically informed faith among the people of God'.[22] Adult faith formation, training for lay leadership and particular lay ecclesial ministries, and ongoing formation for clergy are all essential to any renewal of the Church. *Christus Dominus* says:

> Bishops should present Christ's teaching in a manner relevant to the needs of the times, providing a response to those difficulties and problems which people find especially distressing and burdensome.'

It is part of the responsibility of the ordained to ensure that the laity are sufficiently skilled and formed so that they may competently fulfil their role: 'The ordained have a crucial role to play in the formation of those living in the baptismal priesthood.[23]

Conclusion

History teaches us that the various terms which we use for ministries have changed meaning through the ages, and similarly ministry itself has been constantly evolving. 'What is constant historically is the principle of sacramental order. What changes is how ministries evolve and are ordered.'[24] Church leadership will need to show itself to be flexible enough to adapt to the changing needs of our time.

Notes

1. Richard R. Gaillardetz and Catherine E. Clifford, *Keys to the Council: Unlocking the Teaching of Vatican II* (Collegeville, MN: Liturgical Press, 2012), 112.
2. See John W. O'Malley, *What Happened at Vatican II* (London: Harvard, 2008), 53–93.
3. See Kenan B. Osborne, *The Permanent Diaconate: Its History and Place in the Sacrament of Orders* (New York: Paulist Press, 2007), 75–86.
4. Daniel L. Migliore, *Faith Seeking Understanding: An Introduction to Christian Theology* (Cambridge: Wm. B. Eerdmans Publishing Co., 1991/2004), 298.
5. See *Keys to the Council*, 79.
6. Paul J. Philibert, *The Priesthood of the Faithful: Key to a Living Church* (Collegeville, MN: Liturgical Press, 2005), 19.
7. *What Happened at Vatican II*, 186.
8. William J. Bausch, *The Hands-On Parish: Reflections and Suggestions for Fostering Community* (New London, CT: Twenty-Third Publications, 1989), 28.
9. Margaret Lavin, *Theology for Ministry* (Toronto, ON: Novalis, 2004), 10.
10. *Faith Seeking Understanding*, 205.
11. *The Priesthood of the Faithful*, 54.
12. *Lumen Gentium*, 21.
13. See *The Permanent Diaconate*, 56–72.
14. *Catechism of the Catholic Church*, 1546, 1547.
15. Paul Bernier, *Ministry in the Church: A Historical and Pastoral Approach* (New London, CT: Twenty-Third Publications, 1992, 2006) 211.
16. See *Keys to the Council*, 113–15.
17. Patrick Connolly, 'Priest and Bishop: Implications of the Abuse Crisis', *The Furrow* LVII (2006), 132.
18. Paul J. Philibert, 'Reclaiming the Vision of an Apostolic Church', *Worship* 83.6 (2009).
19. See John Paul II, Apostolic Exhortation, *Pastores Gregis* (October, 2003); also see Philibert, 148–51.
20. *Keys to the Council*, 99.

21. Seán Mac Réamoinn, 'Stoles, Collars and ..', *Ministry, Clerics and the Rest of Us*, Mac Réamoinn, ed. (Dublin: Columba Press, 1998), 25.

22. Dermot A. Lane, 'Vatican II: The Irish Experience', *The Furrow* (2004), 55.2, 76.

23. *The Priesthood of the Faithful*, 127.

24. Susan K. Wood, 'Convergence Points Toward a Theology of Ordered Ministries', *Ordering the Baptismal Priesthood: Theologies of Lay and Ordained Ministry*, Susan K. Wood, ed. (Collegeville, MN: Liturgical Press, 2003), 263.

The Relationship Between Bishop and Priest

WILLIE WALSH

The relationship in theory

The Second Vatican Council opened up for many of my generation an entirely new vision of the Church. It was a Church that was more understanding, compassionate and willing to engage with the human in attempting to make the Kingdom of God a lived experience. It inspired me at the time and continued to do so during my ministry as bishop of Killaloe diocese.

In order to discuss the relationship between bishops and priests, I immediately turn to documents of the Council. *Christus Dominus*, the Decree Concerning the Pastoral Office of Bishops in the Church, sees the role of bishops in terms both of the Universal Church and their own dioceses. I will be addressing here the subject of diocesan bishop and priests and their respective relationship. In this context the decree states:

> Their priests who assume a part of their [bishop's] duties and concerns ... should be the objects of their particular affection. They should regard them as their sons and friends ... always ready to listen to them in an atmosphere of mutual trust ... [Bishops] should be solicitous for the welfare – spiritual, intellectual and material – of their priests. (16)

Pope John Paul II in 2003 reiterated much of the above sentiment in his Apostolic Exhortation *Pastores Gregis*, and gives it a more contemporary tone:

> The bishop will always strive to relate to his priests as a father and a brother who loves them, listens to them, welcomes them, corrects them, supports them, seeks their cooperation and, as much as possible, is concerned for their human, spiritual, ministerial and financial welfare. (47)

In many ways, the above documents say all that needs to be said of the relationship between bishop and priest. I will be attempting to suggest how these ideals might be put into practice in the everyday life of a diocese. I will do so under three main headings drawn from the above documents: supporting one another; mutual welfare; and fraternal correction.

There are two preliminary points I feel must be made before addressing the practical side of the bishop/priest relationship. First, my experience comes from a background of sixteen years as a diocesan bishop, and naturally I tend to see the relationship through the eyes of a bishop. I did of course experience more than thirty years of the reverse relationship as priest to bishop. I was fortunate to serve under two bishops who were basically kind and considerate and were not, despite the times, cut from the authoritarian cloth. In fact, both of them were very involved in the emergence of and implementation of the changes brought about by Vatican II. I was blessed to have been a priest at that time. I often say that, in hindsight, those bishops did not impinge very much on my life. It is very much the reality today as well that the paths of a bishop and his priests don't cross as much as people might think. I mention this simply to underline the fact that the bishop/priest relationship exists within an environment of limited contact, a factor that has its own impact on the relationship.

Second, I think it is important to address the father and son aspects which the quoted documents suggest are at the heart of the bishop/priest relationship. It has its origins in the spiritual parallel of the relationship of God the Father and Son. So often a bishop will speak of 'my priests' and the priests will refer to 'my bishop' and it is analogous with how a parent will refer to a son or daughter as 'my son' or 'my daughter'. Likewise, a son or daughter will speak of 'my father' or 'my mother'. However, rich as it may be, the father/son analogy is not the only way of describing the relationship. In contemporary terms we could as easily describe it as a relationship of respect between two people with a common goal and purpose in life.

Supporting one another

The bishop/priest relationship exists on two levels – a one-to-one level and a group level. Both are important and the relationship is incomplete if one level is preferred to another. Likewise, the relationship cannot be one way. This means that both the bishop and priest must engage with it, work on it and nurture it. The priest must remember that the bishop is as worthy of receiving from the relationship as the priest. The bishop must remember too that the priest has much to bring to their relationship. He must respect the priest's contribution and be humble enough to accept that he has much to learn from his priest. It is this mutual support that is addressed by the Council when it says:

> To ensure an increasing effective apostolate the bishop should be willing to engage in dialogue with his priests, individually and collectively not merely occasionally but if possible regularly. (*Christus Dominus*, 28)

On a practical basis this means that a bishop should have an open door and direct phoneline policy to his priests. There must be an understanding established and honoured that a priest may have access to his bishop at all times. This will cover emergencies as well as create an atmosphere where a priest will know that he can easily arrange an informal meeting with his bishop at relatively short notice. Moreover, a bishop should arrange to meet with his priests individually and formally at least once every two years. However, this should not be a substitute for the open-door, casual arrangement already mentioned.

All of this is founded on a deep respect and indeed love for every priest in the diocese. If as Christians we preach the commandment of love, then surely a bishop is challenged to love his brother priests. Obviously we are talking here about something deeper than a feeling of love over which we have no control. We are speaking rather of a commitment to treat each priest with respect, with kindness and understanding. A goal for both bishop and priest might be to foster a level of deep friendship between them. It should be a friendship robust enough to handle disagreements, occasional rancour and the many ups and downs of any such relationship.

Again, I emphasise that support for one another is something that must be shared by bishop and priest. However, the bishop is but one man and there is more than one priest, which may result in the relationship making too heavy a demand on the bishop. It is important therefore that the bishop outlines to his priests and shows by example that he too is a priest and that their overall relationship will benefit by the normal, healthy interaction of smaller groups of priests who have shared interests and who 'look out' for one another. It is important to respect the reality that a relationship may flounder if forced. Small groups of friends working under the broader umbrella of common purpose and goals is an effective way of deepening the overall relationship between bishop and priest(s).

Relating to the collective body of priests, a bishop offers the support of teacher, leader, inspirer and motivator. In this group interaction, he will share his vision for the diocese and suggest some strategies by which this vision may be put into practice. Likewise, he will listen to their views and take them into account, as well as extending this sense of collaboration to include not only priests but the laity at large in the person of their representatives. Any such vision, of course, must ultimately be rooted in the example and teaching of Jesus Christ and will be adapted to the needs of the diocese at this time.

Mutual welfare

Again, the question of caring for the priests' welfare works out on a personal and group level. It is a two-way street, and the welfare of the bishop should not be overlooked by either himself or the priests. In this sense he once again unites himself with the body of diocesan priests and works in cooperation with them towards their mutual welfare.

A bishop can address effectively many welfare issues in, through and with the collective body of priests. As their spiritual leader he should engage in meaningful consultation with them on a range of issues that may arise, be they human, spiritual, ministerial or financial. The principal vehicle of consultation will be the council of priests. It is important that decisions taken at this level and agreed upon by the bishop be seen to be implemented or acted upon.

A bishop should actively promote a variety of activities that will assist ongoing priestly formation, such as diocesan retreats, days of recollection, pilgrimages, formation and study days, social gatherings and sabbaticals. Attendance at some or all of such activities will help to build up the bonds of friendship between priests and give a sense of unity and purpose to the shared diocesan apostolate of bishop and priests.

The appointment of a priest to a parish or other specific duties within a diocese is a subject that is naturally of great concern to every priest. It can prove to be one of great difficulty for a bishop as he endeavours to appoint personnel suited to the particular needs of various parishes. A happy appointment is very much at the heart of a priest's welfare and a crucial factor in the bishop/priest relationship.

While the final decision regarding appointments must rest with the bishop, such a decision cannot come out of the blue. It requires meaningful consultation between the bishop and the individual priest being considered for an appointment, or 'change' as it is often referred to. That consultation must take into account the needs of a particular parish, the overall needs of a diocese, the strengths and weaknesses of a priest and his suitability for a particular parish. It must also involve an awareness of particular personal needs of a priest.

Such consultation surrounding appointments will benefit greatly if conducted in conjunction with an appointments board, which will assist the bishop and priest through the appointments procedure. If a priest feels he has been sufficiently consulted, listened to and his reservations addressed, it is more than likely that he will accede to the judgement of the bishop or the appointments board, unless he has a strong reason for not doing so. I see no point in appointing a priest to any position if he has strong objections to it. My own experience in this area is that getting agreement on appointments is difficult with or without consultation. However, if genuine consultation is part of the process, it always fosters a good relationship between bishop and priest.

Fraternal correction

Life is not always light and happiness and into every relationship there may come shadows of concern. This is true of the bishop/priest relationship as well, and I feel it is worth mentioning this delicate topic of a bishop correcting a priest or in extreme situations censuring him. If it is done with a heavy hand you can take it that the bishop/priest relationship will be fractured.

No bishop wants conflict between him and a priest, nor indeed does a priest want to be in conflict with his bishop. The reality however is that wherever people are working closely together, there inevitably will be some tensions. The source of such conflict can vary from a priest feeling he has been unfairly treated by his bishop, to a bishop believing that a priest has treated a parishioner or a fellow priest in an unacceptable manner. It may be that the bishop simply feels that a priest is not fulfilling some of his pastoral responsibilities.

There are times when a bishop will have to challenge a priest in relation to behaviour which he deems to be unacceptable. This will often arise from a complaint made by a parishioner. It will be important for the bishop to try to verify that the complaint is true and is not something trivial. Having done so and arranged a meeting with the priest, the priest must be given the right to reply.

Dealing with any such difficult issue in a mature, non-confrontational way can improve and indeed give life to a relationship. A priest will quickly detect whether a bishop's 'fraternal correction' is about helping him to be a better priest or merely punishing a misdemeanour. The obedience a priest promises to his bishop at ordination will be all the more authentic and sincere by virtue of the good relationship that exists between the bishop and priest, one that is constantly strengthened by the exercise of ongoing priestly renewal practices. Obedience exacted by the power of authority alone will not make for a healthy relationship between a bishop and his priests.

Sometimes efforts at 'fraternal correction' can end in failure. A priest may feel that a bishop is more ready to listen to those with complaints against him than to the priest himself. He may feel that the bishop has not treated him fairly. In these situations a bishop needs to be careful not to allow a particular issue to dominate the overall relationship. Even if a priest fails to accept correction in relation to a specific issue, this does not and should not detract from all the good work that he may be doing in other areas of pastoral activity.

Dealing with serious allegations

There may be the very rare occasion when a bishop has to deal with allegations of a more serious nature against a priest. Here I have in mind the type of behaviour which is in total contradiction with one's priesthood, such as sexual abuse, serious neglect of one's pastoral duties and obligations, or financial irregularities. In such cases, the bishop has serious obligations towards the offended against as well as the alleged priest-offender. In terms of the priest, he must see to it that the presumption of innocence until proven guilty is upheld. Likewise, a bishop must be careful that rights to silence and a fair trial are exercised on behalf of the alleged offender just as any citizen is entitled to under the laws of a country.

The way in which allegations of sexual abuse have been handled by some of us bishops over the years has been a cause for serious worry for priests and has led to a significant loss of trust in bishops by many priests. Obviously bishops have a very serious obligation towards victims of alleged abuse, but they must be careful that they do not respond to the alleged abuse in a manner that might be unjust to the alleged abuser before the proper investigation of the allegations has been carried out. It is an area fraught with difficulties and a commitment should be in place for regular reviews of the guidelines of best practices in this area. The rights of all persons involved should be respected according to the law.

An area of great concern to priests is the process of being stood down from ministry when allegations of abuse are made against a priest. Important issues such as the manner in which parishioners are informed and the provision of appropriate accommodation and support are just some issues that priests feel have not been adequately addressed to date.

If a priest is found guilty and is subsequently permanently removed from priestly ministry, what obligations has the bishop of a diocese towards that priest? Different dioceses have different responses to this. I believe that the minimum requirement of any bishop in such a situation is that the priest be treated with respect and compassion. Of course any priest has to take responsibility for his own actions and if proven guilty of serious wrongdoing must be subject to appropriate penalties. However, the imposition of penalties must be balanced by compassion and an overall sense of real care for the offender, and by forgiveness where genuine remorse is shown. This very difficult area of how to respond appropriately both to victims of sexual abuse and to offenders raises questions that are at the heart of our Christian faith.

Conclusion

The complexity of the relationship between bishop and priest cannot be dealt with in terms of rules and regulations alone. Priests at ordination promise obedience to their bishop. I like to think that that obedience is less about implementing in detail every direction from the bishop but more about both bishop and priest responding appropriately and generously to the pastoral needs of those whom it is our common vocation to serve.

Priests' Rights and Responsibilities

PATRICK CONNOLLY

It is no secret that the Church has a certain reserve when using 'rights language' about its own internal affairs, as distinct from when it is speaking to and about the wider society in which it exists. This is perhaps no surprise because service and self-sacrifice are at the very heart of the gospel, and they surely should be primary in any consideration of, for instance, how priests are expected to behave and work. Hence it is predictable that canon law seems to put more emphasis on priests' obligations and responsibilities rather than on their rights. In the 1983 *Code of Canon Law*, Chapter III of Title III (*Sacred Ministers or Clerics*), which is found in Part I (*The Christian Faithful*) of Book II (*The People of God*), deals with the rights and obligations of clerics.[1] There are many more clerical obligations than rights listed, with the rights interspersed among the obligations, and yet nonetheless the Code does attempt to balance the two. The whole area of priests' responsibilities and rights is a very large and indeed nuanced one, and so this essay will focus on three selected themes rather than offer a comprehensive outline of all such clerical rights and obligations. While looking at these three themes, the concentration will be on diocesan priests in general, rather than dealing with the particular rights or obligations which are attached to certain ecclesiastical offices like that of parish priest.[2]

Obedience and its limits

It might be as well to begin with a priestly responsibility which can be challenging for both priest and bishop.[3] Canon 273 states that clerics are bound by a special obligation to show reverence and obedience to the supreme pontiff and to their own Ordinary. In the Code there is a general obligation of obedience pertaining to all Catholics, both laity and clergy: c. 209 §2 (they are to fulfil with great diligence the duties which they owe to the universal Church and to the particular Church); c. 212 §1 (they are bound by Christian obedience to follow what the pastors declare as teachers of the faith or determine as leaders of the Church); and 218 (the *obsequium* owed to the Magisterium). Canon 273 distinguishes between that general obedience and the one required of clerics by referring to the latter as a *special* obligation.

Interestingly, the equivalent canon in the 1917 Code made no mention of the pope, and in the preparation of the 1983 Code it was decided to make this obligation explicit given the Code Commission's emphasis that the Roman pontiff possesses the power of an Ordinary with respect to the universal Church.[4] The obligation to obey the pope is not explicit in the ordination promise. At a presbyteral ordination, one explicitly promises obedience only to one's Ordinary and his successors. And on a practical level, the issue of obedience for a priest arises more directly with his bishop.

With respect to his bishop, for the priest the obligation to obey stems from three factors. First, there is the nature of the jurisdiction of the bishop: he is the Vicar of Christ in the diocese, the visible foundation of the unity of faith and charity, and therefore needs to be obeyed.[5] Second, priests are necessarily cooperators with the bishop and depend on him in their exercise of power.[6] Third, there is the priest's promise of obedience made at ordination. In many ways, this promise simply affirms that which is already implicitly required of a priest by reason of his ordination.

The obedience mentioned by c. 273 is not supposed to be a mere external servile compliance with orders. Rather, it involves at least an attempt to comprehend the thinking lying behind the bishop's decisions. On the other hand, canonical obedience need not be unquestioning nor indeed does it have to be joyful. It does presuppose an active obedience in which the priest called upon to obey has had the opportunity for personal input into decisions affecting his life, as befits one collaborating with the bishop.[7] Canonical obedience doesn't imply a mere passivity on the part of the priest but a co-responsibility for ministry involving personal initiative and fraternal dialogue, provided he is ultimately willing to follow the judgment of those who have the primary governing function. As the Directory on the Life and Ministry of Priests says, 'nothing should take away from the intelligent capacity for personal initiative and pastoral enterprise.'[8]

This obedience owed to the bishop is not all-encompassing and has its limits. We must distinguish *canonical* obedience from the more general virtue of obedience. Only canonical obedience is juridically enforceable and it is restricted to those matters that are prescribed or governed by canon law. Canonical obedience is defined by the person's clerical status (and his ecclesiastical office, if he has one), but also by the limits of the bishop's jurisdiction. Accordingly, canonical obedience cannot be invoked when the bishop is commanding anything prohibited by canon law or prohibiting something that is clearly permitted by canon law. Moreover, canonical obedience does not interfere with a priest's right to take advice before responding to any allegation of impropriety and it cannot be used to force a revelation of conscience, that is, being forced to reveal matters known only in the person's inner sanctuary or conscience.[9] It likewise could not be invoked when dealing with a private matter or a matter not directly connected with the government of the diocese. In that regard, it contrasts sharply with the much more extensive *religious* obedience that obligates members of institutes of consecrated life in all parts of their life, and not just with respect to their state.[10]

The scope of canonical obedience is determined by the scope of priestly ministry and those things which have a direct relationship with that ministry. In other areas of life, a priest has a reasonably wide autonomy, for example, his cultural activities, administration of his personal property, his spiritual life and social relationships.[11] An example might be a bishop ordering a priest to quit some organisation. Does c. 273 require the cleric to obey? While a bishop could invoke canonical obedience to prohibit a cleric from involving himself in an association to the extent that involvement conflicted with ministerial responsibilities or which advocated positions clearly in conflict with the Church, he could not obligate the cleric to quit the association merely because it advocated positions which the bishop did not personally hold. The priest might obey out of a sense of goodwill and *ex virtute obedientiae*, but he could not be canonically bound to do so. In all of these matters, the cleric would always have the right to administrative recourse to the Congregation for Clergy in Rome.

Related to the general obligation of canonical obedience, c. 274 §2 speaks of the cleric's responsibility to undertake and to fulfil a function (*munus*) which has been entrusted to him, unless excused by a legitimate impediment. The 1917 predecessor of this canon specified that this obligation was binding only as long as the bishop judges that the needs of the Church demand it. At the 1981 plenary meeting on the revision of the Code, it was suggested that a reference to the 'needs of the Church' be added to the present canon. The response was that this addition was unnecessary given that it was already understood.[12] One has the duty of obedience because of the needs of the Church. Accordingly, it would seem that the bishop should accept a resignation of an office or assignment, unless there is some grave reason for rejecting it, keeping in mind the objective needs of the Church. Where the bishop decides that the resignation should not be accepted because there is no one to replace the priest in his role, the resignation should be accepted once someone comes along who could be a suitable replacement.

Canon 274 §2 speaks of a 'legitimate impediment' enabling a priest to decline an assignment – what is meant by this? Sickness could be one impediment. It is ultimately up to the bishop to judge the validity of the excusing cause. The greater the ecclesial necessity to be met by the proposed appointment, the greater should be the priest's justifying reason for declining it. A priest could obey the bishop's command under protest and subsequently make administrative recourse to the Congregation of the Clergy that he has a legitimate impediment to undertaking the assignment. What could happen to a priest who refuses to accept or fulfil a function lawfully entrusted to him? Canon 1371 §2 provides for punishment with a just penalty for a person who *wrongly* does not otherwise comply with legitimate precepts or prohibitions and who persists in disobedience.[13]

Remuneration and support

Canon 281 §1 provides that when clergy dedicate themselves to the ecclesiastical ministry, they deserve a remuneration (*remuneratio*) which is consistent with their condition in accord with the nature of their responsibilities and with the conditions of time and place. This remuneration should enable them to provide for their own life and for equitable payment of those services they need. The second paragraph of c. 281 states that provision must be made for those priests who are ill, incapacitated or elderly. The canon doesn't speak of any right (*ius*) to remuneration, though such a right is clearly implied. There seemed to be a concern that to speak explicitly of a right to remuneration would make priestly ministry sound too much like a business or a job. Certainly, there is no strict correlation between ministerial service and payments; it is not a contract in that sense. On the other hand, the 1990 Oriental Code explicitly enunciates the right of clergy to a just remuneration for carrying out the office or function committed to them.[14]

Who is to provide this remuneration? Canon 222 §1 says that the Christian faithful are obliged to assist with the needs of the Church so that it has what is necessary for the decent support of the clergy, while in canons 1261 §2 and 384 there is placed an onus on the bishop to remind Catholics of this obligation and to make provision for the financial support of his priests.[15] How much should a priest receive? The canon sets forth two primary factors: the nature of the responsibility/office; and the conditions of time and place. Vatican II indicated that remuneration should be fundamentally the same for all living in the same circumstances.[16] With respect to the conditions of time and place, the canon suggests two further questions: what amount is necessary to ensure that the priest is able to meet the needs of personal life (e.g. food, clothing, studies, vacation), and how much is necessary to pay those who carry out needed services for the cleric? Vatican II, moreover, indicated that the level of remuneration should also allow the priest to assist personally those who are in need (this was not included in the canon). Remuneration should be adequate to allow a priest to live in a reasonable manner in line with the general economic conditions surrounding him. As reflected in the emphasis on circumstances, while large differentials are unwarranted, there is no need that all clergy receive exactly the same remuneration: 'uniformity in remuneration for all priests is not an unassailable principle and justice may advise that both the nature of the office as well as the work actually performed by the priests may be taken into account, for economic purposes.'[17] Finally, canon law does not cover the remuneration situation of clerics who perform secular jobs or professions.

Note that c. 268 §1 suggests that the term 'remuneration' applies to those priests who exercise ministry. The Code implicitly distinguishes between *remuneratio* ('remuneration') and *sustentatio* ('decent support or sustenance'); the distinction is stated explicitly in the Oriental Code.[18] Priests receive *sustentatio* on account of their being members of the clergy incardinated in the diocese, whereas they receive *remuneratio* because they perform the ministry assigned to them. Therefore, *remuneratio*, which provides for the normal support of a priest in his ministry, may be more substantial than *sustentatio*, which provides for his vital needs. While a priest is remunerated on the basis of his dedication to ministry, decent support is always due to a priest, even if he is not exercising ministry for some reason. His bishop is obliged to see that this support is provided for, because ordination and incardination are the basis for a priest's right to decent support, rather than his performance of ministry.

Lifestyle

The fundamental responsibility in regard to a priest's lifestyle is set forth in c. 282 §1, which says that clerics are to cultivate a simple style of life and are to avoid whatever has a semblance of vanity. Pretension, ostentation and extravagance are the very antithesis of the priestly life. This avoidance of showiness and luxury should manifest itself in all aspects of the priest's personal life. When it comes to housing, it is not necessarily a matter of the size of the parochial house but rather that people feel welcome and are comfortable going to visit it. Vatican II said that the priest's residence should never appear unapproachable.[19] Nothing about it should be off-putting.

This canon does not impose a juridical requirement of poverty, and yet should be read in the light of Vatican II, which called on priests to embrace voluntary poverty, while not mandating it.[20] The canonical emphasis on a simple and modest clerical life doesn't mean a priest is to dress shabbily and not look after himself appropriately in terms of food, accommodation and indeed planning for the future. Taking a proper holiday is likewise not contrary to a simple lifestyle. Indeed c. 283 §2 states that clergy are entitled to a due and sufficient period of vacation each year, to be determined by universal or particular law. For instance, parish priests and curates may be absent on holiday each year from the parish for a maximum period of one continuous or interrupted month; the annual retreat doesn't count as part of this vacation time (cc. 533 §2, 550 §1). The Code is in these instances setting an outer limit, and diocesan law may specify things further.

The concern that priests avoid both a worldly lifestyle and anything that might in any way distance the poor finds itself expressed, for instance, in the prohibition of priests engaging in business or in a trade, either by themselves or through others (c. 286). Vatican II taught that the priest must always avoid avarice and carefully refrain from all appearance of trafficking.[21] Historically, canonists have made distinctions between various activities, one *leitmotif* being that there must be a habitual profit-making intent for an activity to fall under this prohibition, whereas the simple investment or safeguarding of one's own assets wouldn't. What was historically called 'household business' (*negotiatio oeconomica*) involving the profitable management of the priest's own goods was and is permitted, because there's no intention of profit for profit's sake – only the intention of prudently managing his assets (to serve his needs or the needs of those entrusted to his care) and no question of improving the goods with his own work.[22] What is forbidden is activity which seeks something more than the normal preservation of one's own assets. Finance is a complicated area, and yet the view of ordinary sensible people is important: if they regard an activity as a business or as a quasi-business, then that should ring alarm bells for clergy. The long-standing bar on priests engaging in business has a spiritual purpose – the prohibited commercial activities are bound to affect ministry and pastoral care, create a bad impression, not to mention the possibility of exposing the priest to the temptation of cupidity in contradiction to the call to lead a simple lifestyle.

Conclusion

In 1975, Pope Paul VI memorably said that the modern person listens more willingly to witnesses than to teachers, and if the modern person does listen to teachers, it is because they are witnesses.[23] That thinking about witness to the gospel is perhaps the best context in which to view and interpret priests' responsibilities and rights. Canon law is one, albeit imperfect, way of trying to articulate and lay down how priests should live out their responsibilities and rights as they attempt to witness to the truths of the gospel.

Notes

1. The term 'cleric' also includes deacons, but our discussion will deal only with presbyters.

2. See, for instance, E. A. Sweeny, *The Obligations and Rights of the Pastor of a Parish according to the Code of Canon Law* (New York: Society of St Paul, 2002).

3. See G. Ghirlanda, 'L'obbedienza dei chierici diocesani nel nuovo codice', *Rassegna di Teologia* 24 (1983), 520–39.

4. See the thinking of the Commission for the Revision of the Code in *Communicationes* 14 (1982), 169.

5. See *Lumen Gentium*, 27a and 23a.

6. See ibid., 26.

7. See ibid., 28, *Christus Dominus*, 15, *Presbyterorum Ordinis*, 7.

8. Congregation for the Clergy, *Directory on the Ministry and Life of Priests* (Rome: Libreria Editrice Vaticana, 1994), 24.

9. See P. Connolly et al., 'Accused but Innocent: What Should a Priest Do?', *The Furrow* 57 (2006), 193–204.

10. See the discussion in J. E. Lynch, 'The Obligations and Rights of Clerics', *New Commentary on the Code of Canon Law*, commissioned by the Canon Law Society of America, J. P. Beal, J. A. Coriden and T. J. Green, eds (Mahwah, NJ: Paulist Press, 2000), 345–7.

11. However, a priest must avoid activities which are unbecoming and foreign to the clerical state, and exercise prudence in regard to persons whose company could endanger their obligation to celibacy or cause scandal to the faithful: see cc. 277 §2, 285 §1-2.

12. See *Communicationes* 14 (1982), 168.

13. Furthermore, c. 1373 indicates that an interdict or other just penalty may be imposed for stirring up hostilities against the Ordinary because of some act of ecclesiastical power or ministry, or for inciting subjects to disobey.

14. See c. 390 §1 of the 1990 *Code of Canons of the Eastern Churches*.

15. The obligation of the diocesan bishop and the faithful to sustain their clergy is discussed at greater length in *Presbyterorum Ordinis*, 20.

16. See *Presbyterorum Ordinis*, 20.

17. J. de Otaduy, Commentary on c. 282, *Exegetical Commentary on the Code of Canon Law*, Á. Marzoa. J. Miras, and R. Rodríguez-Ocaña, eds, English language ed., general ed. E. Caparros (Montreal: Wilson & Lafleur; Chicago, IL: Midwest Theological Forum, 2004), Vol. II/1, 369.

18. Canon 390 §1 of the 1990 Oriental Code states: 'Clerics have the right to a suitable sustenance and to receive a just remuneration for carrying out the office or function committed to them.'

19. See *Presbyterorum Ordinis*, 17.

20. See ibid., 17, and also c. 282: 'After they have provided for their own decent support and for the fulfilment of all their duties of their state of life from the goods which they receive on the occasion of exercising an ecclesiastical office, clerics should wish to use any superfluous goods for the good of the Church and for works of charity'.

21. See *Presbyterorum Ordinis*, 17.

22. See J. de Otaduy, 382–3; J. E. Lynch, 378–9.

23. See Paul VI, Apostolic Exhortation, *Evangelii Nuntiandi: On Evangelization in the Modern World* (Rome: Libreria Editrice Vaticana, 1975), 41.

The Ministry of the Priest:
A Lay Perspective

NUALA O'LOAN

A challenging calling

Priesthood has always seemed to me a wonderful, yet very challenging calling. The essence of Christianity is that we are called to give as Christ gave for us; to give not when we feel like it, not when it suits us, but always and in full measure. We celebrate the priestliness of all people, the consequence of Baptism in Church, parish and the wider world. Yet we recognise too that Jesus Christ gave to some of his followers a very specific calling, sending them out to be evangelisers of the world, to celebrate Baptism and the Eucharist, and to forgive sins. We also know that he gave his disciples authority over the people. Thus it is that men who become priests must leave behind the attachments of family and secular life, and enter into a life which is not only always centred in Christ, as indeed we should all be so centred, but whose whole *raison d'être* becomes their priesthood. For those of us outside priesthood, it is extraordinary, and if we think about it, we will begin to understand something of the sacrifice made by these men.

Daniel O'Leary writing in *New Hearts for New Models* says:

> ... to be a priest today takes all the life we have left to live. To be a priest today takes the heart of a hermit, the soul of a mountain climber, the eyes of a lover, the hands of a healer,

the compassion of one who sees the whole world as part of himself. It requires total immersion in the life of Christ.[1]

What people expect

To some degree, this encapsulates what people expect of their priests. However, in some ways, the appreciation of the essence of priesthood is limited by the lived experience of community and parish, and by the culture and practices of that community. Most people regard priests as being people who have specific responsibilities given by Christ. Living in parishes they expect that certain things will happen almost automatically – there will be a local church building; it will be sound, warm and well lit; it will be clean and will probably have nice flowers on the altar; there will be sacramental celebrations, worship and beautiful liturgy. There should be parish schools and someone to ask about the time of Mass and the various parish activities that are ongoing, as well as someone on whom they can call in moments of crisis, at any time day or night: all the responsibilities, ultimately, of the priest.

It is of course the case that not all priests work in parishes. Some work in social justice issues, in education, in chaplaincies in prisons, in hospitals, in the armed forces, and some work in church administration. Some combine such work with work in parishes. For the most part, however, the most common everyday interactions are between people and priests working in parishes.

There is undoubtedly an ongoing appreciation of the value of priesthood. Indeed, through all the difficulties of the clerical abuse scandals, I have heard people talk generally of the failings of priests, but they always seem to differentiate 'their priest' from those who have failed. People talk with love and respect, recognising the particular talents of individual priests, and acknowledging the consequences of age, sickness and reducing numbers of priests for those who minister to them.

The danger of disconnecting

However, there is a mystique attached to the priesthood that seems to have the effect of disconnecting in some way the priest from the people. It is in part an appreciation of the sacredness of ordained priesthood, but it is also simply a product of history. Tradition and canon law indicate that the priest has both authority and decision-making powers, and so, over time, many people became, perhaps unwittingly, passive – leaving responsibility to others, content to allow the priest to run the show so long as he was there when they needed him. Others were frustrated by the clerical culture which evolved, leaving laypeople, both men and women, largely excluded from involvement in any meaningful way in the governance of their Church. The view evolved that in order to protect the Church it was necessary that the clergy keep control of everything from catechesis to worship to parish finances. This is no longer the case, but its echoes still resound in our Church. Ultimately, the result was an experience and understanding of priesthood among many of the people that was limited and in some ways distorted.

It had the effect of enhancing division between priests and people, and of consolidating clericalism. Assumptions were made about the people of God: that many of them were 'simple' and not to be disturbed or challenged, but rather consolidated in their faith; that they would not have the capacity to do so many of the ancillary tasks which became attached to the priestly function; that they were not formed so as to be capable of contributing in any significant way to the running of the Church, because they could not have the wisdom which resulted from ordination. For priests there were complementary frustrations. Just as power was given to them, so too it was given over them to their bishop or religious superior. They were also limited by tradition and by what seems to have been unqualified obedience.

The ultimate effect of this rather dysfunctional, rigid and *ad hoc* approach to Church governance, in which priests did not perceive themselves as having the power to create real change, was to limit the effectiveness of priests in their sacred work 'of recognising the holiness of others, of soul making'.

Changing role and identity

There is no doubt that there has been huge change since Vatican II, but such has been the simultaneous pace of change in the world that necessary change in the Church seems to have been very slow, and it has also seemed that one of the things that Vatican II created was uncertainty. At first, there was a sense of exhilaration, as altars were turned so that the priest faced the people and lay ministries began to emerge. New spirituality and a consciousness of the need for social justice and the engagement of the Church with the people where they were on their journey also brought a sense of change and hope. There were new translations of the Bible, and unprecedented access by the laity to scripture.

However, this change brought with it a questioning about the role and identity of the priest. Many priests declared that they were not just functionaries and that they needed to be involved in more than word and sacrament. This is true, and my experience was that it was always thus. As Benedict XVI stated in 2010:

> I would say we know the ... three pillars of our being priests. First the Eucharist, the Sacraments. The Eucharist – to make possible and present the Eucharist ... so that it becomes the really visible act of God's love for us. Then the Proclamation of the Word in all its dimensions: from the personal dialogue to the homily. The third point is *caritas*, the love of Christ: to be present for the suffering, for the little ones, for the children, for people in difficulty, for the marginalised; to make really present the love of the good shepherd. And then a very high priority is also the personal relationship with Christ.[2]

Changes have occurred, and we have seen a minor division of labours between clergy and laity – the introduction of the ministries of the Eucharist and the Word, the creation of parish finance committees and parish pastoral councils, though all change is dependent on the approval of the parish priest.

Training and formation of the laity to undertake some of the tasks that could rightly be done by them was not always easily accessed. In an increasingly complex world, many people also felt that they did not have time or energy to devote to these matters. People would engage for a period in some activity, but for a myriad of reasons could cease to be so involved, leaving others to continue the work where possible. Thus, we see parish websites developed with enthusiasm, on which the last entry was five years ago; we have seen initiatives for sacramental preparation and children's liturgy developed, and then in some cases abandoned, because there was nobody left to take responsibility for them. There has been a lack of sustainability. There are many priests now who long to be able to share the burdens, but who know that the people they involve will really need to understand that they must commit to the project at least for a defined period, and who know also that ultimately it is the priest who is responsible. In many situations priests and people work really well together. There are many priests who are very happy in ministry, though most would probably want to see supportive structural changes. Almost inevitably, many good priests have become overworked, stressed and frustrated as they sought to discern how best to live their priestly vocations.

Facing challenges

There are questions about the need for compulsory celibacy. We embrace men who were previously Anglican priests and who are already married and able to live out their vocation as priests within marriage, as well as men coming to priesthood late in life after becoming widows. We also observe other religions and remember that priestly celibacy is not a dogma. Is it not possible that we will come to understand that compulsory celibacy may be a choice made by some men who are called to priesthood, whilst others may actually be called to live their priesthood within marriage? I cannot see a situation in which the ordination of women will occur, though I find that the arguments against women priests are certainly limited and there is an evolving critical shortage of priests in some parts of the world.

It is not good to generalise, but looking on priesthood from the outside, I have seen a clergy, many of whom have in some ways become demoralised, tired, uncertain and unsure. Yet for many of them their uncertainty is not faith-related, but rather it relates to the world in which they must operate and the consequences of some of the activities of some of their fellow priests. They have undoubtedly been deeply shocked and shamed by the abuse crisis. Many have felt diminished and marked by the crimes of others. They see that men are not coming forward to serve as priests in the same numbers as before, and they may wonder how they will manage as they are required to assume responsibility for more and more churches and parishes, with few young curates to help and to bring vitality and youth into their lives.

Priests today face many challenges. Traditionally priests were involved in the business of real estate; building schools, parish centres and churches was an activity which was necessary in a world in which there was a growing Catholic community and a lack of facilities. It must have been satisfying too, to have a monument that would survive their passing, particularly a church built for worship, a place of prayer. Now many priests face the difficult and sensitive task of modernising those churches to make them fit for today's worship and liturgy, often in the face of resistance to change among parishioners who are comfortable with what is, and who fear loss in the process of change and modernisation.

The world in which we live has become infinitely more complex and priests today must deal with a whole range of practical matters: hiring and firing, maternity and sick leave, pension issues, health and safety issues and compliance with equality and human rights laws. They have responsibility for catechesis in a world of diverse ethnic backgrounds and multiple different languages. They may have to be part of processes for caring for the elderly and sick clergy. They must organise fundraisers in a world of recession and economic uncertainty, when the numbers in congregations are falling and income may well be declining. They must try to bring their people closer to God in a world of increasing secularism and competing attractions. People question compliance with rules, and even question the rules themselves. Paradoxically, although they have so little time to engage with the Church, they want to be more involved, and above all to be heard by their Church. Priests and laity both seek a forum for debate and discussion that does not yet exist.

It has also seemed that there are those who have moved beyond a sense of wonder and awe at sacrament and word, into a place where what was understood as the sacred may be regarded as old-fashioned. We have seen a disconnection between those who yearn for the familiarity of well-known ways, and those for whom there is an urgent need to change so that the Church can remain connected to the young and hence to the future.

Companion on life's journey

In all this the essence of priesthood remains as it always has been – an essential part of our Church. Daniel O'Leary describes priesthood through a series of images: 'the farmer of hearts, watching the spiritual seasons of life, knowing that there is no short cut to happiness, no cheap grace to salvation'; the 'prophet of beauty' so that we will be 'moved by our own inner splendour, by the bright divinity that makes us sons and daughters of God'; the 'healer of fear'; the 'mid-wife of mystery' – drawing 'out from hearts and souls ... the innate wisdom and healing waiting to be released'; the 'soul-friend of the community' 'holding up the mirror of the true self of another, gently revealing the carefully concealed flaws and the strong subtle veins of shadow'; the 'weaver of wholeness' 'through pastoral leadership', the 'voice of the silent' and 'the sacrament of compassion'.[3] Richard Rohr writes: 'We need people who understand darkness and by their presence can hold us through to the light.'

I have experienced all these on my journey. A man does not become capable of engaging at this level and of doing the work of the Lord unless he is paying attention to the Lord of the work, and is grounded in prayer, not just the prayer of doing, but also the prayer that is time spent being present to the Lord, worshipping, asking, thanking and above all just being still. People talk of holy priests, and they recognise men of God when they meet them. Holiness is palpable. They can also detect those who seem not to believe, but carrying on in ministry perhaps because they do not know what else to do, or because they are afraid to do something else.

Some of the holiest people I have met have been priests who live their daily lives in the present moment with God, unselfconsciously, capable of speaking of him and engaging with him, sometimes in the simplest and most direct terms, but fed always by a diet of reading and prayer which, with their experiences in priesthood, deepens their knowledge and understanding whilst still preserving in them the absolute sense of mystery and the sacred which is he who said, 'I am.' They have walked part of my journey with me, as they walk with others, making Christ so real at times of great happiness when it is not hard to see the face of God in all his works, but also when he seems to have gone away from us, when the darkness threatens to overwhelm, when we feel lost. I will always remember with gratitude the patience and the compassion that made getting on with life as wife and mother possible at such times.

It is the lot of a priest to walk with us on the difficult and challenging parts of these journeys of ours and very often they do not know the good that they have done. Very often, I suspect, we do not go back and tell them when all is well again. Is it because they have sacrificed family and children that we feel that they are there and can be called upon? I wonder often too how open we are to their moments of darkness and desolation, and whether we should be doing more to help, and if so, how we could help. We all blossom when we are affirmed and recognised for what we have been able to do. It seems to me that such affirmation, such confirmation is not articulated sufficiently to our priests who work alone and are on call constantly, very often with no defined working day that starts and finishes with regularity, leaving time free for other things. They must make their own schedules, devise their own initiatives, try to persuade parishioners to engage with new ideas, and accept the unfairness and adverse comment of those who criticise without just cause, all the while acknowledging that like their very human parishioners, they too are human, with all the fallibility that is part of our humanity. They must move from a funeral Mass with its grieving mourners to a wedding with its congregation of joyous family and friends within hours. They must sit beside the dying and then move across a hospital to rejoice in new birth. Through all this they must bring Christ.

That above all is the role of the priest, to walk with us on our journey in love to enlighten, inform, enable, support and encourage us through Eucharist, Word and sacrament. Jesus told his people, 'Be not afraid, I am with you always.' I thank God for the gift of priesthood and for those who answer the call and live it faithfully.

Notes

1. Daniel O'Leary, *New Hearts for New Models* (Dublin: Columba Press, 1997), 110.
2. Benedict XVI, Vigil on the Occasion of the International Meeting of Priests.
3. *New Hearts for New Models*, 38–96.

Prophets of the Eternal

NIALL AHERN

What is absolute about priesthood?

Antoine Givre is the name of the young man who encountered the Curé d'Ars as he tried to find his way to his first parish appointment. The Curé realised he needed help and in the very asking for assistance he defined for Antoine, and for all of us, the heart of priesthood. 'Show me the way to Ars,' he said 'and I'll show you the way to heaven.'[1] The point of the story is that the meaning of priesthood is fundamentally one of sustaining belief in the eternal vision of life. The priest needs to remember this as he schools himself in all aspects of his ministry so as to minister more effectively in these confusing and challenging times. The priest is primarily the spiritual leader of his community.

In the context of rapid change in our world, the priest as spiritual leader is a more vital constant than ever before. Although aspects of his traditional role have been taken over by other elements in society, many people still turn to him for direction and solace. He is called on especially nowadays to respond to an ever-increasing sense of angst and disillusionment, and this with a competence and skill for which he may not be specifically trained. If he engages in ongoing personal accompaniment and learning, he is much more able to respond with fresh authority to the eternal longing at the heart of his people's journey. There is an urgent need for us as pastors to accept the key role of our ministry as leaders in faith and to articulate our mission in a manner that is contemporary and in touch with the lived experience of our people. Yesterday, today and tomorrow, we are prophets of the eternal.

The current financial crisis has shown how fragile are the institutions on which we depend for our security and prosperity. It has been quite a shock. I think that the uncertainty and insecurity now evident in our financial institutions reflect something in our society as a whole – namely a lack of secure and trustworthy institutions in which people can really put their faith. Related to this is a strong sense many people have that we live in something of a moral and spiritual vacuum. Certainly people tend to be both critical and sceptical of those who hold any kind of moral or spiritual authority. It is a culture in which choice is paramount but we necessarily wonder about what values and principles inform people's choices. I suggest that it is in precisely this kind of society that the priest has a vital role to play and his continuing education must keep this in mind as he leads people on their faith journey. The ongoing education of the priest is fundamentally the deepening of his own faith in order that he might deepen the faith of his community.

There is something absolute about priesthood, something which runs directly counter to the prevailing culture. The most important task the priest has is the celebration of the Eucharist. In doing this, he situates himself within a tradition of worship that reaches back in history, to long before the development of our modern culture and ethos. The Eucharist finds its roots in the Old Testament and finds its meaning in the death and resurrection of Christ.

The priest, therefore, is a sure and reliable reference point. His ministry provides life – life which brings stability here and now as well as for eternal life. In himself, the priest embodies a deep confidence about the value of his role and his work in the world. It is a confidence grounded in faith, nourished by hope and expressed in love of people, especially those entrusted to his care. The presence of a priest in a local community provides a level of security that no political organisation or social service can provide. In the context of ongoing formation for the priest, it is necessary that this sense of continuity and permanence be at the core of any new expressions of priestly service.

The priest, by his whole life, should be a sometimes silent, and sometimes not so silent, reminder to everyone that God exists; that God is creator and that we are his creatures. 'Know that the Lord is God. It is he that made us, and we are his; we are his people and the sheep of his pasture' (Ps 100:3). To God we owe everything: our creation, health, success in undertakings, redemption, call to the Christian life or to the priesthood, and so forth.

To proclaim the greatness and fidelity of God is the duty of the priest. Even more, it is his honour and joy to give this witness. God is greater than we could ever think or imagine. To him we owe our debt of thanksgiving. From him we request all we need. To him we call to assist our being faithful in every detail of our lives. This is what belief is all about. It is the recognition of God with our mind, our heart and our actions. His will, his eternal law guides us. In this sense, belief is not optional. The Second Vatican Council testifies: 'Without the creator the creature would disappear ... When God is forgotten ... the creature itself grows unintelligible' (*Gaudium et Spes*, 36). Every Sunday many millions of people, speaking in hundreds of different languages, join together to say the words, 'I believe in God'. There are also millions who will not or cannot join in this great profession of faith. In some countries, belief is increasing and strengthening, in others it is fading and becoming weaker. In some countries believers are persecuted and discriminated against; in others they are given complete freedom. But belief cannot be controlled by laws. Indeed belief is sometimes stronger and more active in places where it is forbidden than in places where it is allowed.

Belief and unbelief can exist side by side in the same country, in the same town, in the same street, in the same household. They can even exist side by side in the same person. Every believer has to face the temptation to disbelieve. Every unbeliever has to face the temptation to believe. It is at this crossroads that the priest today can point the way. Whatever new approaches he may take in ministry, he is first called to be there to assist each person as they decide for themselves whether or not to join in an act of faith in God. It is the most fundamental decision a person can make. It affects the whole shape and direction of life. We need courage to make that decision and we need strength to live with it. This is the great challenge of ministry today. It is the core challenge of the priest in the modern world. He is the *anam cara*, the spiritual guide, the man of God for others. Through his ongoing theological training; his spiritual and human formation, through contemplative action and constant renewal, he reinvigorates his vocation and engenders belief.

The priest, as prophet of the eternal, exposes secularism as unacceptable. To live and act as if God did not exist is a mistaken and poorly formulated ideology that does not hold up under examination and is harmful in private and public life. It is the central challenge of our time that the priest cannot ignore. On 8 March 2008, Pope Benedict XVI said at the plenary assembly of the Pontifical Council for Culture that secularism, which presents itself in cultures by imposing on the world and humanity a future without reference to the eternal, is invading every aspect of daily life and developing a mentality in which God is effectively absent from human awareness. Any ongoing formation that benefits the ministry of the priest should be a way of declaring to people: 'Lift up your voices.' If the people can sincerely reply: 'We have lifted them up to the Lord', then the priest has succeeded. It is the priest who preaches that God is the eternal and transcendent one; that, in spite of all of its vicissitudes, the invisible hand of God is never absent from human history. It is the priest who finds in the Christian faith the reassuring word to say to the terminally ill person or the young widow or the poor or those suffering because of the errors of an inefficient government. It is the ministry of the priest today, as always, to help all such people realise that God has not forgotten or abandoned them. In order to carry out this delicate and difficult ministry, the priest needs to be in solidarity with people who suffer, so that he shares with them his faith, hope and trust in God. He should become a minister of eternal values and he needs to underpin all his ongoing formation on the ground of belief in the transcendent.

Restless hearts

Many people today seem disorientated. They are not sure from where they come, or why they exist on earth, where they are going, and how they can get there. They want to see meaning in their life on earth. If the priest does not witness to them the answers to these fundamental questions, who will do it for them? If he does not face the fundamental questions at the core of ministry, he misses the point. The priest will be rendering to them an important service if he makes it clear to them that life on earth can be lived in terms of eternal life and that only God can give to the human heart the fully satisfying response. As Augustine said, God has placed in all our hearts an eternal longing and our hearts are restless until they rest in him. Life on earth is not one monotonous activity after another. It is not a heap of scattered mosaics without unity, meaning or design. The doctor, the dockworker, the factory labourer, the specialist surgeon, all need to see a clear meaning in their lives and in the details of their daily work, which may seem like those of the day before but are lived with eternal significance.

Against a background of drudgery, deep recession and unemployment it is understandably difficult for both priest and parishioner to sustain in faith. And no matter how much we may seek clarification and use modern methodologies, there is essentially a mysterious quality to faith, and the priest is the one called to declare the mystery of faith. It is a gift given by God and does not lie within our competence to control. We can celebrate it but we cannot command it.

On one occasion, a man asked Jesus to cure his son who was suffering severely from epileptic fits; Jesus asked the father, 'How long has this been happening to him?' 'From childhood,' he replied, 'and it has often thrown him into the fire and into the water in order to destroy him. But if you can do anything, have pity on us and help us.' 'If you can?' Jesus retorted. 'Everything is possible for anyone who has faith.' Immediately the father of the boy cried out, 'I do have faith. Help the little faith I have' (Mk 9:21-24).

The prayer of the father has been repeated by believers all down the ages. Even the greatest saints have felt the weakness of their faith and their need for God and a spiritual guide to help and strengthen it. 'I do have faith. Help the little faith I have.' We must not expect that our faith will always be free from difficulties. There will be times when misfortune will afflict us, or morality seems too heavy a burden to bear. There will be times when prayer is a torture and God seems to have vanished from our lives. These are the times when the strength of our faith is put to the test. These are the times when we must cry out to God for help. These are the times when the priest as the man of belief and understanding will direct our hearts.

The priest today must stand beside those who are torn between belief and unbelief in our world. He must stand beside those who find it difficult to accept the explanation of the world that is given to them by religion, yet find it just as difficult to accept that the world has no explanation. This difficulty is often most sharply felt by young people. They tend to rebel against the values that are taught to them by believers in religion but they find no comfort in the values that are taught by unbelievers. A word that is often used to describe this condition is alienation. An alien is a foreigner and alienation is the feeling of being a foreigner, an outsider, of not really belonging, of not fitting into the world in which one lives. The alienated person cannot find a meaning for life and has a heart filled with restless desires but does not know how these desires can be satisfied or this restlessness set at peace. It is here the priest is the one who reminds all that the heart of humankind is restless until it rests in God. This condition of alienation is not anything new. It was described by Saint Augustine fifteen hundred years ago in his *Confessions*. Here he tells us of his struggle to reject belief but that he knew no peace of mind until he returned to God. 'You have made us for yourself,' he wrote, 'and our hearts are restless until they rest in you.'

The priest, as prophet of the meaning of our earthly life, should always help people see clearly that authentic practice of Christianity relates life on earth to life in the world to come. *Gaudium et Spes* reminds us that 'While we are warned that it profits a man nothing if he gain the whole world and lose himself, the expectation of a new earth must not weaken but rather stimulate our concern for cultivating this one. For here grows the body of a new human family, a body which even now is able to give some kind of foreshadowing of the new age' (43).

Our faith gives joy to our life on earth. It gives our life a meaning and a sense of direction. It helps us to avoid the feeling of monotony in our daily work. It shows us how the universal call to holiness should be concretely lived according to each person's vocation and mission. The priest is the announcer, the indicator, the prophet of this life of hope, this clarity of vision, this limpidity of action, and this sincere joy.

Priesthood as life-giving

All of this applies to those ordained in the sacrament of Holy Orders. It is significant that we nowadays see the character of this sacrament less as a stamp imprinted once-for-all and more as a life-long process set in motion by ordination into a special covenant relationship with Jesus Christ and his people. This call is for a continual programme of living the qualities of the God of the covenant, the God whose love is strong and who is true forever. This programme of love and continuing truth calls for the continual renewal of those ordained. This renewal must essentially be one that brings the priest into an ever-deepening communion with Christ, the author of life. The search for suitable renewal programmes and support groups for the ordained is a striking expression of this need for rededication. The Chrism Mass on Holy Thursday, at which the presbyterate join their bishop in the sacrament of unity and oils are provided again for the many anointings of the people of God, is not only an eloquent expression of the reconsecration of the ordained but a call to renewal and evangelisation for the priest. Whatever supports him and offers him fresh clarification as prophet of the eternal must be employed.

This is, therefore, the central call of the priest: to give primacy to the transcendent in his life through his ongoing formation. His spiritual growth and ever-deepening awareness of his call as one who points beyond himself to the eternal must never be lost or unattended. The priest mediates the eternal meaning of life. His ongoing formation must underpin the reality of the eternal for which every heart has an insatiable longing. And he must do it in each age in a manner that is understood and speaks to each generation.

If priesthood is involved in the essential quest of humankind, why are there so many people today who say they are tired of the language of priesthood and mediation? There would seem to be as many answers as there are people. It is good to remember that there is a very real sense in which Christians do not need mediators. The great work of redemption has been done, once-for-all, in Christ. Yet the ministry of the ordained is a kind of immediate mediation. The task of all Church ministry is to make transparent the work of our redemption, the work of Jesus Christ. Without this transparency, priests could give the impression that they are acting on their own right. This would be a negation of their ministry. Without pointing to the transcendent, the work of the ordained minister would seem like brokering in one's own name. This happens when the servant leaders have, without realising it, come across as a caste, an elite, a chosen few who have forgotten that they are chosen to point to the eternal by their own self-emptying and service. *Kenosis* is the kernel of ongoing formation for the priest and the key to his role as prophet of the eternal. All authentic ministry is a call to generously give and to be given away.

In a priestly ministry that is continually giving and being given away, there is essential room for priests who are willing to remain open to renewal at every level of their priesthood. We lay down our lives only to take them up again. The Church and its mission demands this renewal of us. Each of its ministers is called, like its founder, to help recognise the presence and action of God in this particular place, with this people and at this time. Under the admonition of Saint Paul, as we journey, 'let us keep eyes for the invisible!'

Note
1. Bartholomew O'Brien, *The Curé of Ars* (USA: Tan, 1956), 30.

Dissent and Dissension

PÁDRAIG MCCARTHY

Jesus prayed: 'May they all be one, just as, Father, you are in me and I am in you ... so that the world may believe it was you who sent me' (Jn 17:21). It is a great challenge to his disciples. Every disciple in whatever position in the Church is called to this. As Jesus and his Father are distinct but united, we are called to live united in the Body of Christ (cf. Rm 12:4-8; 1 Cor 12). 'I appeal to you: make my joy complete by being of a single mind, one in love, one in heart and one in mind' (Phil 2:2).

How we deal then with dissent in the Church is central to our mission. Those called to teaching in the Church can serve as a focus of unity. Talk of dissent may immediately conjure thoughts of disloyalty and confrontation. In terms of priests, one might think of King Henry II and Thomas Becket: 'Will no one rid me of this turbulent priest?' The media, mobile communication and the internet are tools useful for unity, but also for speedy dissemination of turbulence.

Priests and hierarchy have a particular responsibility here. There are dangers. In a lecture in June 1962, Karl Rahner said:

> We must face the possibility, with fear and trembling, that we could be the ones who stifle the Spirit (1 Th 5:19) – stifle him through that pride of 'knowing better', that inertia of the heart, that cowardice, that unteachableness with which we react to fresh impulses and new pressures in the Church.[1]

Bishop Christopher Butler OSB wrote in relation to the Second Vatican Council: 'Let us not fear that truth might endanger truth.'[2] And the then Cardinal Bergoglio, now Pope Francis, wrote:

> The great leaders of the people of God were men that left room for doubt ... The bad leader is the one who is self-assured and stubborn. One of the characteristics of a bad leader is to be excessively normative because of his self-assurance.[3]

Should we seek as far as possible to eliminate dissent, or can we incorporate the energy of dissent to bring new life to the Church? Is 'optimal dissent' possible? To what extent does dissent affect Catholic priests in Ireland today? This brief chapter will touch on some lines of relevant thought.

Some factors involved

Unity in diversity is impossible unless we acknowledge that there may be many ways of expressing a truth, and that the richness of human language varies over place, time and culture. Translation is not just a matter of converting one language to another word for word. Did Jesus lay down his life 'for all' or 'for many'? Dialogue is necessary so that dissent may not be too easily presumed.

Also important are words of Vatican II: 'In Catholic doctrine there exists a "hierarchy" of truths, since they vary in their relation to the fundamental Christian faith' (*Unitatis Redintegratio*, 11). It is clear for instance that the existence of a loving God and the existence of a college of cardinals are not equally central truths; nor are the place of forgiveness and the place of recitation of the Rosary. Agreement on their varied 'relation to the fundamental Christian faith' may not be easy to achieve. But the hierarchy of truths invites us to consider expressions of truth as a means of unity in diversity rather than of dissension.

With an eye on Cardinal John Henry Newman's *On Consulting the Faithful in Matters of Doctrine* and his *Essay on the Development of Christian Doctrine,* we need to keep in view a commentary on the *Professio Fidei* issued by the Congregation for the Doctrine of the Faith on 29 June 1998 in regard to certain doctrines: 'Whoever denies these truths would be in a position of rejecting a truth of Catholic doctrine and would therefore no longer be in full communion with the Catholic Church' (6).

Dissent and power

Dissent may lead to dissension, a rupture within the communion of the Church. How can we find a 'Catholic' embrace so that dissent could be a valuable dimension in the Church? We need to understand it better in a Christian context, so that diversity of gift and understanding will enrich the life of the whole Church.

Dissent is not a simple function of divergence of understanding. Very human factors such as authority and power also come into play. A person in authority may feel threatened by dissent, and react to protect both the position of authority and the doctrine which is perceived as threatened.

Where there is no clear established channel to address serious differences, fear can inhibit some people from contemplating confrontation. For a priest, it can affect his whole future.

To dissent from a teaching of those in a position of leadership poses a challenge to that leadership. Any organisation which does not provide channels for managing dissent fails to deal with the reality of human life. Authority which excludes discussion is not 'management'. However 'correct' the position of authority may be, the manner of exercise of authority may be destructive of true communion, resulting in dissension and a breach in relationships. Saint Augustine wrote that the City of Man, in contrast to the City of God, 'is ruled by the lust for domination (*libido dominandi*)'. This can operate too, unintentionally, in each of us who aspires to live in the City of God, however intelligent and well-intentioned we may be. It may be difficult for a person in authority to allow for the fact that sometimes there can be a variety of theologies, each making a valuable contribution.

Dissent may take varying forms.

1. *Articulated dissent* is expressed openly in a constructive fashion to other members of the organisation, including those in authority. This may be done where there are avenues by which to express the dissent; or even in the absence of such avenues. This last can take considerable courage.
2. *Latent dissent* is either wholly unarticulated, or is expressed only to others within the organisation who have no authority to effect change. This may occur even when avenues for expression exist, but are perceived as ineffective or cosmetic.
3. *Displaced dissent* may be expressed to external audiences, or by obstruction or lack of cooperation within the organisation, or by withdrawal, or by forms of illness. A destructive cynicism can develop.

The extent to which dissent is present among Catholic priests in Ireland in any of these or other forms is a question I cannot answer. In relation to core doctrines of Catholic faith I have not encountered dissent.

As well as 'vertical' dissent in relation to authority, there is also a continuum of 'horizontal' dissension among priests and people. There are those of the *Gaudium et Spes* culture who absorbed the heady hopes of Vatican II and who see it as a work which has met resistance and is still to be enacted. There are those who have almost lost hope of this. There are those who want to restore some of the glories of the Church which they feel they have lost since Vatican II. There are those who perceive the slightest deviation from liturgical or other norms as a threat, to be reported immediately to the highest authorities. Dissent is not confined to one end of the spectrum. In the face of mutual incomprehension, our challenge is to be fully Catholic. Paul's admonitions in 1 Corinthians 12 and 13 still apply.

Dimensions of the situation

Difference of viewpoint is normal in human society. We have examples at the very beginnings of the Church. Paul could be very forthright in addressing situations where Christians were going wrong. The spread of the gospel to non-Jewish peoples sparked divisions about whether non-Jews should be bound by Jewish laws. At the beginning of the letter to the Galatians, having greeted them with 'grace and peace', he immediately addressed his concern: 'I am astonished that you are so promptly turning away ...' He even confronted Peter (Cephas) as recounted in Galatians 2:11-14. I wonder how Peter responded! Who was the true dissenter here? Was this 'loyal dissent'?

However, in 1 Corinthians 8, Paul deals with the question of eating food offered to idols. This was a cause of scandal for new converts with newborn faith. Paul's delicate solution is to affirm the freedom of those of stronger faith, but to counsel that they exercise their freedom so as not to become 'an obstacle to trip those who are vulnerable'.

Christians need a way to establish what is core to Christian faith, and how suitably this can be expressed in varying ages and cultures, languages and situations. There are obstacles to good management of dissent.

Poor communication

We may too easily presume we are understood by another party. However sophisticated our language skills, clear communication can never be reasonably sure unless we build in feedback and confirmation. Language carries both meaning and cultural function and association.

Pope Benedict XVI quoted Byzantine emperor Manuel II Palaiologus in Regensburg in September 2006. His words may have been unexceptional to a western mind, with Greek thought categories where words express concepts. In Semitic languages, however, a word may be more like an event bringing about what is expressed. The violent reaction, in word and deed, to Pope Benedict's speech is a cautionary reminder that in cases of dissent within the Church, the words of another person may not always carry the intent we presume to understand. There is danger of polarisation if we conclude too quickly that views are mutually exclusive.

How Magisterium is exercised

Pope Paul V, in 1605, showed discernment when he dealt with the dispute between Dominican and Jesuit theologians about grace and human freedom. They had begun to accuse one another of heresy. Paul V ordered that, while they could continue to hold their positions, they should desist from condemning one another. He reminded them of the need for humility in seeking to understand the mysteries of God. Such delicacy from the Magisterium is good to bear in mind.

Similarly, the value of dissenting voices experienced by those taking part in Vatican II may underlie the encouragement of 'fraternal rivalry' in arriving at deeper understanding in the Decree on Ecumenism, *Unitatis Redintegratio* (21 November 1964):

> When comparing doctrines with one another, they should remember that in Catholic doctrine there exists a 'hierarchy' of truths, since they vary in their relation to the fundamental Christian faith. Thus the way will be opened by which through fraternal rivalry all will be stirred to a deeper understanding and a clearer presentation of the unfathomable riches of Christ. (11)

Cardinal Newman, in his *Essay on the Development of Christian Doctrine*,[4] also says dealing even with heresy may yield benefit:

> No one doctrine can be named which starts complete at first, and (which) gains nothing afterwards from the investigations of faith and the attacks of heresy.

Richard Gaillardetz, editor of *When the Magisterium Intervenes*, writes that current ways of exercising Magisterium are recent:

> ... the 'magisterium', as we understand it today, emerged largely as a part of an ecclesiological framework that was first constructed in the nineteenth century.[5]

317

In this book, Bradford E. Hinze lists ten 'lamentations' theologians have about the procedures of the Congregation for the Doctrine of the Faith (CDF). The present operation of the system, where the CDF is the investigator, the CDF is the prosecutor, the CDF hands down the judgment and the penalty, and the CDF is the court of appeal, does not present good practice in administration of justice.

The 1971 Synod of Bishops on Justice in the World said:

> While the Church is bound to give witness to justice, she recognises that anyone who ventures to speak to people about justice must first be just in their eyes. Hence we must undertake an examination of the modes of acting and of the possessions and lifestyle found within the Church herself. (40)

Styles of leadership

The style of leadership affects the way dissent is managed. The late Fr Desmond Forristal, in a talk given some years back in Clonliffe College, described the administration of the Church as 'a Byzantine autocracy, mitigated by inefficiency'. Newman reminds us that the precise shape of the institutions of the Church may be more time-conditioned than we may sometimes assume:

> Christianity ... came into the world as an idea rather than an institution, and has had to wrap itself in clothing and fit itself with armour of its own providing.[6]

Early Christianity clothed its community in the model of administration which seemed best at the time, emulating many of the trappings of civil society. Without compromising its mission, the Church can equally learn from what is good in society today. Pope St Pius X (*Vehementer Nos*, 1906) expressed one model of leadership:

> ... with the pastoral body alone rests the necessary right and authority for promoting the end of the society and

directing all its members towards that end; the one duty of the multitude is to allow themselves to be led, and, like a docile flock, to follow the Pastors.

Benedict XVI called for a quite different model at the International Forum of Catholic Action in August 2012:

> This responsibility requires a change in mentality concerning, in particular, the role of the laity in the Church. They should not be considered as merely 'collaborators' of the clergy, but as people truly 'co-responsible' in the work of the Church.

True co-responsibility is destroyed by some styles of leadership. Such styles may be variously described as autocratic, democratic, *laissez-faire*, bureaucratic, transformational, charismatic, collaborative, transactional, servant leadership, and so on. Different times and situations may call for different styles. An autocratic style may be appropriate in a particular crisis, but is unwise on a permanent basis. In dissent situations, it can be disastrous. Martin Luther's intention was not to start a breakaway Church, but to call the Church back to its mission. Church authorities felt threatened, reacted rather than listened. Politics saw an opportunity and we still live with the consequences.

Dissent without dissension?

Jesus had important principles. In Matthew 18:15-17:

> If your brother does something wrong, go and have it out with him alone, between your two selves. If he listens to you, you have won back your brother. If he does not listen, take one or two others along with you: whatever the misdemeanour, the evidence of two or three witnesses is required to sustain the charge. But if he refuses to listen to these, report it to the community (*ekklesia*); and if he refuses to listen to the community, treat him like a gentile or a tax collector.

The first step, 'between your two selves', is vital, but may be the most neglected. Sometimes the first step taken is a report to the bishop or higher.

The further steps indicate need of a local structure in Ireland, perhaps a theological commission with transparent procedures. Archbishop Diarmuid Martin suggests some such body, and the Association of Catholic Priests in Ireland in February 2013 asked the hierarchy to initiate such a body.

The ultimate step sounds like the final blow: 'Treat him like a gentile or tax-collector.' But before we jump to hasty conclusions, we need to ask: how did Jesus himself treat gentiles and tax-collectors?

Jesus called Matthew, a tax collector, to be an apostle. He is criticised for eating with these reprobates (9:11), and described as a friend of tax-collectors and sinners (11:19). He praised the faith of a gentile woman (15:21). He spoke of tax collectors and prostitutes entering the kingdom before chief priests and elders (21:28-32). In 13:24-30, he warned of the damage that could be done by removing the darnel from the wheat.

Following this gospel guidance, we would have no guarantee of peaceful resolution of dissent, but we would be closer to living the wise counsel:

> *In essentialibus, unitas*: In what is essential, let there be unity.
> *In dubiis, libertas*: In what is debateable, let there be freedom.
> *In omnibus, caritas*: In all things, let there be charity.[7]

Notes

1. *Theological Investigations* VII (1971) 'Do Not Stifle the Spirit', TI vol. VII, 1971, 80.
2. AS III/3 (CG XCV), 353–4.
3. Cardinal Jorge Bergoglio and Rabbi Abraham Sorka, *On Heaven and Earth: Pope Francis on Faith, Family, and the Church in the Twenty-First Century* (New York: Random House, 2013), chapter 5.
4. Cardinal Newman, *Essay on the Development of Christian Doctrine*, chapter 2, 2.

5. Richard Gaillardetz, ed., *When the Magisterium Intervenes: The Magisterium and Theologians in Today's Church* (Collegeville, MN: Liturgical Press, 2012), viii.
6. Cardinal Newman, chapter 2, 2.
7. The source of this extract is uncertain, and often misattributed to St Augustine. It is quoted in John XXIII's *Ad Petri Cathedram* (1959), 72 (with *necessariis* in place of *essentialibus* – both versions are common).

Sign and Sacrament

Presiding at Eucharist: The *Ars Celebrandi*

TOM WHELAN

> The best catechesis on the Eucharist is the Eucharist itself, celebrated well.[1]

The Eucharist brings together all that is at the heart of Christian belief. It does not just sum up the salvific work of Christ; it is the ritual and sacramental environment within which the redeeming work of God in Christ continues to operate for us today. It sums up what Christian living aspires to be. For Eucharist describes the way of the cross and its self-emptying as constituting the way to life and the foundation of our hope. It models reconciliation and inclusion, and allows us glimpse our completion in Christ. Here we find the context within which we must situate the ordained priest and his ministry of leadership. This ministry finds its highpoint in the Sunday celebration of the Eucharist of the community within which he serves.[2] This is not so because of any sacramental 'rights' that he has over others on account of Orders, but because Sunday Eucharist is the 'source and summit' of the life of all the baptised, himself included.[3] It is the food for the mission journey. Ordained priesthood, as cooperation with the leadership ministry of the bishop in the local church, serves the baptised priesthood of the Church, and his participation in the priesthood of Christ is for the sake of the priesthood of all in Christ. Together all in the Church are ultimately called to participate actively in the mission of God (*missio Dei*).

Presiding is less about the detail of gestures and postures and more about the understanding of Eucharist and Church the minister brings to bear on his ministry of leading worship. Pope Benedict XVI used the term *ars celebrandi* to speak of the care with which an ordained priest presides in the eucharistic assembly.[4] As an 'art', presiding does involve certain skills, but to the extent that it relates to the sacramental life of the Church, it also requires a faith-informed understanding of what is happening. This essay will delineate something of the ritual and theological context useful for an understanding of what it means to preside at Eucharist before exploring in the second part some elements of the leadership of the local liturgical assembly. It will consider this by employing the framework of the triple office of Christ, applying this also to the presiding ministry of the ordained person, as well as to the community's celebration of the Eucharist, noting that it too participates in the triple ministry of Christ.[5]

The faith-world of eucharistic ritual

The origins and final purpose of the Eucharist is to be found in mission. It is in Eucharist that the Church experiences itself most intensely as Body of Christ given for others. Thus, ordination is not for its own sake, nor is it a private possession, and there is no such thing as 'the priest's Mass'. Ordination is ordered to the priesthood of the baptised and the priest celebrates Eucharist 'for the sake of the world' (Jn 6:52) – therefore relating to the mission of God in Christ – and a personal eucharistic devotion emerges from, and informs, a way of being Church.

Students of ritual often make a useful distinction between what might be called the surface level of a rite and its deep structures. The surface level of a rite serves and reveals the deep structure where the meaning of the event can be uncovered. Unfortunately we either get caught up with the surface level, through a concern akin to rubricism, and give exaggerated importance to how we 'do' the liturgy, or, at the other extreme, we dismiss ritual as providing an artificial and stylised way of acting that is somehow untruthful. Either way we tend to be uncomfortable with ritual. Whether we like it or not, we are ritual beings. From greeting people, to how we dine, or how we engage at sporting events, State and social happenings … all of these involve ritual behaviour. We cannot but act ritually.

Surface-level ritual relates not just to how we stand or sit, or to how a presider gestures, intones prayer, or oversees the interflow of activity in a liturgy: these elements serve to enable the full participation of the assembly in the celebration of the Paschal Mystery of Christ. We err when we judge a liturgy to have been 'good' if it managed to keep the attention of people and 'give them a lift', or if it were celebrated merely with rubrical accuracy. 'Ritual truth' occurs when the surface level of a rite carries participants to its deeper structure. A good liturgy is one that enables us to experience the Paschal Mystery of Christ in all its depth, and challenges us to live out of the Mystery and allow it to shape our lives.

Good presidency in the liturgy will be helped by a move away from doing only what is deemed to be minimally necessary for valid celebration of the sacrament, thereby ignoring the power of the ritual enacted and the symbols employed.[6] Such reduction in an understanding of Eucharist and sacrament borders on magic and does not allow for an engagement with the ecclesial and faith context of sacramental action that has the Mystery of Christ at the centre. Examples of this can be found in how we deal with the distribution of the Eucharist. Employing ritual practices that are faithful to our tradition means that the assembly will receive, by preference, the eucharistic species that are consecrated at that Mass, for the same reason that the priest is bound to do so, rather than from the Tabernacle. Likewise, Eucharist ought to be offered to the assembly under both species (permission for which has been granted in Ireland since 1991), so that 'by means of the signs Communion will stand out more clearly as a participation in the sacrifice actually being celebrated'.[7]

We need to allow symbol to speak, and learn to be generous in gesture, bodily movement, dialogue, biblical reading and in use of song. How liturgical space is utilised is crucial, as is the cultivation of a deep sense of beauty. Presiding skills are important. They concern the surface level but must flow from, and lead back to, the mystery which is Christ.

The ritual truth of a presider relates to the overall 'truth' in his ministry when this is rooted in human experience, in empathy that flows from prayer, and in a familiarity with scripture as a lived faith-reality. The incarnational principle becomes important here. Christ, as the human face of God, embodies human experience. Only one who can see God through the lives and experiences of others in their human suffering and joy can preside with some degree of ritual integrity and authenticity. Central to this is a capacity to be private in public. As one leading the assembly's insertion into Paschal Mystery, the message communicated cannot be that of the presider's own personality and current angst. Unhelpful is the tendency to comment at every point in the liturgy thereby disabling symbolic and ritual language. There is a need to respect boundaries and not to ritually and emotionally manipulate an assembly. Authentic and truthful ritual behaviour is lodged in the ministry to which the presider is ordained, and in his groundedness in prayer, scripture and pastorally sensitive care.

The deep structure of liturgy, to which surface level ritual refers, is to be found in the Paschal Mystery. If we speak of liturgical participation, then we must affirm that the purpose of the 'full, conscious and active participation' (*Sacramentum Caritatis* [SC], 14) is that, engaging through liturgical ritual, we become more deeply part of the living Body of Christ in 'this' local assembly and beyond. But its full meaning points to our participation, through the liturgy, in the life of the Trinity. The various ritual aspects of liturgy have as their purpose this deepest sense of the term. Presiding with care and devotion at the Eucharist means that the ordained priest 'through rites and prayers' (SC, 48: *per ritus et preces*) facilitates the liturgical participation of the assembly, which reaches its deepest point in Trinitarian life.

Eucharistic presidency and the ordained priest

The role of the ordained priest is not merely functional. A balanced understanding of liturgical presidency at the Table of the Lord can be achieved by seeing how this is intimately linked to both the presbyter's and community's sharing in the triple office of Christ in the Church.

Eucharist and prophetic office

The third edition of the Roman Missal now contains among the final dismissals, 'Go and announce the gospel of the Lord.' This brings to the fore the 'mission' dimension of Eucharist. However, to reduce the dismissal rite to a mere 'sending' or 'missioning' at the end of Mass, as is often done in catechetical material, is to misunderstand that the very celebration of Eucharist is itself a participation in the *missio Dei*. Orthodox Christians help us to appreciate that Eucharist is essentially an act of mission, a proclamation of the wonders of God. The way in which we engage with Eucharist and allow it to engage us in life requires a prophetic expression that is rooted in the salvific preaching of Christ.

Liturgical gathering responds to a call to be something new and different. From the earliest times, Christians assembled in their baptismal faith around the Tables of Word and Eucharist in order to be sustained by the mystery of Christ's saving death. Assembling in its baptismal faith the early community strove to embody a radical form of egalitarianism (cf. Gal 3:26-29) and a service based not on power, but on love (cf. John 21:15-17). Within this 'culture' the presider exercises his ordained priesthood of leadership at the Altars of Word and Meal. A clericalism that pronounces privilege and authority is not only wrong; it is sinful, because it blocks the work of the Kingdom. Clerics cannot 'lord it over others'. The Church is called to be a sacrament of Christ, and cannot exercise authority in the way 'the world does'.[8]

Dining on the Body and Blood of the Lord, freely given for us for the forgiveness of sins, we are formed into a new way of existing that places the sharing of bread broken at the heart of human discourse, self-offering as a model for building human relationships, and forgiveness as being a non-negotiable in the building of a society inspired by the Kingdom. In this, the baptised are 'rehearsed' by liturgy to live by gospel standards, but must present this to wider society as a model of the 'new community' of Jesus Christ. Thus, the liturgical assembly should itself help shape how welcome is made to the stranger, how the drug addict and immigrant are brought to the centre of the community, how forgiveness is made, and how the weak are given support. It could be said that John 13, the washing of the feet, is the way that the institution of Eucharist is portrayed in the fourth gospel. If a community refuses to wash feet, then its Eucharist is inauthentic and a blasphemy (cf. 1 Cor 11:27).

The ministry of the presider is to lead the assembly to discover the graced presence of God in the world around and to allow Christ be shown forth even in the most unlikely of places and circumstances. For as Body of Christ we are tasked with revealing the Kingdom in our midst, and with bringing about a society that is ever more just, equitable and honouring of the poorest and marginalised. The liturgical assembly is able, in a privileged way, to 'manifest to others the mystery of Christ and the real nature of the true Church'.[9]

Word

The Introduction to the Lectionary asserts that the connection between liturgies of Word and Eucharist is so close that they form, in fact, but one single act of worship (see SC, 56). Such is this unity that 'whatever we can say of the Eucharist we can also say of the Word' (Introduction to Lectionary, 5). Thus the Liturgy of the Word is not simply a nice thing to do before the 'real' part of the Mass. It constitutes an integral component of the sacramental action of the Eucharist.

The homily therefore has sacramental qualities. It allows the Word to penetrate the life of 'this' assembly as it opens it up to the continued salvific workings of the God of Jesus Christ in its midst, which helps it, in faith, to make sense of its own life issues. When done well, the assembly can be brought through a poetic and imaginative experience to a place where a revisioning of how to live becomes possible. The great challenge remains the underdeveloped biblical culture of many Catholic Christians. One way to address this would be for the ordained presider to participate in a weekly *lectio divina* (based on the following Sunday's readings) with members of the assembly, and then to treat this as part of his homily preparation. There are two potential outcomes to this. First, all learn to become a listening Church, carefully discerning the prophetic movement of God in our midst. Second we become practiced, as a local assembly of which the priest-presider is a member, to read the Word in the context of the society to which we belong, as well as in its liturgical context. In this way the prophetic Word, which finds its most authentic and privileged interpretation in the liturgical eucharistic assembly, will become a source of hope for those who engage with it. The homily will reflect a meeting between the real presence of Christ in the Word proclaimed (see SC, 7) and assembly as it seeks to live its Kingdom vocation.

If the ordained priest is called to a eucharistic piety that finds nourishment through participation in the consecrated species on the altar, then he is equally called to a piety that is informed by a prophetic reading of the transforming Word of God in which he also encounters the real presence of Christ (see SC, 7). The quality of his ministry to the Word will be dependent on his personal and ecclesial sense of scripture.

Eucharist and priestly office

The priestly character of the Eucharist is clear: in it the baptised unite themselves, in and with Christ, to Christ's self-offering, and proclaim his death until he comes (cf. 1 Cor 11:26). This aligns the assembly with the salvific event of Christ, through which a new era was swept in. Participation in Christ's high priesthood requires of the entire baptised community that it lives out in its collective and individual lives the self-emptying of the cross so that the salvation offered in Christ may become evident to those around.

For others

The transubstantiation of the eucharistic species has as its purpose the transubstantiation of the lives of those who participate in the eucharistic celebration. The sacramental Body of Christ transforms the Church assembly into the living Body of Christ. Eucharist is best understood as a verb rather than a noun, as an action that is self-implicating rather than a static reality or object of prayerful adoration that can be left behind in church.

A strong sense of Church as sacrament allows us to appreciate the eucharistic action of the local assembly as being part of a life-long salvific process that helps believers discover the graced presence of Christ around them. As transubstantiation transforms from the core outwards, a presider imbued with a sacramental sense of Church will bring to the fore a transformative approach to liturgical ritual.

Intercession for the world

The community does not, in the first place, celebrate simply for itself so that it might become more holy. Yes, holiness is very important because we cannot become 'living Eucharist' in the society of which we form part unless we are somehow transformed and sanctified by it. However, the purpose of eucharistic transformation goes beyond us. As a priestly people, whose lives are to be 'a living sacrifice of praise' (Rm 12:1), we must exercise this priesthood by continually interceding for the salvation of the world. The assembly brings to public prayer its concerns for our political, social, ecological and economic environment. Through Word and sacrament we seek an empowerment to address the human needs of the world that are, by that fact alone, part of the salvific mission of Christ. The concerns of the Prayers of the Faithful are Kingdom-related, and while these will be rooted in the lives of the local assembly, they should not be trivialised by simple desires and 'wants' of private individuals.

Ordained presider

The role of the presider in the assembly must be carefully articulated in the actual ritual of the liturgy. It can best be described as being almost like a hinge in that it relates the assembly to Christ (in its discipleship and prayer) and the Lordship of Christ to the assembly in its obedience in faith. This particular iconic role finds clearest expression in the priest's liturgical presidency as does no other aspect of his ministry.

Ecclesial eucharistic piety includes adoration of the Risen Lord really present in the communion on the altar, whose priesthood continues to mediate on behalf of all. Relating the role of the presider to the Kingdom mission of God suggests that the focus of the liturgy is not the ordained priest but the assembly, in Christ. His eucharistic devotion will require of him that he serve the liturgical rituals of the Christian community in a way that is not idiosyncratic, and that offers adoration to Christ present in the living ecclesial Body of Christ in and over which he presides. For example, the presider's role will be enhanced by learning that rituals and symbols do not require explanation, and that introductions to various parts of the liturgy should only be given when absolutely necessary and should never become mini-homilies. There is need to trust the ritual, and to engage with it selflessly so as to allow the assembly be brought directly into the action through its participation. Liturgy does not function well with 'personalities' – be they ordained or not.

Eucharist and pastoral office

How we celebrate Eucharist has implications for the pastoral character of our participation in Christ's ministry as a baptised people. The Lord's Supper is already an anticipation of the Reign of God which reveals God's plan for us. As root metaphor it is something more than simply a ritual moment in our daily and weekly lives. Rather it is a 'faith-event' which defines our very existence and lifestyle as Christians. In this sense we can state that the Eucharist, and all that it means, becomes a paradigm for our pastoral guidance and ministry.

Presiders will take seriously the implications of celebrating Eucharist faithfully: as a sign of the Reign of God it requires the development of a deep eucharistic piety around the real presence of Christ which is to be found also in the hungry, the stranger, the naked and the rejects of society (cf. Mt 25:32-46). Participating in this sacred meal is self-implicating and has ethical consequences. It requires a lifestyle in the assembly that overflows in justice and care for the earth. Eucharistic real presence is a sign of the inauguration for us, now, of God's Reign.

No different to all the baptised, ordained priests are called to a eucharistic piety that involves a full commitment to transformation at personal, ecclesial and social levels – and that sees in the Mass a paradigm for a new way of political, social, economic living that places justice (in all its dimensions) at the centre. Through nourishment it roots the Church in its call to be a symbol of the unity of humanity as it journeys towards its completion in the fullness of the Reign of God.

Conclusion

Through sharing in the bread of life and cup of salvation we are helped to define God as love, as self-giving, as outreaching, and as the One who invites to communion. Eucharistic dining helps us to define all other meals we share. For the ordained priest, presiding at the Eucharist is a ministry to the assembly so that the community of believers will become present to the saving Lord, have its brokenness healed and its deepest yearnings satisfied. Good presiding enables the assembly to frame its Christian existence with the root metaphor of the Paschal Mystery. Transformation by the Spirit of God flows from the Eucharist into the life of the assembly, thereby transforming society.

Notes

1. Benedict XVI, Post-Synodal Apostolic Exhortation, *Sacramentum Caritatis* (SC), (2007), 64.
2. See Hervé-Marie Legrand, 'The Presidency of the Eucharist According to the Ancient Tradition', *Living Bread, Saving Cup*, R. Kevin Seasoltz, ed. (Collegeville, MN: Liturgical Press, 1987), 196–221. He states that in earlier tradition, an ordained priest presided at the Eucharist because he was first of all the one who presided over the life of the assembly.

3. See SC, 10 and *Lumen Gentium*, 11.
4. SC, 38–42.
5. See *Lumen Gentium*.
6. See SC, 11.
7. See General Instruction of the Roman Missal, 85.
8. See Mark 10:42-45; John 13:12-17, etc.
9. SC, 2.

Speaking From Within: More Effective Preaching

KIERAN J. O'MAHONY

The use of the Bible has been strongly promoted, at least at official level, since the Council of Trent.[1] That Council said that every diocese should employ a biblical scholar for the better understanding of the scriptures among the clergy. Vatican II and many subsequent documents have said the same, encouraging insistently the increased use of the Bible for prayer, for pastoral life, for liturgy and so forth. One of the encouraging signs – if not quite of spring, at least of new shoots – is the awareness of the Word among the people of God. Formal encouragement seems finally to have found a place in people's own journey of faith. We read scripture no longer because we ought to, but because we want to. We want to because the regeneration of the Church can have no other genesis than in the Word of God. The move from the ideal to the real, from the official to the felt, does bring hope in the current Church climate.

In many parishes, there are Bible study and *lectio divina* groups, following the Lectionary. There is a corresponding raising of expectations regarding the homily. Not everyone but certainly some are really hungry for the Word. They expect an informed, engaged and life-giving exposition in the homily. How can this happen?

Praying the Word

The title of this essay indicates the direction of the content: speaking from within. Speaking from within means speaking from my experience of life and my experience of praying the scriptures. There are many different ways of praying the scripture and many ways of conducting *lectio*. The destination is always the same, but the route will vary. One such route is offered here, acknowledging that it may not suit everyone.

Before preaching on the Word of God, the preacher begins by listening to the Word. This can open very simply: a set place and time, a moment of quiet, perhaps some reflective music and certainly a prayer. For example:

> Merciful God, anoint me with your Holy Spirit. As I read your Word, let me hear your voice speaking to me from within. Give me wisdom to understand your message to me. Let your word be the joy of my heart and a lamp for my steps. May I rejoice in the blessedness of those who hear your Word and keep it. Speak, Lord, your servant is listening ...

For the first step in this prayer of listening, take up the passage chosen and read it slowly. Pay attention to how your feel as you hear the Word. There are three worlds at play here, the world before the text (yourself and your concerns), the world behind the text (the context and background) and the world in the text (whatever it is saying). It is important to begin with where you are and how you feel. When the various steps of reflection have been undertaken, the hope is that you will have heard a Word, that addresses your experience, a Word that will penetrate your heart and change your life. Letting the Word resonate with your personal experience should not be rushed. Let the Word summon up feelings, memories, images – really anything at all in your own life which is evoked by the images, words and events.

Only after adequate time has been devoted to the first step should the second be taken. Read it again slow and notice whatever is not clear to you. This could be anything: a word, a custom, some historical background, the religious teaching of the passage as a whole. It is very useful at this point to have more than one translation at your disposal. The version in the Lectionary is the original Jerusalem Bible, which has itself been updated to the New Jerusalem Bible. A very popular current translation is the New Revised Standard Version, especially its study edition, the HarperCollins Study Bible. The notes and essays are excellent. The New English Translation (see www.bible.org) offers a fine translation, with very complete explanatory notes. It is good to have more than one translation, given that the majority of preachers will not be reading in the original languages.

At this point we encounter two other 'worlds' of the text, the world behind it and the world within it. Today there are many methods and approaches, conveniently summarised and assessed in *The Interpretation of the Bible in the Church*.[2] For us as Catholics, convinced of the coherence of faith and reason, the historical critical method (really a collection of methods) poses challenges but no threat to our faithful reading of the Bible. In the words of the Commission:

> The historical critical method is the indispensable method for the scientific study of the meaning of ancient texts. Holy scripture, inasmuch as it is the 'Word of God in human language', has been composed by human authors in all its various parts and in all the sources that lie behind them. Because of this, its proper understanding not only admits the use of this method *but actually requires it*.[3]

It means that a responsibility devolves upon the preacher to be adequately informed about the text, its context and meaning. This does not have to be burdensome scholarship; it is sufficient to use standard resources regularly and well. Naïve interpretations, which take no account of historical questions and literary forms, serve no one. My own personal experience in adult faith formation tells me that many people are ready for something more grown-up than that.

A good study Bible with decent notes will satisfy many questions. Any of the standard one-volume dictionaries of the Bible would also be very serviceable. As a larger general resource it would be really hard to beat *The New Interpreter's Dictionary of the Bible*. It is certainly comprehensive, in five volumes, but also pastorally accessible.

Eventually we return, in a spirit of prayer, to the text once more. It should be read slowly, as always, with a view to noticing how I, at this moment in my life, find myself addressed by the reading. After about an hour or so, these first steps can be drawn to a conclusion. The suggestion is to return to the same passage for a period each day for the next while. A practical way of doing this may be to schedule it as part of your regular prayer. It can surprise how our reading of a passage changes and grows over even only a few days. Two more steps are proposed.

The second last step is to read the passage once more, slowly, and in the silence which follows to spend time reviewing what came up for you over the last few days of reflection. How different was your final reflection from your first? Did any particular point emerge as a special word for you, now, at this moment? It might be helpful to keep a diary or note of your reactions the better to discern the message for you.

The very last step is prayerful contemplation. It would be appropriate to read the passage one more time, as a way of entering the prayer moment. Verbal prayer may help – using words and phrases from the scripture. As we harvest the extended reflection, the time of quiet leads naturally to simply resting in God's presence. This slow prayer is not merely homily preparation but a regular and nourishing part of the life of prayer. The risk among 'professional' users of the scriptures is a certain instrumentalisation of the Word of God. If we as preachers are to have a word of life for those who hear us, we ourselves must have heard that word to begin with. We are called to speak from within, that is, from within my own encounter with the Lord, through his living word, in the Holy Spirit.

Preparing the homily

Our word 'homily' comes from the Greek verb *homilein*. Its meaning is captured in these passages in Luke:

> Now on that same day two of them were going to a village called Emmaus, about seven miles from Jerusalem, and talking [*homilein*] with each other about all these things that had happened. While they were talking [*homilein*] and discussing, Jesus himself came near and went with them, but their eyes were kept from recognising him. And he said to them, 'What are you discussing with each other while you walk along?' (Lk 24:13-17; cf. also Acts 20:11, 24:26)

The range of meanings of this verb is: to be in a group and speak, to speak, to converse, to address. The associated noun – *homilia* – is close in meaning: to be in a state of close association with others, to engage in talk, either as conversation, speech or lecture. The classical root means to be in company with, to consort with (from the adjective *homos* meaning one and the same, common, joint).

A homily means 'to be with others'; it should be as natural as having a conversation. This does not mean, however, that it needs no preparation or presentation. Such illusions from the 1970s – perhaps in reaction to the stylised or theatrical preaching of the past – constitute the myth of spontaneity, as if only that which is spontaneous is authentic. A comparison with music may help to make the point. Nothing sounds more natural than the music of Mozart. As you listen you feel this is the only way this music can be. At the same time, nothing is more full of artifice than such music, carefully calibrated with astonishing, though concealed, sophistication, with the result that it sounds 'natural' on an altogether other plane. In that sense, artifice (that is, skilful preparation and presentation) does not at all mean artificial or lacking in authenticity.

The first and most important step is to figure out what needs to be said in this situation. It helps to know the congregation really well, what is affecting their lives and what is going on for them. Nothing is more important that this first sitting down to think. After all, the hope is to deliver a word of life into a particular setting, and the preacher has to know this context before anything else. Saint Paul illustrates this. Before dictating any of his letters, he first of all informs himself thoroughly. For example:

> But Timothy has just now come to us from you, and has brought us the good news of your faith and love. He has told us also that you always remember us kindly and long to see us – just as we long to see you. For this reason, brothers and sisters, during all our distress and persecution we have been encouraged about you through your faith. For we now live, if you continue to stand firm in the Lord. (1 Th 3:6-8)

Often when presenting his teaching, he uses the slogans of the groups he confronts ('It is well for a man not to touch a woman') as a measure of just how well informed he is. Of course, it may well be that over all the Sundays of the year there is nothing particularly dramatic happening in the faith community (a welcome prospect in these difficult days). Often, however, there are things happening in the community, to the community, in the wider society – things which provide the link between the Word of God and life today. Otherwise, we may find ourselves speaking into the air (cf. 1 Cor 14:9).

Having landed on the core topic or context that needs to be addressed, the next step is to provide a sequence that is engaging and interesting. Without wishing to be over-prescriptive, I would suggest the following moments, each meriting distinct consideration.

The beginning of a homily

All beginnings are important and so the opening couple of sentences need to be carefully chosen and calibrated. There are two goals here. The first is to get people's attention, for without that you will indeed be speaking into the air, or worse to yourself. An anecdote, a personal story, something you have observed may serve to get started. The second goal is to get people on your side, so to speak, so that they will want to listen to what you are about to say. The key here is brevity and wit. A long introduction may not simply delay engagement with the main issue, it may even obscure it.

The main point

It would serve both the homilist and the hearers if the preacher could offer in one simple sentence whatever it is they want to get across. This does not have to be complete – it would be to risk tedium by saying it all at the start – but it does have to be clear and serviceable. Some such one-liner early on would be an act of mercy towards all concerned. Saint Paul is a good example. In 1 Thessalonians 1:9-10 he gives the message of the letter, to be unfolded in detailed over the next five chapters.

Argument(s)

The word 'argument' is used here in the positive sense of persuasive reasons. The current preaching style (if there be such) may be a reaction to desiccated theological sermons of old and that is understandable. A reaction depriving the homily of ideas would be extreme. Most people can handle a degree of sophistication these days. A more common risk is to exhort, without adducing arguments or evidence. Such 'persuasion' depends more on forceful presentation and personality than reasoned conviction. Furthermore, moral exhortation places the speaker in the role of judge. When people feel they are being morally assessed they do pay attention, but the distancing effect of assessment causes them to withhold consent and receptivity.

Arguments can be of many kinds. Certainly one can use scientific evidence wherever appropriate. For example, in the case of care for the earth, the catastrophic melting of the polar ice cap could be an effective illustration. Evidence from developmental psychology helps in dealing with stages of life and faith. Or when addressing values and attitudes in society, polls and surveys can help. For example, it emerged in a recent survey that 17 per cent of Australians think Jesus never existed.[4]

There are also examples from personal experience – some personal context in which a particular insight came to mind. Such 'I' witness can be powerful and usually holds people's attention. Depending on who you are speaking to, recent illustrations from films or novels, or occasionally a phrase from poetry, can be effective.

From time to time it would be good to attempt a more biblically focused homily. This would most likely not work all the time, but certainly some of the time it could be effective. For example, paying attention to the special occurrence of the word 'compassion' in the gospels – used exclusively of Jesus or of God in the parables. This can illuminate its use in the Prodigal Son. Or take a word like *shalom*, which means something rather more in its biblical wealth of resonance than our pedestrian peace of mind.

To challenge common unexamined presuppositions in our contemporary culture is surely needed today. The prophetic word is there to disturb and destabilise. We live in a culture of distraction, a culture that tends to close out time for reflection on those things that really matter. The unease can be deeper. In a postmodern frame, there can lurk a conviction that there is no point whatsoever in looking at the deeper questions, a kind of counsel of despair, a conviction that chance and absurdity are the marks of human existence. And yet the hunger for something more is part of the spiritual DNA of being human. The biblical picture of God, both faithful and true, could not be more different.

One could go on, but the point has been made that the conversation – which the homily is – should engage more than the feelings of the believer. Only abstractly can we separate mind and heart: we can feel our thoughts and we can think our feelings.

At the centre of our faith stands the person of Jesus and his Good News. The different arguments brought to bear lead eventually to some faith affirmation precisely about Jesus and his teaching. The words of Benedict XVI retain their significance:

> Being Christian is not the result of an ethical choice or a lofty idea, but the encounter with an event, a person, which gives life a new horizon and a decisive direction.[5]

In the end, all our preaching should bring the hearers to a renewed and deeper encounter with the Risen Lord. The quality of relationship, of encounter, of horizon, of direction – this is what is at stake. There is no need for homilies to be the last word on anything; they are part of a longer conversation and that conversation or *homilia* is being with others and with Jesus, which transcends the particular occasion.

Concluding a homily

Every oral communication requires a conclusion, the purpose of which is threefold: to win the attention of the hearers yet again, to summarise what has been said, and to touch the hearts of all assembled. The summary can again be a sentence or two to pull it all together. There are many wonderful summaries in Paul. Again, one example may suffice:

> Welcome one another, therefore, just as Christ has welcomed you, for the glory of God. For I tell you that Christ has become a servant of the circumcised on behalf of the truth of God in order that he might confirm the promises given to the patriarchs, and in order that the Gentiles might glorify God for his mercy. (Rm 15:7-9)

Careful examination reveals that the grand sweep of Romans is summarised intellectually and yet presented practically and emotionally in these few words. A homily should leave people slightly unsettled, their minds not quite at rest.

As a practical guide to effective communication, the following outline may help:

1. Introduction: to raise people's attention and interest.
2. Main message: in one sentence, fairly early on (it can be repeated in the conclusion, with some added enrichment).
3. Arguments: the goal is persuasion by combining conviction and reason.
4. Conclusion: to summarise, to encourage, to move and to unsettle.

Rigid adherence to such a schema would be artificial and constricting. Nevertheless, being aware of what you are trying to achieve in the different moments will promote clarity for the speaker and the hearers. Often, the best effect is achieved by cutting out whatever clutters up or obscures the chief line of persuasion.

Writing and delivering the homily

A homily, however brief, will benefit from the discipline of writing. It helps to see the ideas in their actual sequence. It is also an opportunity to eliminate anything awkward in expression or any technical terms that might put people off. Much of the energy of preaching is and should be given over to finding new language for faith convictions. Much of the old language lost its resonance long ago (*pace* the new Roman Missal). An example would be the word 'redemption'. Does it mean anything to people today? Writing affords an opportunity to review language, making it more attractive and appealing.

Lastly, effective communication means eye contact. For a real *homilia* or conversation with people, nothing can replace speaking directly and with conviction. It is essential to memorise what you are going to say. Occasionally for more formal or more difficult occasions, a homily may of course be read, but for the ordinary Sunday the preacher should look at the listeners. While we cannot take on the high quality of communication in the media, people are accustomed to professionalism. For the sake of the gospel and for the sake of our fellow believers, we owe them our best. The habit of praying the text, with its gradual 'harvesting' of teachings over time, should be a good help in memorising because it will be based on direct experience of the biblical text.

Conclusion

Our topic is one aspect of a larger project: handing on the faith. Evangelisation, to give it its formal name, is central to the life and well-being of the Christian community. Preaching is only one aspect of evangelisation but an important part. It takes time and personal engagement. The benefit of good preaching is enormous in the life of God's people. It is not that everyone goes away every Sunday newly informed and on fire. Rather, Sunday after Sunday the hearers are convinced of the Good News, that it makes sense and that it connects to life. When their time of need arises, they will know where to turn.

Notes

1. J. O'Malley, *Trent: What Happened at the Council* (London: Harvard University Press, 2013), 99–102. See also the Decrees of Trent, Fifth Session, Decree on Reformation, Part 1.
2. *The Interpretation of the Bible in the Church* (Pontifical Biblical Commission, 1993).
3. Ibid., 1a. Emphasis added.
4. 'Spirituality and Christianity in Australia Today', Crindle Research (April 2012).
5. Benedict XVI, *Deus Caritas Est*, 1.

Ministering Healing and Forgiveness

HUGH CONNOLLY

The centrality of forgiveness and reconciliation

One suspects that for many modern Christians, the words 'conversion', 'repentance' and 'penance' carry with them unsavoury resonances of bygone times. For some they connote attitudes and practices and an image of God with which they are no longer at ease. Nowhere is this unease more apparent than in the crisis which has surrounded the Sacrament of Penance.[1] Yet at the heart of our faith remains the conviction that confessing our sins is part and parcel of the moral life and of our own personal dialogue with Jesus Christ. Since the Second Vatican Council, the Church has sought to emphasise that it is the compassionate, merciful and forgiving Christ whom we encounter through the mediation of the priest.[2] In the Sacrament of Reconciliation we recall Jesus' summing up of the entire Christian message as love of God and love of neighbour. We attempt therefore in the moment of Confession to put behind us everything that has wounded, damaged or even broken those key relationships and to put in place a new commitment to the Great Commandment. Each of the sacraments takes place in the context of human life and of the journey of Christian faith. They validate and nourish our Christian identity in the world and they mark important stages in life's journey to the kingdom. The priest then has the privileged role, in the name of the Church, of reconciling the penitent with God and with the community. Just as sin weakens

347

or ruptures our relationships with God and with others, through this healing sacrament fractured relationships are restored.[3]

Unfortunately, even where the sacrament is celebrated today, what should be an important moment of healing encounter with Christ is frequently marred by an excessive 'mechanism', or what some have called an 'absolution mentality'. In its starkest form, this sees the priest and penitent stressing absolution to the exclusion of a more profound reflection on personal conversion and healing.[4] A key aspect of confession which makes it a nodal point, an encounter with Christ along our faith journey, is thus neglected and reduced to an unhealthy legalism. Confession too easily becomes an exchange of words where the penitent, having recounted their sins, hears the confessor almost invariably prescribe a verbal act of satisfaction. Perhaps an over-emphasis on the requirements for validity has skewed our understanding of this sacramental encounter away from its rich heritage of healing and mercy.[5]

The biblical basis for reconciliation and forgiveness

It is salutary perhaps to recall that Christ 'came into the world to reconcile all things to himself' and that the gospels show him issuing his call to repentance within the context of proclaiming the Good News of God's kingdom among us. Scripture and tradition have always seen the Christian life in terms of a continual conversion, a turning back to God who is author and sustainer of our lives. Such a view is in keeping with the traditional understanding of the law of growth or gradualness.[6] Seen in this context, the goal of the conversion journey is to experience afresh our graced and intimate relationship with God and our relatedness to one another in Christ. In the process, we – as the people of God – are to become living signs of conversion.

The biblical backdrop is worth reflecting on here because we can sometimes get lost in the 'tactics' of the sacraments – the when, where, how and the specifics of a sin or group of sins. In so doing we lose sight of the deeper reality of conversion to God's ways and will. Turning to one's self alone and turning one's back on others only leads to the hardening of the heart, spoken of by the prophets (Ez 11:14-21) and the insensitivity of the priest and the Levite (Lk 10:30-37).

As people of God who believe that we live in the interim time between the already and the not yet – on the one hand redemption is accomplished and on the other redemption is not yet complete – we see ourselves as having 'no abiding city'. We are a pilgrim people. To engage in penitential activity, to celebrate repentance and to undertake true conversion is to demonstrate and remind ourselves of this pilgrim status. Pilgrimages, however, cannot be static. They must be dynamic, ongoing and far-reaching, for they are in themselves an act of witness. We celebrate sacraments so that we too might become real and effective signs of conversion while living in an imperfect world. If our celebration is to be truly sacramental in the broader meaning of that term as a living and efficacious sign, then we need to strive to become living and efficacious signs of reconciliation and conversion to the Good News.[7] Similarly, mono-dimensional conceptions of repentance, which see repentance entirely as momentary, static acts, must give way to understandings which emphasise conversion as an attitude of life. We may think of it figuratively as 'wiping the slate clean' but that very image is of something static and unvarying, something done at periodic moments only to be set aside or even forgotten about until the next appointed time.[8]

Conversion as a process

To be sure, the practice of periodically taking stock, of reflecting on one's life in the presence of the priest at the appointed times is essential. But this reflection will only bear fruit if sufficient emphasis is given to the life context, and the follow-up and the follow-through. Ultimately it is our day-to-day efforts at conversion that the sacramental celebration of conversion draws upon. It is the ongoing aspect of our conversion which grounds the sacrament in a particular human context. This is what is perhaps most central to our understanding of healing and forgiveness. A signpost is static – a pathway by contrast is dynamic and accompanies us along the journey. Healing, if it is to be real, takes time. While the moment of absolution does indeed wipe away our sins from a human perspective, time is needed for us to alter our sinful patterns of behaviour. Our pastoral praxis therefore must take due account of this.

The moral life may be seen as a task of becoming human, becoming whole, a task in which we are called to be co-creators with God. We are invited to accept responsibility for our lives, and to gradually realise agapeic love both in our own person and in communion with others. Understood in this light, sin is, above all, the failure to incarnate love and to cooperate with God in giving birth to a new *koinonia*. The re-creative, regenerative and ultimately healing process of repentance takes place primarily in the human heart. What is needed is the cooperation of human free will – the willingness to surrender our aspirations to self-sufficiency and to accept God's love and the implications of that love in outreach to others. This dynamic and synthetic view of creation and of the human person sees the *imago Dei* as at once gift and task.[9] Each human being has been created in the image and likeness of God and is therefore conferred with an undeniable dignity but each is also called to make real that 'communion of love' which is the hallmark of the same God in his or her own life. This is the awesome adventure of human nature. Sin therefore represents one possible expression of that freedom which is ultimately a refusal, whether small or great, of human destiny in its noblest reach.[10]

Columbanus, the great Irish pilgrim monk and author of a penitential handbook, once suggested in one of his sermons that each human being may ultimately determine the 'picture' that is to be painted in and through their lives:

> Let us not be the painters of another's image ... for righteousness and unrighteousness ... are opposed to one another. Then lest perhaps we should import into ourselves despotic images let Christ paint his images in us.[11]

According to this view the moral life works gradually either to confirm the imprint of the *imago Dei* upon one's entire existence or else to slowly replace it with the image of the 'tyrant' which enslaves us.

Even in these earliest theological reflections there was evidence of a synthetic, integral and holistic approach. There was also keen awareness of the continuous as well as the immediate aspects of moral behaviour. Indeed it has also been the tenor of the vast learning and practical wisdom of the Christian tradition to regard both the immediate and continuous dimensions as co-essential aspects of the moral life. In other words, one has to allow each of these dimensions to co-exist in a creative and complementary tension.

Recent theology has understandably sought to root its reflections on sin in a more adequate synthetic and integral understanding of the human person. It has rediscovered the dramatic and incredible assertion at the heart of Matthew's account of the final judgement that 'as often as you did this to one of the least of these my brothers and sisters you did it also to me!' To love others is therefore to love God and conversely to fail others is to fail God. Sin is therefore not alone a moral fault, it is also a religious failure. Recovery from sin challenges us in turn to a renewal of faith, to a renewed acceptance of the fact that the path away from sin and toward healing and wholeness cannot be travelled alone. Growth out of sin becomes but another way of describing our own personal part in the ongoing story of humankind as it continues its struggle toward the realisation of the Kingdom of God.[12]

Celebrating the sacrament today

What does all of this mean for the way in which we celebrate the sacrament today? The Sacrament of Reconciliation[13] is an efficacious 'sign' from God who comes into our sinful situation to bring us back into his family, and on each occasion gives us new hope. Therefore, we have to find ways to emphasise that the initiative comes from the gratuitous outreach and generosity of our loving Father. Our celebrations need to encourage a radical change of mentality, a move away from a primitive religious thinking that believes that the predisposition of God somehow rests in the way we encounter him. Instead, what is needed is to present confession as an act of faith that allows us to discover the tenderness of the Father as well as our own desire for rebirth and renewal.[14] Our celebration should render us open, available and able to recognise the most powerful moment of the whole process: the Word of God revealing to us God's unfathomable love. One might say then that our examinations of conscience should be first and foremost examinations of trust and of faith, and indeed renewal of our trust and hope, in the All-Merciful Father.

There are of course a few practical points worth making about the celebration itself. In terms of the lived and shared faith of a parish, the ritual of the sacrament has two forms. The first emphasises the personal approach where the moment of confession is celebrated with an individual priest and entails: an acknowledgement of sins, a request for forgiveness with expression of contrition, a prescription of a concrete penance by the priest, and finally the granting of absolution/forgiveness by the priest through the ministry of the Church 'in name of the Father, the Son and the Holy Spirit'. The second form is integrated into the worship of the community where all assembled jointly listen to the Word of God, aimed at enlightening their awareness of sin and often amplified by the reading aloud of a carefully prepared examination of conscience with common prayers of intercession and then personal approach to one of several priests present. As we know, in exceptional cases of necessity determined by the law and with approval of the bishop, this form can also be celebrated with confession and general or collective absolution.[15]

Whatever the form to be used, 'those who approach the Sacrament of Penance obtain pardon from God's mercy for the offence committed against him, and are, at the same time, reconciled with the Church which they have wounded by their sins and which by charity, by example, and by prayer, labours for their conversion'.[16]

With regard to the first form, there is a pastoral imperative that quality resources to aid the examination of conscience be provided, which should have the aim of thoroughly renewing and reviewing our lives. For individual confessions this can be as simple as a helpful leaflet outside the confessional. The confessional itself should provide penitents with a choice of either face-to-face or anonymous confession of sins, as well as an opportunity to select a reading from Holy Scripture.[17] Where possible, the penitent should also hear the priest's prayer of absolution in its entirety without having to shout their own act of contrition over it. Penances should be clear, definite and doable and ideally with some reference to the need for ongoing conversion, commitment and resolve. But care should be taken to adapt this for special categories of penitent, such as the scrupulous, the infirm, children and so forth. Indeed it goes without saying that the entire approach to the sacrament needs to consider carefully the needs of the particular faithful presenting at any particular celebration.

For the communal celebration, a thoughtful and prayerful reflection, preferably done by two lay voices and based on a carefully chosen reading from sacred scripture, can be a powerful moment of catechesis.[18] When publicly proclaimed this should be done in a spirit of prayerful reflection and never accusation. The examination should be aimed at arousing contrition, repentance and sorrow in our hearts. The aim is to be comprehensive and yet succinct whilst using plain, simple and accessible language. So as not to be an entirely passive experience, an opportunity could be afforded for the congregation to periodically respond with a prayerful refrain. The great communal prayers of contrition and petition for God's mercy, such as the Confiteor and the Kyrie, should also be prayed together. They can be recited simply and without elaboration.

Individual confessions usually need to be allotted a period of at least twenty minutes. Because of the length of time involved it is best that careful provision be made for music, light, singing and, insofar as possible, a good number of confessors. The prayerful atmosphere can be augmented by having muted lighting for this phase of the celebration, with some meditative and unobtrusive sacred music. After confessing their sins and receiving absolution, penitents could be invited, for instance, to go to the altar and bless themselves from a container of Holy Water as a reminder of their baptismal calling. The ceremony ends with a proclamation of praise and penitents duly return to their places while priests return to the sanctuary. The main celebrant then leads the people in a psalm, Magnificat or other suitable prayer. It is preferable, however, that the people be familiar with the words of the prayer to be used or to have the text in front of them. Where there is doubt, it is probably best to use familiar prayers such as the Our Father, Hail Mary or Glory Be to the Father.[19]

The confessor's preparation and disposition

Regarding the confessor's own preparation, a few points are worthy of note. Chief among these perhaps is the observation that 'being an effective confessor is not primarily a matter of mastering theological principles on the one hand or acquiring a lengthy inventory of pastoral techniques on the other'. While competence in both principles and practice is needed, 'theological expertise without sound pastoral application has little use outside the classroom. But a pastoral practice that is not informed and guided by sound theological study and reflection is dangerous'.[20] It is fair to say that celebrating the Sacrament of Reconciliation remains for every priest a privileged and humbling experience. A genuine disposition on the confessor's part to receive the penitent's sincere acknowledgement of their sins is key. On the other hand, a 'scrupulous over concern for the integrity and matter of the sacrament is not required for the confessor to discharge his duties faithfully'.[21] General guidelines as to how a confessor is to approach particular pastoral situations are set out in the so-called Vademecum for Confessors. With a little adaptation however, these observations hold good for all celebrations:

In dealing with penitents, the confessor should keep four aspects in mind: a) the example of the Lord who 'is capable of reaching down to every prodigal son, to every human misery, and above all to every form of moral misery, to sin'; b) a prudent reserve in inquiring into these sins; c) help and encouragement to the penitents so that they may be able to reach sufficient repentance and accuse themselves fully of grave sins; d) advice which inspire all, in a gradual way, to embrace the path of holiness. The minister of Reconciliation should always keep in mind that the sacrament has been instituted for men and women who are sinners. Therefore, barring manifest proof to the contrary, he will receive the penitents who approach the confessional taking for granted their good will to be reconciled with the merciful God, a good will that is born, although in different degrees, of a contrite and humbled heart (Ps 50:19).[22]

Finally, to paraphrase a further observation from the same document, 'the pastoral practice of confession will be more effective if it is united to an ongoing and thorough catechesis on the Christian vocation to love and on its joyful and demanding dimensions, its grace and personal commitment'.[23] When all is said and done, conversion and repentance are demands of God's kingdom so that we can enter that kingdom worthily and fully as God's sons and daughters. As such, far from being momentary or static acts of worship, they are, or at least should be, a life-long project.

Notes

1. 'We have to recognise the present difficulties facing the ministry of penance due to a certain loss of the sense of sin, a certain disaffection towards this sacrament, a certain blindness to the usefulness of the confession of sins and also the exhaustion suffered by many priests because of their manifold duties.' *The Priest, Minister of Divine Mercy: An Aid for Confessors and Spiritual Directors* (Vatican Press: Congregation for the Clergy, 2011), 21.

2. Pope John Paul II in the Post-Synodal Apostolic Exhortation *Reconciliatio et Paenitentia* (1984), 31. III teaches: 'The sacramental formula "I absolve you" and the imposition of the hand and the Sign of the Cross made over the penitent show that at this moment the contrite and converted sinner comes into contact with the power and mercy of God. It is the moment at which, in response to the penitent, the Trinity becomes present in order to blot out sin and restore innocence. And the saving power of the passion, death and resurrection of Jesus is also imparted to the penitent as the "mercy stronger than sin and offence", as I defined it in my encyclical *Dives in Misericordia*.'

3. Cf. 2 Cor 5:18.

4. *Reconciliatio et Paenitentia*, 15: 'The mystery of sin is composed of a two-fold wound which the sinner opens in himself and in his relationships with his neighbour'.

5. 'If the forensic approach is not carefully modulated it runs the risk of turning the sacramental experience into an inquisition.' Jerry McCarthy, 'Forming Confessors with Grateful and Compassionate Hearts', *Seminary* (Winter 2011), 22. *Seminary Journal* is published three times a year, in Spring, Fall and Winter. It is a scholary journal for Catholic seminary faculty, administrators, formation directors, field education directors and vocation directors.

6. See here Pope John Paul II's masterly reflection in *Familiaris Consortio* (1981), 9; and also *Vademecum for Confessors Concerning Some Aspects of the Morality of Conjugal Life* (Pontifical Council for the Family, 1997).

7. A sacrament is an 'efficacious sign of grace, instituted by Christ and entrusted to the Church, by which divine life is dispensed to us through the work of the Holy Spirit' (*Catechism of the Catholic Church*, 774, 1131). 'The seven sacraments touch all the stages of Christian life: they give birth and increase, healing and mission to the Christian's life of faith. There is thus a certain resemblance between the stages of natural life and the stages of the spiritual life' (CCC, 1210). 'The purpose of the sacraments is to sanctify men, to build up the body of Christ, and finally, to give worship to God, because they are signs they also instruct. They not only presuppose faith, but by words and objects they also nourish, strengthen, and express it; that is why they are called "sacraments of faith". They do indeed impart grace, but, in addition, the very act of celebrating them disposes the faithful most effectively to receive this grace in a fruitful manner, to worship God duly, and to practice charity' (*Sacred Constitution on the Liturgy*, 59).

8. The Priest, Minister of Divine Mercy, describes the journey of reconciliation and the Christian life which 'forms a cornerstone and foundation for a society which lives communion' (13).

9. For the Church Fathers, man is born as God's image, but he has to complete the *imago Dei* through his free yes to God. Blessed John Paul II shared in this vision. The divine image is seen as both a gift and a task: 'The likeness is a quality of the personal being ... and is also a call and a task' (see *Mulieris Dignitatem* [1988], 7). Insofar as it is a task, and not just a gift, the image of God takes time – indeed, a whole lifetime – to unfold its riches.

10. Pope Benedict XVI explains: 'Thus the meaning of sin – which is a different thing from "guilt feelings" as these are understood in psychology – is only grasped in discovering the meaning of God', First Sunday of Lent, Angelus message (13 March 2011).

11. Saint Columbanus, Sermon XI.

12. See K. O'Kelly, 'Saints or Sinners?: Towards a Spirituality of Growth Out of Sin', in his *From a Parish Base: Essaus in Moral and Pastoral Theology* (London: DLT, 1999), 166.

13. Note I have used the terms Sacrament of Penance, Reconciliation and Conversion almost interchangeably here in line with the observation in the *Catechism of the Catholic Church*, 1423–4.

14. CCC, 1424: 'It is called the sacrament of confession, since the disclosure or confession of sins to a priest is an essential element of this sacrament. In a profound sense it is also a "confession" – acknowledgment and praise – of the holiness of God and of his mercy toward sinful man.'

15. 'The third form however – reconciliation of a number of penitents with general confession and absolution – is exceptional in character. It is therefore not left to free choice but is regulated by a special discipline.' *Reconciliatio et Paenitentia*, 32.

16. *Lumen Gentium*, 11.2 and CCC, 1422.

17. The *Code of Canon Law* sets out the arrangements for confessions thus: 964 §1. The proper place to hear sacramental confessions is a church or oratory. §2. The Conference of Bishops is to establish norms regarding the confessional; it is to take care, however, that there are always confessionals with a fixed grate between the penitent and the confessor in an open place so that the faithful who wish to can use them freely. §3. Confessions are not to be heard outside a confessional without a just cause.

18. See, for instance, Thomas Richstatter, 'How to Celebrate the Sacrament of Reconciliation Today', http://www.americancatholic.org/Newsletters/CU/aco800.asp (accessed 1/4/2013).

19. An excellent online resource by the Liturgy Office of the Bishops' Conference of England and Wales can be found at http://www.liturgyoffice.org.uk/Resources/Penance/Advent-Resources.pdf (accessed 1/4/2013).

20. See Kurt Stasiak, 'The Making of a Confessor' in 'Forming Confessors with Grateful and Compassionate Hearts: Seminary Formation and the Renewal of the Sacrament of Reconciliation', *Seminary* (Winter 2011), 12. Kurt Stasiak, *A Confessor's Handbook* (New York: Paulist Press, 1999) is also thoroughly recommended.

21. 'Forming Confessors with Grateful and Compassionate Hearts', 24.

22. Pontifical Council for the Family, *Vademecum for Confessors Concerning Some Aspects of the Morality of Conjugal Life* (1997), 3.1.

23. Ibid., 3.17.

The Priest and Ministry to the Sick

LA FLYNN

Sickness and infirmity are a constant in human experience. When illness or trauma strikes us we experience ourselves as needy. Even a relatively light brush with infection or injury can leave us feeling vulnerable. The experience of finding ourselves physically, emotionally or mentally wounded or unwell in any significant way is isolating and raises existential and religious questions. We find ourselves facing the contingency of our human condition. Dependency and pain raise issues of meaning. Priests, especially those in pastoral ministry, regularly find themselves engaged with people who are facing illness, both critical and chronic. What can we usefully say about this aspect of the ministry of the priest in Ireland today?

Two texts from the earliest stratum of the New Testament are foundational for any consideration of priestly ministry to the sick. Mark 6:13 recounts that when Jesus sent out the Twelve, two by two, with authority over the evil spirits, they anointed many sick people with oil and healed them. In the Letter of James we read:

> Is there anyone sick among you? Let him send for the presbyters of the church and let them pray over him, anointing him with oil in the name of the Lord. The prayer of faith will save the sick person, and the Lord will raise him up. If he has committed any sins they will be forgiven. (Jas 5:14-15)

Together, these two texts are read by the Catholic Church as testimony to the institution by Jesus of the Sacrament of the Anointing of the Sick. This does not imply in a crude and a historical way that Jesus of Nazareth invented a rite. The language borrowed from the Council of Trent and used by Paul VI in the 1972 Apostolic Constitution, by which he approved the revised rite following Vatican II, is somewhat careful. The sacrament is 'intimated' in the text from Mark and 'recommended to the faithful and made known' in the Letter of James.[1]

But it is the interaction of Jesus with the sick that is truly foundational for the Christian response to those who from time to time or in a chronic way must face and struggle with illness. Clearly, in his personal practice of prophetic and life-giving ministry among the diseased, the disturbed and the tormented, Jesus is the model and inspiration for Christian disciples of every age, including especially those ordained to service as bishops and priests.

Jesus and the sick

The historical fact is beyond doubt: Jesus was devoted to such people above everyone else. As his reputation for compassion and healing spread, people flocked to Jesus. Apart from the individual stories of healing that come to mind, the gospels offer several summaries of his ministry among the sick and the broken.[2] It is important that we be clear that the engagement of Jesus with the sick was from a religious viewpoint, not from a medical one. They had to be the first to feel the Father's mercy and to experience the arrival of God's reign. Direct and indirect references to the Hebrew scriptures throughout the gospels highlight the prophetic quality of this aspect of his ministry.

While the gospels refer occasionally to medical professionals,[3] the Galilean population, among whom most of Jesus' ministry unfolded, would have had little access to professional healthcare. The conditions from which these people suffered are reflected in the language of the texts as they were understood in the culture of the time. Leprosy, for example, covered most forms of troublesome skin conditions. In reaching out to lepers with his healing power, Jesus was addressing social and religious exclusion. Epileptic and psychotic episodes were understood as manifestations of demonic possession. Jesus also thought in this way: 'His struggle to liberate these unhappy people was a victory over Satan and the best sign of the coming of the reign of God, who wants a healthier, more liberated life for his sons and daughters.'[4] Contemporary western society thinks of 'diabolic possession' as an illness. Professionals tend to say that people who become convinced that they are 'possessed' are dramatically projecting onto an evil spirit the repressions and conflicts that fragment their inner world.

Although Jesus shared the general sense of the nature of illness that was current in his time, he clearly challenged any implication that sickness or misfortune was a direct punishment from God for moral wrongdoing.[5] A full exploration of the newness in the attitude of Jesus to sickness and mental disturbance is beyond the range of this essay. What cannot be gainsaid is that the Christian community, led by its ordained ministers in terms of strategy as well as by example, is called to make present the prophetic compassion and the healing ministry of Christ in every time and in every culture, in ways that are complementary to best current medical practice, but with a focus on the religious implications of illness in its many forms.

The priest and the sick

From the gospel accounts it is clear that Jesus had a unique ability to connect at a profound level with the sick. This is how he made such a difference in terms of their condition, their sense of self and of where they stood before the awesome mystery of the God whom Jesus called Father. I suggest that the heart of the charism of healing that was so distinctive in Jesus of Nazareth lies in the quality of his presence to sick people. Not every Christian or priest is blessed with a special charism of healing, but we can learn to become present in ever more deeply human ways to others. We can engage with opportunities that help us to become more self-aware, and so unmask the unhelpful responses that prevent us from being really available to others and especially to those whose condition can trigger these responses. This is the kind of self-work that is undertaken in clinical pastoral education training programmes, which are now a standard part of seminary formation. Spiritual direction, pastoral supervision and reflection, and other practices in the area of self-care will also have much to offer. This also arises in terms of the value of debriefing after traumatic experiences like attending the scene of a road traffic accident or a violent death. As demands on priests increase, issues around self-care become ever more critical.

'The old priest, Peter Gilligan', in the well-known poem 'The Ballad of Father Gilligan' by W. B. Yeats, 'was weary night and day' because of the demands of his faithful ministry to the sick and the dying.[6] One of the frustrations experienced today by priests is around the difficulty of keeping in touch with the sick, amid the wide range of other calls on time and diminishing energy. In urbanised settings it is simply impossible to know which parishioners are sick and in need of a visit. Even in rural parishes, repeated appeals to the church-going population to let the priest know when a family member or neighbour is sick can have limited success. The parish pastoral council can come into its own in these situations by developing the ministry of care for the sick in a team approach, planning for appropriate visiting in a gospel spirit and directing the attention of the priest to the cases where his presence and sacramental ministry are more needed. In this context, the priest needs to address the ongoing task of formation for parishioners and for pastoral leaders in relation to ministry to the sick.[7]

The anointing of the sick

A brief review of the historical development of the anointing of the sick can be helpful.[8] Between the New Testament and the eighth century, what survives are formulas of blessing over oil. These texts are supplemented by references in writing of the period. In his letter to Decentius of Gubbio (416), Pope Innocent I states that oil blessed by a bishop may be used not only by priests but by all

Christians for themselves and for their loved ones.[9] The principal effect expected is an improvement of bodily health, although later we begin to find references to the remission of sins. In this period, priests are far from being the only ministers of God's healing grace. The oil was for the sick, not the dying, and there was no clear distinction between the sacrament and the use of the oil as a sacramental.

From the eighth to the twelfth centuries many rituals survive, testifying to the increasing interest of the Church in regulating the practice of anointing the sick. The focus gradually shifts over this period. Initially the prayers ask for bodily health and strength; then we find references to the particular body part being anointed, sometimes with a request for forgiveness for any wrong use of the sense in question; and finally we have rituals in which the prayer asks only that the Lord may forgive whatever wrong you have done through your eyes, and so on. The rituals move to detail, for example, entry of priest, sprinkling holy water, prayer, sacramental confession, litany of saints, anointings, Holy Communion. We begin to find deathbed rites where the person is commended to God's eternal care. We note that these developments gradually focus more on the role of the priest and we can parallel them with the increasing clericalisation in the Church over the medieval period as well as with a more spiritualised and sin-focused understanding of salvation.

The scholastic theology of the sacrament was conditioned by these developments. The effect of the sacrament was understood ever more as the remission of sins, to the point where Scotus suggests that for maximum benefit it is best to defer anointing until the dying person has become unconscious, so that they may be unable to sin further.[10] We had certainly arrived at Extreme Unction. Aquinas is more balanced: the sacrament was instituted to address 'the sickness that is sin' – bodily healing will be granted by God where this is useful for spiritual healing.[11]

The Council of Trent treated Extreme Unction in response to Protestant objections, mainly that what is mentioned in the

Letter of James described was not a sacrament but a charism of the apostolic period. This is the context for the careful wording used by Trent.[12] In fact, Trent widened the understanding of the sacrament, including reference to what we would now call its psychological and physical effects. It said, 'This anointing is to be given to the sick, especially those who ... appear to have reached the end of their life.' However, it would take four centuries and the developments of the liturgical movement as well as in scripture and patristics in the early twentieth century before Vatican II would say that Extreme Unction may also and more properly be called 'anointing of the sick'.[13] The essence of our current catechesis on this sacrament is well summarised in the Constitution on the Church:

> By the sacred anointing of the sick and the prayer of its presbyters, the whole Church commends the sick to the suffering and glorified Lord so that he may raise them up and save them (see James 5:14-16). The Church exhorts them, moreover, to contribute to the welfare of the whole people of God by associating themselves willingly with the passion and death of Christ.[14]

The 1972 ritual Pastoral Care of the Sick systematised the vision of Vatican II. It is a wholesome discipline for priests to revisit the *praenotanda* or General Introduction in the Rite of Anointing, with an eye to how well their practice matches up to the vision and theology outlined there.[15] The *Catechism of the Catholic Church* 1499–532 offers the essence of the contemporary theology of the sacrament of anointing.[16]

The value of this outline of historical and theological development is to invite us to a healthy sense of how liturgy, pastoral care and the theologies that underpin our practice are living realities. Essential and unchanging elements find new expressions as culture changes but these need to be evaluated critically since experience teaches that not all development is positive.

Among our experiences with the present ritual, the communal celebration of the sacrament of Anointing of the Sick has been particularly rich in meaning and in pastoral effectiveness. Those who have had the experience of such celebrations at Lourdes, in Knock or at the 2012 International Eucharistic Congress in Dublin have seen how they place the sick at the centre of the liturgical assembly, and how sick people appreciate the opportunity of celebrating the sacrament in this context. Usually presided over by a bishop and concelebrated by several priests, with the assistance of supporting ministries, these celebrations offer a distinctive experience of Church and an antidote to the isolating effect that is part of sickness and disability. We think too of many diocesan pilgrimages to Lourdes that have the participation of youth pilgrims to accompany and help the invalided and less mobile pilgrims, and how both the young people and those they assist value this aspect of the overall experience.

It is also good practice that at least annually there would be a communal celebration of anointing at parish level, ideally accompanied by a social occasion. World Day of the Sick on the feast of Our Lady of Lourdes offers one opportunity, but mid-February may not be the best time of year. In our parish we try at least to have an autumn celebration of this kind, before winter settles in.

These celebrations offer opportunities for catechesis on the place of the sick in the Christian community, on what the sick can offer to us in their prayer and the example of their patience in union with the suffering Saviour, on the mystery of infirmity, vulnerability and pain, on Christ's identification with those who suffer and on his invitation to recognise his presence in the sick and the wounded. Cumulatively, these recurring celebrations can make a significant catechetical contribution at parish level. The National Directory for Catechesis in Ireland, *Share the Good News*, has a particularly thoughtful, accessible and sometimes challenging section devoted to catechesis in relation to people living with illness.[17]

Before the mystery of death

As we said at the beginning, the mystery of infirmity ultimately brings us to face the mystery of our mortality. In this sense, the logic of the medievals was impeccable. However, our culture tends towards denial in the face of death. Developments in medical science and in surgery continually reduce mortality rates for specific conditions and increase life expectancy. We rejoice that palliative care can offer effective management of pain and other symptoms right to the end of life. At local level, we support the many volunteers who fundraise for research into cancer and other conditions in order to broaden the delivery of respite and palliative care, and we encourage them to see their commitment as part of their response to the invitation of Jesus to share his ministry to the sick and the needy. As chaplaincy, once a ministry entrusted exclusively to priests, becomes a ministry often delivered by skilled and prayerful laity and religious, good working relationships and mutual support become a key contribution that priests make in facilitating this vital service in hospitals and residential care settings.

Still it is a particular privilege for the priest to accompany the terminally ill and their families before the mystery of death. It is also an opportunity of grace for the priest. The priest-poet Gerard Manley Hopkins puts it tellingly as he ponders his experience with Felix Randal, the farrier, through his final illness when he writes: 'This seeing the sick endears them to us, us too it endears.'[18] As treatments inevitably decline in effectiveness, the Paschal Mystery of the dying and risen Christ comes into its own. This is a costly grace, however. Truisms and pious language will not suffice. Only humility and prayerful respect before the mystery will be up to the situation. Our earlier reflections around presence are particularly relevant here. The witness of Pope John Paul II in his final illness spoke very powerfully. We may think also of the generosity of the late Fr Martin Tierney in sharing the journey of his final illness with us in his writings shortly before his death.[19] As priests themselves become an ageing cohort (some might say 'a dying breed'), more and more of us face declining health and feel the burden of the years. We are finding ourselves increasingly as receivers of the ministry we have offered to others.

It is false religion that promises that if we trust in God, God will not let the things we fear happen to us. True religion recognises that the things I fear may well happen to me, but trusts that since God is with me these things are not after all anything to fear. The mystery of God-with-us in Christ is the heart of all Christian ministry to the sick, or as Paul puts it: 'The mystery is Christ among you, your hope of glory'.[20] Acting *in persona Christi capitis ecclesiae* it is the call of priests to lead the Christian community in making this mystery available and effective in regard to those who need it, and to embody it in a personal way themselves.

Notes

1. See Paul VI, Apostolic Constitution (30 November 1972) in *Pastoral Care of the Sick* (Dublin: Veritas, 1983), 5; CCC, 1510 and footnotes.
2. See, for example, Mt 4:23-24; Mk 3:7-11; Lk 6:17-18; Jn 6:2.
3. Mk 2:17, 5:26.
4. José A Pagola, *Jesus: An Historical Approximation* (Miami: Convivium Press, 2011), 173. Chapter 6, 'A Healer of Life', offers a fresh look at the ministry of Jesus to the sick from a historical perspective.
5. Jn 9:1-3, cf. Lk 13:2.
6. W. B. Yeats, 'The Ballad of Father Gilligan', *Anthology of Irish Verse*, Padraic Colum, ed. (New York: Boni and Liveright, 1922).
7. For an outline of key elements, see General Introduction, 32–7, in *Pastoral Care of the Sick*, 18ff.
8. A full account can be found in *Anámnesis*, 3/1: La Liturgia, I Sacramenti, Part III: Unzione degli Infermi (Marietti, Genova: Pontificio Istituto Liturgico S. Anselmo, 1986).
9. *Letter Si instituta ecclesiastica*, DS, 216.
10. See *Anámnesis*, 3.1, 229.
11. *Summa Theologiae*, Suppl., q. 30, a. 1 and 2.
12. See note 1 above.
13. Vatican II, *Constitution on the Liturgy*, 73.
14. Vatican II, *Dogmatic Constitution on the Church*, 11.
15. *Pastoral Care of the Sick*, 10–22.

16. CCC, 336ff.

17. *Share the Good News*, Irish Episcopal Conference (Dublin: Veritas, 2010), 126–8. The paragraph on 181 beginning 'Those who have become ill' offers a helpful outline of the range of faith stances that may be met among sick people.

18. 'Felix Randal', Gerard Manley Hopkins, *Poems and Prose* (London: Penguin, 1953), 47.

19. See various publications in *The Irish Catholic*, as well as *Battling the Storm: A Cancer Patient's Diary* (Dublin: Veritas, 2009).

20. Col 1:27.

Supporting the Sacrament of Marriage

RIK VAN NIEUWENHOVE

Theological reflections

Marriage has an iconic value in Christian theology. More so than any other sacrament it reveals the covenantal nature of the relationship between God and his people. In the Old Testament this covenant or relationship between Yahweh and his people is expressed in a number of texts which adopt the analogy of marriage – a marriage in which Israel often proved unfaithful (cf. Hos 2:21; Jer 3:6-13; Is 54):

> Does a man cast off the wife of his youth?
> For the mountains may depart, the hills be shaken,
> But my love for you will never leave you
> And my covenant of peace with you will never be shaken.
> (Is 54:6, 10)

Marriage is the first sacrament, instituted before the Fall in the Garden of Eden. The narrative of Genesis relates how the earth was a 'formless void', with 'darkness over the deep'. The climax of the creation story is the creation of humankind in the image of God: 'male and female he created them' (Gn 1:26). In the second creation story (Gn 2:5ff) Eve is created from the side of the sleeping Adam, and he rejoices when he wakes: 'This at last is bone from my bones, and flesh from my flesh.' The narrator adds, 'This is why man leaves his father and mother and joins himself to his wife, and they become one body' (Gn 2:24).

In the Letter to the Ephesians, St Paul quotes this text, and adds, 'This mystery has many implications; but I am saying it applies to Christ and the Church' (Eph 5:32). The Vulgate translated the Greek *mysterion* as *sacramentum*, which contributed to the inclusion of marriage as one of the seven sacraments – a move which finds its origins in the theology of St Augustine but which was only finalised by Peter Lombard in his twelfth-century *Sentences*.

Thus, the symbolism of marriage as denoting the relationship between God and God's people acquires an even deeper dimension through the Word becoming flesh, and living and dying among us. Indeed, the Letter to the Ephesians suggests that Christian marriage reflects, participates in and makes present the love of Christ for his Church, the bride. As Christ came to serve us unto his death on the Cross, so too the husband should serve his wife: 'Husbands should love their wives just as Christ loved the Church and sacrificed himself for her' (Eph 5:25). The text has traditionally been used as a legitimisation of a patriarchal understanding of marriage. There is, however, a different reading possible. For in St John Chrysostom's understanding, the text does not imply that the husband can 'lord it over his wife'. On the contrary: modelling your life on that of Christ is not an invitation to domination or abuse of power but to a life of humble serving. The wife will then respond lovingly and honour the husband who serves her like this. As St John Chrysostom admonishes the husbands in his congregation:

> For when he [Paul] says, 'Husbands, love your wives', he does not stop with this, but gives a measure for love, 'as Christ loved the Church'. And how did Christ love the Church? Tell me. 'He gave himself up for her.' So even if you must die for your wife, do not refuse. If the master loved his servant so much that he gave himself up for her, all the more you must love your fellow servant as much.[1]

In short, a more nuanced reading of the Letter to the Ephesians makes clear that Christian spouses are called to a life of humble service, in which they are requested to be 'subservient to one another' (Eph 5:21) – a counsel which only makes sense in a Christian understanding of power, which is about empowering others to grow in humanity, rather than overpowering them. As *Gaudium et Spes* states:

> [I]t is in the spousal love of Christ for the Church, which shows its fullness in the offering made in the cross, that the sacramentality of marriage originates. The grace of this sacrament conforms the love of the spouses to the love of Christ for the Church.[2]

This strong sacramental understanding of marriage does not just merely affirm an analogy: marriage as a sacrament makes the love between Christ and the Church *present* between the Christian spouses. It *causes* it, or rather Christ causes it through the sacrament.

As *Gaudium et Spes* suggests, the intimate link between the Church, the bride, and her bridegroom, Christ, who offers himself up for her, suggests that sacrifice, or self-gift, is at the heart of Christian marriage. This is a message that is all too often forgotten, in a society in which marriage is often perceived to be a mere lifestyle option of two loving people. The link with the gift of self of Christ, which the text from Ephesians alludes to, also explains why the sacrifice of the Mass is at the heart of a Catholic wedding. Through the Eucharist we are invited to become Christ-like, to imitate and share in a life of self-giving and sacrifice. The Eucharist re-enacts the self-gift of Christ on the Cross, which can be best understood as an act of penance on behalf of humanity or, in more modern language, restoration of a broken relationship with God. As St Augustine made clear in Book X of *The City of God*, through participation in the eucharistic bread the community of the believers shares in this self-gift of Christ, and, in faith, hope and love, becomes itself an offering to God.[3]

While sacrifice may at times involve self-abnegation, this should not be viewed negatively. Indeed, it is 'first and foremost the most beautiful and sublime fulfilment of a human being's life'.[4] Generally, it is only by giving ourselves away, and identifying ourselves with an ideal or project that is truly fulfilling, that we find true meaning. Similarly, sacrifice is at the heart of marriage, and this too does not have to be construed in oppressive terms. True human freedom is not so much freedom from, but freedom for – and nowhere does this observation apply as much to laypeople as in marriage and its commitments (monogamy, mutual support in bad times, and so on). Spouses are to find their genuine personal fulfilment by following Christ's life of self-giving love, and in doing so they will acquire their true identity as Christians and human beings.

In short, there is, in theological terms, a powerful connaturality between key aspects of Christian doctrine: the covenant of God with his people, which reaches its climax in the Incarnation of the Word made flesh who gives himself up on the cross (a gift of self which is re-enacted during the Sacrifice of Mass), on the one hand, and marriage as a sacrament, on the other.

It will have become clear that Christian marriage is more than love between two people: it also involves God, and it is only in the explicit recognition of the presence of God that our love for one another reaches its fulfilment (see the beautiful prayer by Tobias and Sarah in Tobit 8:4-9). This is the distinction between 'contracting' a marriage in the secular sense (with mutual obligations, which can be withdrawn or dissolved by the two contracting parties by mutual consent) and marriage in the religious sense in which a man and a woman take vows. Taking a vow implies involving God, inscribing your life into God's eternity. The vows we take can only be fully understood within a religious perspective. Given the ambiguities, temptations and unpredictability of life, it is – from a purely calculating or 'contractual' perspective – bordering on insanity to promise 'to hold and to cherish' another person 'until death'. This kind of 'contract' only makes sense if it transcends itself, and becomes a vow before God, who can heal our ineptitude and failings and strengthen us in our resolve to continue against our worse judgement. Only (religious) marriage does justice to this self-transcending nature of love. For to say you love somebody amounts to saying: 'you will not die' (Gabriel Marcel; cf. Songs 8:6). In the words of *Gaudium et Spes*:

> Authentic married love is caught up into divine love and is directed and enriched by the redemptive power of Christ and the salvific action of the Church, with the result that the spouses are effectively led to God ... Fulfilling their conjugal and family role by virtue of this sacrament, spouses are penetrated with the spirit of Christ and their whole life is suffused by faith, hope and charity.[5]

This analysis, incidentally, opens perspectives in a more secular Ireland. While pastors are often confronted with wedding candidates who have no sympathy or even understanding of the Christian teaching on marriage, a reflection on the dynamic of their own mutual love may open up the possibility to make more explicit the implicit religious dimension present in all true human love.

Having said this, we should be careful not to reduce the sacrament of marriage to mere interpersonal love between the spouses – as if the sacrament of marriage is only 'real' insofar as the Christian spouses still love one another. Bernard Cooke, for instance, criticises the view, expounded in the *Catechism of the Catholic Church* that

> by reason of their state in life and of their order, [Christian spouses] have their own special gifts in the People of God. This grace proper to the sacrament of matrimony is intended to perfect the couple's love and to strengthen their indissoluble unity.[6]

According to Bernard Cooke this kind of theology may mislead people into thinking that there is a 'bank of grace' from which they can make withdrawals if needed, and this kind of theology, he argues, is utterly meaningless to ordinary Christians.[7] However, the problem with Cooke's view (known as the 'personalist' view) is that it is in danger of reducing the operation of divine grace in the sacrament of marriage to nothing but the interpersonal love between the faithful couple.[8] This is a disturbingly reductionist view of divine grace, which ultimately denies the reality of the Incarnation (for the sacraments are an extension of the divine presence in Christ). Moreover, the personalist approach, ironically, often becomes a romanticised version of the contract-thinking which it denounces: when marriage is being reduced to the love between two people, the evaporation of love then naturally results in the dissolution of the marital bond – just like contracts can be dissolved by the contracting parties.

Again, M. G. Lawler has enthusiastically endorsed a paradigm shift in our thinking about marriage, from marriage as a 'procreative institution' to 'interpersonal union'. Following this logic, he considers marriages between 'baptised unbelievers' as valid but not sacramental. This is a genuine pastoral issue. Undoubtedly, priests in today's Ireland are increasingly confronted with couples who, although baptised, have become utterly alienated from the life of the Church, and who, at worst, may just be looking for a nice venue for their rite of passage. How should a priest deal with a couple who, although baptised, are not practising Catholics, and may actually have little or no faith at all? Is their marriage truly sacramental (as traditional teaching has it)? This brings us to a discussion of some pastoral issues with which I will conclude.

A glance at some pastoral issues

Estranged Catholics and marriage

At first sight, the proposals of Cooke and Lawler are attractive. After all, according to traditional Catholic theology, the spouses themselves are the ministers of the sacrament of marriage. In postmodern times we often reduce reality to meaning, and we usually understand meaning in terms of experience. So if we cannot perceive any difference in the lived experience of the spouses, we are inclined to conclude that there is no difference in reality. Again, while the efficacy of the sacrament does not depend on the faith of the minister of the sacrament (usually the priest – cf. *ex opere operato*) it does depend on the faithfulness of the recipient. If one accepts the eucharistic bread without sharing in the Christian faith, it will bear no fruit.

In a traditional understanding, however, it will still be sacramental. For instance, in Catholic teaching, Christ is really present in the bread and wine, and the lack of faith of the recipients does not affect the real presence. So too we must say: the marriage of two 'unbelieving Catholics' is still sacramental and not just valid. Indeed, the very desire of a couple to seek marriage in the Church is 'a sign of true, if only minimal, faith'.[9] The onus is on the Church, through proper theologically informed marriage courses, and indeed the wedding ceremony itself, to explain to prospective spouses how their commitment to each other is already an implicit affirmation of obedience to God's will, and a participation in divine love and grace. As John Paul II puts it:

> They have thus already begun what is in a true and proper sense a journey towards salvation, a journey which the celebration of the sacrament and the immediate preparation for it can complement and bring to completion, given the uprightness of their intention.[10]

The commitment of the couple towards one another (even if it is not framed in explicitly Christian terms) in fidelity, participates in the faithfulness of Christ towards his Church. While the indifference towards the Church and its message amongst today's young Catholic couples is deeply problematic, their own commitment towards one another may nonetheless prove a vantage point which the priest (or committed lay teachers within the parish) can seize upon as an implicit participation in, and embodiment of, Christian faith.[11] As Robert Barry has argued, the view that a marriage between 'non-believing Catholics' is not sacramental, effectively means that they are excluded from active participation in the true lay ministry that marriage constitutes.[12]

Marriage and procreation

Moreover, Catholic marriage has always been linked to procreation, and the personalist model is in danger of downplaying the central role of children in Catholic marriage. According to *Gaudium et Spes*:

> By its very nature the institution of marriage and married love is ordered to the procreation and education of the offspring, and it is in them that it finds its crowning glory.[13]

This link is crucial. If two Catholics marry one another with the explicit intention not to have children, their marriage falls sadly short of the Catholic ideal of marriage. Their love for one another remains self-enclosed – utterly at odds with a Christian understanding of love. While the Magisterium has consistently maintained the view that every act of intercourse should be open to new life (see *Humanae Vitae*), many Catholics have adopted contraceptive practices which limit the number of children they hope to have. This discrepancy between the teaching of the Magisterium and the vast majority of practising Catholics is an ongoing issue for the Church today. However, even those Catholics who do not subscribe to the full teaching of *Humanae Vitae* must recognise that the widespread availability of contraception has contributed to a social climate in which the connection between sexual activity and personal, long-lasting commitment has become severed; and this is not in the best interest of society (especially women and children).

'My own private wedding ...'

While it is correct that the ministers of the sacrament are those marrying one another, this should not open the door for a kind of 'privatised' celebration of the church ceremony. Some priests, perhaps attempting to appeal to young couples who have little or no affinity to the Church, may be tempted to indulge them on 'their special day'. Indeed, it is ironic that it is generally exactly those Catholics who have become estranged from the Church who usually most want to revamp the wedding ceremony in accordance with their own personal tastes. This is a symptom of a deeper malaise, in which marriage is considered a mere lifestyle option. The result of this is, at times, a ceremony with tacky music ('their song', often with no religious significance whatsoever) and equally inappropriate secular readings. Undoubtedly, couples should be encouraged to get involved in the celebration of their church wedding. However, while the couple are the ministers of the sacrament of marriage they are not the principal cause or source of grace bestowed through the sacrament. God is. As Carlo Rocchetta writes:

> The spouses do not 'administer to each other', nor do they even merely 'receive' the sacrament of marriage as if it were a 'thing', but they celebrate an act which – by virtue of their Baptism – makes them participants in the mystery of the covenant which takes place for them and in them.[14]

Moreover, a wedding is a public celebration of the whole community. Therefore, the choice of unusual times or venues to celebrate weddings should be discouraged.

Divorce and second unions

Unlike the Orthodox Church, the Catholic Church does not allow for divorce and second unions, as this is seen as being in breach of the Christ's prohibition of divorce (cf. Mk 10:9-12). It contravenes the indissolubility of the sacrament of marriage, which reflects the fidelity of God to his covenant, and that of Christ to his Church.[15] It is debatable, however, whether barring persons who are in second unions from full participation in Communion (especially if they are not the primary cause of the break-down of their marriage) is a pastorally sensitive or appropriate manner of dealing with this issue.

Same-sex marriage

It should be recognised that the Christian Churches have, in the past, often used language which was hurtful to people of homosexual orientation, and may have contributed to a climate in which they suffered. While this must be acknowledged, it is not sufficient reason to welcome a radical redefinition of marriage, effectively revamping it into some kind of gender-neutral union, rather than a union between man and woman.

On 22 November 2010, the European Court of Human Rights, in a case known as Schalk and Kopff v. Austria, decided that the right to marry (art. 12 of the Convention) does not extend to same-sex couples. In other words, Ireland is under no legal obligation to introduce gay marriage, and the claim that the absence of gay marriage constitutes discrimination against gay people is simply incorrect. If, however, Ireland were to give full marital status to same-sex unions, opposition to same-sex marriage would become punishable by law, and people who object on religious grounds to celebrate these unions could find themselves penalised or even dismissed (e.g. registrars).

There are effectively two lines of arguments being put forward in favour of gay marriage. The first line of argument states that all that matters for a marriage is the *love between the two partners.* Whether these partners are homosexual or heterosexual is a matter of indifference. Nor do children matter in this understanding of marriage. Marriage is simply a private union of two people who love one another.

In this line of reasoning there are two crucial errors. This view ignores that marriage is not simply a private transaction between two individuals but it is also a *public institution*, with rights and responsibilities. The reason why state and society, even in pre-Christian times, have taken an interest in marriage is quite simply because the intrinsic fruitfulness of traditional marriage can lead to the birth of children. Moreover, those who argue that marriage is nothing but a loving union between two people, with no reference whatsoever to the common good, are actually undermining the status of marriage in society. If marriage is based only on the feelings of love, and nothing else, then it will become harder to maintain marriages that are in trouble. The second problem with this line of thinking is that it undermines the nature of marriage as a union in which man and woman beautifully *complement* one another. This harmony in difference, between man and woman, is effectively being written out from this new understanding of marriage. The new understanding of marriage, which proponents of 'same-sex marriage' promote, effectively undermines the *otherness* at the heart of heterosexual marriage. This is ironic, at a time when culturally, difference and diversity are being promoted as values in society. Ultimately, the gay marriage position is based upon a flawed understanding of the human person. It holds that it does not matter whether you are male or female. But this fails to acknowledge that we are embodied beings, and that our sexual identity (male or female) goes to the heart of who we are as human persons.

A second line of argument in favour of gay marriage claims that gay marriage does involve a concern for children. Of course, these children will either be adopted, or be the biological child of just one of the two partners. The proponents of this view are not arguing that marriage is simply about a loving union between two gender-neutral people but, like traditional marriage, it involves social responsibilities, especially in relation to children. They claim that they are actually supporting traditional values of marriage, rather than subverting them.

The problem with this view is that it makes an understanding of marriage normative in which the link between the two biological parents and their children becomes severed. There is, however, a considerable body of research to back up the view that children are best raised in families consisting of the two biological parents united in a loving marriage. The Fourth National Incidence Study of Child Abuse and Neglect (edited by Andrea Sedlak et al.) which reported to the US Congress in 2010 showed that the rate of harm and abuse for children living with two married biological parents is significantly lower than the rate for children living in all other conditions of family structure and living arrangements (such as single parent; single parent with partner; unmarried persons). In short, society has an interest in encouraging mothers and fathers to raise their own children together. Every society has developed the institution of marriage mainly for that purpose. The biological bond between the two parents and the child is of immense importance. This bond is non-existent in gay marriage, with at least one of the parents, if not both. Now the ideals we promote in society matter, for they determine our behaviour. So, it is not in the best interest of society to promote an ideal of marriage in which the biological bond between the parents and the children becomes incidental.

Conclusion

Marriage, between man and woman, is one of the most iconic sacraments of the Catholic faith. It symbolises the covenantal love between Christ and the Church, and as a sacrament it makes this love present between the spouses. As such it involves a radical gift of self of the spouses, sharing in Christ's sacrifice – a deeply counter-cultural notion in a consumerist society which pursues individualist and instant gratification. It is through marriage that laypeople can begin to learn how daily sacrifices can be truly life-giving. By living the sacrament of marriage they can begin to appreciate some of the central mysteries of the Catholic faith (covenant, Incarnation, sacrifice of the Cross, Eucharist), and vice versa: by sharing in the central mysteries of the faith they will be enabled to persevere in their marital life, and be true to each other 'in good times and in bad, in sickness and in health'.

Notes

1. Saint John Chrysostom, 'Third Sermon on Marriage: How to Choose a Wife', *On Marriage and Family Life* (New York: St Vladimir's Press, 1986), 91.
2. *Gaudium et Spes*, 48.
3. It is the role of the priest to act *in persona Christi capitis ecclesiae*, in the person of Christ as Head of the Church. In the words of R. J. Daly,

'The full axiom points to the ecclesiological fullness of the Eucharistic celebration not just as the prayer and action of a priest, but as the prayer and action of the Body of Christ, and specifically of a particular assembly of the body of Christ.' See Robert J. Daly, 'Marriage, Eucharist, and Christian Sacrifice', INTAMS 9.1 (2003), 69–70.

4. Ibid., 73.

5. *Gaudium et Spes*, 48.

6. *Catechism of the Catholic Church*, 1641.

7. Bernard Cooke, 'Christian Marriage: Basic Sacrament', *Perspectives on Marriage: A Reader*, K. Scott and M. Warren, eds (Oxford: OUP, 2001), 48.

8. See Bernard Cooke, *Sacraments and Sacramentality* (New London, CT: Twenty-Third Publications, 2002) and M. G. Lawler, *Marriage and the Catholic Church: Disputed Questions* (Collegeville, MN: Liturgical Press, 2002).

9. Robert Barry, 'Marriage as a Sacrament for Young Adult Catholics', INTAMS 14.2 (2008), 190.

10. *Familiaris Consortio*, 68.

11. Pope Benedict's intuition that there is a profound connection between monogamy and faith in one God may prove pastorally fruitful in this regard.

12. See Robert Barry, 181–94. Canon 1012.2 states that 'a valid marriage contract cannot exist between baptised persons without its being by that very fact sacramental'.

13. *Gaudium et Spes*, 48.

14. Carlo Rocchetta, 'Marriage as a Sacrament: Towards a New Theological Conceptualisation', INTAMS 2.1 (1996), 12.

15. *Catechism of the Catholic Church*, 1647.

The Priest and the Permanent Deacon

MARTIN BROWNE

A chapter on the topic of the permanent diaconate may seem like a strange thing to include in a book on the priesthood. Clearly, permanent deacons are not priests. And despite the fact that many other countries have had them for decades, permanent deacons are pretty much a novelty in Ireland. So, if they aren't priests and are so few in number, why discuss them in a book like this? The answer is simple: now that the permanent diaconate is becoming a more visible dimension of the Church's ministry, the priests of today need to understand what deacons are about.

It cannot be taken for granted that the formation received by most priests before ordination has equipped them to work fruitfully and wisely with permanent deacons. This is despite, or perhaps because of, the very obvious fact that all priests were themselves ordained as deacons once upon a time. In almost all cases, they served as deacons for a year or thereabouts, and were then ordained as priests. For many priests, particularly in recent years, their 'diaconal year' involved very little time in seminary and concentrated on placements in parishes and hospitals or other locations. Being a deacon was very much like partaking in a kind of apprenticeship or internship. Such placements, which provide for limited public ministry, backed up by appropriate supervision and feedback, are certainly a useful part of a seminarian's formation and preparation for his role as a priest. But they do not reflect what a deacon is meant to be.

I am reminded of the traditional account of the martyrdom of the deacon Saint Lawrence in Rome in 258, which holds that he was killed by being burned on a grid-iron. After a while over the coals, he is alleged to have joked with his executioners: 'I'm done on this side now. Turn me over!' True or not, this pious legend sums up how many people, clerical and lay, understand deacons: as apprentices, who need to be 'cooked on the other side' by priestly ordination in order to be made complete. However, a deacon is not a 'half-baked' priest.

It is also worth acknowledging that not all priests are particularly enthusiastic about the idea of ministering alongside permanent deacons. Some see the introduction of the permanent diaconate as a late and inadequate response to the crisis in priestly vocations. Some argue that it further clericalises Church life at the expense of lay ministry in an already excessively clerical institution. Some others are frustrated that another male-only form of ministry is being promoted and worry that it will have a negative impact on the Church and further marginalise or alienate women. These are not unreasonable comments, and any honest appraisal of the evolving ministerial landscape will need to take them seriously. If we are honest, there are some priests around too who might feel threatened by the arrival of deacons on the scene, or who may resent the way they are allowed to combine family life with ordained ministry.

What are deacons?

Chapter 6 of the Acts of the Apostles has traditionally been understood as describing the origin of the diaconate: as the Church of the apostolic period grew, in order to see to the needs of Greek widows, the apostles instructed the Greek believers to 'select from among yourselves seven men of good standing' (Acts 6:3). Those chosen were Stephen, Philip, Prochorus, Nicanor, Timon, Parmenas and Nicolaus, and 'they had these men stand before the apostles, who prayed and laid their hands on them' (Acts 6:6). This episode is recounted in the Prayer of Consecration in the rite for the ordination of deacons used to this day. In the Church's tradition, St Stephen has been venerated as the first deacon as well as the first martyr.

Because the word deacon comes from the Greek word *diakonos*, meaning 'servant', the idea of service has always been central to most understandings of what deacons should be about. Also, because the episode in Acts 6 refers to the seven men waiting tables in order to make sure that the Greek widows weren't left hungry, the diaconate has come to be very closely associated with charitable service to the poor. In some quarters, the renewed (and permanent) diaconate has been seen almost entirely in these terms, to the virtual exclusion of ministry at the altar and ministry of the Word. However, much contemporary biblical scholarship challenges the view that the ministry of deacons should be identified so particularly or exclusively with this kind of charitable work.[1]

The Second Vatican Council's great document on the Church, *Lumen Gentium*, made it clear that *all* ordained ministry needs to be understood in the context of the prior mission of the whole People of God:

> For the nurturing and constant growth of the People of God, Christ the Lord instituted in his Church a variety of ministries, which work for the good of the whole body. For those ministers, who are endowed with sacred power, serve their brethren, so that all who are of the People of God, and therefore enjoy a true Christian dignity, working toward a common goal freely and in an orderly way, may arrive at salvation. (LG, 18)

It is a short paragraph, but it provides a rich answer to the question of why we have ordained ministry at all. It asserts the divine institution of the threefold ordained ministry and speaks of 'sacred power' stemming from ordination – to the diaconate as well as the priesthood and the episcopate. But these strong claims are balanced by the reminder that the power of orders is given for 'the nurturing and constant growth of the People of God', and that the ordained are to serve, respecting the innate dignity of all of God's people. The life of the People of God is presented as a harmonious pilgrimage, where all, ordained and lay, complement and cooperate with each other, as they journey towards the kingdom.

It is in this context that the particular service of the deacon is best understood. We can only understand the mission of deacons if we understand the mission of the Church, and we can only have a vision for the ministry of deacons if we have a vision for the ministry of the Church. Cardinal Walter Kasper has written of priests and deacons as 'two separate arms'[2] of the bishop. That a formal ordained ministry of service exists at all is a reflection of the attitude of service which the Church as a whole is called to embody.

> The Church is seen to exist, not for its own sake but for others: for human beings, for a world in need of unity, reconciliation and peace. The Church is a servant Church. In its broadest sense, then, *diaconia* is not just one dimension of the Church: it is its essential dimension.[3]

As one Irish-born deacon serving in the USA says, 'service in terms of building up the Church that, in turn, is building up the world towards greater and more aware communion with God is what not only the diaconate but the Church itself is all about'.[4] In this understanding of the Church, the particular vocation of the deacon, asserts Kasper, 'is to represent the specifically diaconal dimension of *all* Church ministry, i.e. the servant-ministry of Jesus Christ in the Church'.[5] Pope Francis has made it clear in both words and deeds that he identifies with this intuition, kneeling to wash and kiss the feet of young offenders during his first Holy Thursday liturgy as Pope and urging the Church during his Inauguration Mass to '... never forget that authentic power is service, and that the Pope too, when exercising power, must enter ever more fully into that service which has its radiant culmination on the Cross'.[6]

Underlining this key theme of his pontificate, when washing feet during the Mass of the Lord's Supper, he re-arranged his stole in the manner of a deacon.

Such a rich understanding of the office of deacon may all be very well, but the reality up until Vatican II was quite different. The diaconate was one of several major and minor orders through which a seminarian graduated on his way to the presbyterate. In some cases, ordination to these offices took place in rapid succession with little or no opportunity for the minister to serve in them in any meaningful way. Perversely, with so few actual deacons available, when the rubrics of a solemn liturgy required the ministry of deacons, more often than not, priests were vested to function as deacons instead. It is no wonder that some priests have struggled to take deacons seriously. Up until 2012 in Ireland, because the diaconate was exclusively a 'transitional' state, its meaning was largely lost. Those communities which did experience the ministry of deacons had little sense of them as anything other than apprentice priests who wore their stoles sideways and did some things priests normally do.

Lumen Gentium paved the way for the restoration of the diaconate as a permanent ministry in the Church. The paragraph dealing with the question is odd, in that it sketched a rich vision of what the diaconate might be, but then stopped short of specifically formally mandating its re-introduction as a permanent office. Instead, it asserted somewhat weakly that it could be re-introduced:

> At a lower level of the hierarchy are deacons, upon whom hands are imposed 'not unto the priesthood, but unto a ministry of service'. For strengthened by sacramental grace, in communion with the bishop and his group of priests they serve in the diaconate of the liturgy, of the word, and of charity to the people of God ... Dedicated to duties of charity and of administration, let deacons be mindful of the admonition of Blessed Polycarp: 'Be merciful, diligent,

walking according to the truth of the Lord, who became the servant of all.' Since these duties, so very necessary to the life of the Church, can be fulfilled only with difficulty in many regions in accordance with the discipline of the Latin Church as it exists today, the diaconate can in the future be restored as a proper and permanent rank of the hierarchy. (LG, 29)

The Council's decree on the missionary activity of the Church, *Ad Gentes*, developed this further however, stating that where Bishops' Conferences 'deem it opportune', the diaconate *should* be restored.[7] Thus, it was Vatican II which restored the permanent diaconate to the life of the Church. In 1967, Pope Paul VI began the implementation of this restoration with the publication of the Apostolic Letter, *Sacrum Diaconatus Ordinem*. Further official documents were issued over the following years, culminating with two key regulatory documents in 1998: *Basic Norms for the Formation of Permanent Deacons* issued by the Congregation for Catholic Education; and the *Directory for the Ministry and Life of Permanent Deacons* issued by the Congregation for the Clergy.

Since the late 1960s, the diaconate has been reintroduced as a stable ministry in many countries. There are currently over 17,000 deacons serving in the United States alone. However, the Irish bishops did not opt to introduce the permanent diaconate until much later. The Bishops' Conference only began looking seriously at the question in 1996, and it was ten years before a national directory and norms were published. The first group of men in formation were formally 'admitted to candidacy' in 2010, and the first ordinations took place in June 2012. Interestingly, only a minority of dioceses have yet established diaconate formation programmes.

The long period between Pope Paul VI providing for the re-introduction of the permanent diaconate and its actual introduction in Ireland has not been helpful. It gives the impression that the office was and continues to be seen by bishops mainly as a last resort when there is a shortage of priests. That Ireland is only seeing its first permanent deacons now, more than forty years after the ministry was restored, suggests that it is seen as second-best and that it is only being introduced now because of falling numbers of priests. This is not healthy. If we do not have enough priests, the Church needs to look at why this is so and at how we might have more or order our ministry differently. Tough questions about what exactly priests need to do and who exactly can and may be ordained priests need to be addressed. These are bigger questions than a short chapter like this can address, but seeing deacons as a sort of second-division auxiliary force to stop a few gaps is no solution.

Why?

I am in the unusual position of being a deacon in a monastery. Being ordained deacon without the intention of being ordained priest a year later was a difficult concept for many people to grasp. They couldn't see the point in 'not going the whole way'. I regularly meet people who see me ministering as a deacon and ask politely when I am going to be ordained. That I already am ordained and have been for several years is perplexing to them. The other question I am often asked – and I am sure I am not alone in this – is what I am 'able to do' as a deacon. Though it is a genuine question, it clearly comes from an understanding of diaconate which sees deacons as half-baked priests. It will take time for this new – or to be more precise, newly restored – ministry to become embedded in the life of the Church in Ireland. During the intervening period of reception it will be very important that priests, and the new deacons themselves, show by their deeds that deacons are more than functionaries who can do some of the things priests do. Otherwise, the argument that sees the permanent diaconate merely as a clericalisation of existing (male) lay ministry will be proven correct.

Yes, deacons are clergy. They are just as much clergy as transitional deacons on the way to priesthood. (The term 'lay deacons' used in some quarters to describe married deacons is nonsensical.) And yes, there are certain ministerial and liturgical roles which are proper to deacons, as well as certain roles which may be given to them as needs be, and these are clearly laid out in the *General Instruction of the Roman Missal* and elsewhere. However, just as a priest is more than his functions, so too is a deacon. *Lumen Gentium* underlined the significance of the deacon being 'strengthened by sacramental grace'. The International Theological Commission (ITC) developed this further, noting in the process that many of the things deacons do are things which they were already doing before ordination. This invites the question as to why the Church should bother ordaining them at all then. The ITC's answer is that sacramental ordination provides 'a confirmation, a reinforcement and a more complete incorporation into the ministry of the Church of those who were already *de facto* exercising the ministry of deacons'.[8] That sort of thinking needs to get into the Church's bloodstream if we are to move beyond a merely functional and pragmatic understanding of the diaconate. The very fact that deacons do nothing whatsoever that cannot be done by others in the Church speaks volumes about who and what they are called *to be*. This was presented most eloquently by the Anglican Bishop Mark Santer at the ordination of one Rowan Douglas Williams in 1977:

> The deacon is one who waits. He is never in charge. He is the servant of others – of God, of his bishop, of the congregation. He is a voice: it is his task to read the Lord's Gospel, not his own. He is a servant: it is his task to wait at the Lord's table. It is others who preside. He is the waiter, the attendant. Is there anything at all that is peculiar to the deacon? Is he given powers that are given to no-one else? The answer is 'No'. There is nothing he can do which nobody else can do. But that is just what is distinctive about him. He has no power. He is a servant. He is entrusted with the ministry of Christ who washes his servants' feet. He embodies the service of the Lord who has made himself the servant of us all.[9]

Conclusion

It will take some time for the Church in Ireland to get used to the regular presence of deacons. There will undoubtedly be teething problems. There will be tensions about the balance between liturgical ministry and other forms of service. Deacons will sometimes struggle to balance their clerical status with their roles 'in the world'. There will be tensions about the relationship between the ministry of deacons and lay ministry. There will be sadness and anger that this ministry is not open to women, although some theologians see potential for change in this area.[10] Nevertheless, the recovery of this ancient order, in which candidates are ordained 'unto a ministry of service', sacramentally embodying the servant nature to which the whole Church is called, is surely an important development for our times. However, it needs to be thought about and talked about not in isolation, but in the context of the wider mission and ministry of the Church, lay and ordained. In such a 'process of mutual discussion, the interrelationality of ministry becomes very evident. It is no longer a question, for example, of what the permanent *deacons* can do, but what the permanent deacons *together with* the bishop, the priests, and the lay ministers can do'.[11]

Notes

1. John N. Collins, *Deacons and the Church: Making Connections Between Old and New* (Leominster: Gracewing, 2002), Ch. 2.
2. Walter Kasper, *Leadership in the Church* (New York: Crossroad, 2003), 18.
3. Ibid., 25.
4. Owen F. Cummings, 'The State of the Question', in Owen F. Cummings et al., *Theology of the Diaconate* (New York/Mahwah, NJ: Paulist Press, 2005), 12.
5. *Leadership in the Church*, 21.
6. Pope Francis, *Homily at Mass for the Beginning of the Petrine Ministry of the Bishop of Rome*, 19 March 2013 http://www.vatican.va/holy_father/francesco/homilies/2013/documents/papa-francesco_20130319_omelia-inizio-pontificato_en.html (accessed 1/4/2013).
7. Second Vatican Council, *Ad Gentes*, 16.

8. International Theological Commission, *From the Diakonia of Christ to the Diakonia of the Apostles*, Ch. V http://www.vatican.va/roman_curia/congregations/cfaith/cti_documents/rc_con_cfaith_pro_05072004_diaconate_en.html (accessed 1/4/2013).

9. Mark Santer, 'Diaconate and Discipleship', in *Theology* 81 (May, 1978), 181–2.

10. Gary Macy et al., *Women Deacons: Past, Present and Future* (New York/Mahwah, NJ: Paulist Press, 2011).

11. Kenan B. Osborne OFM, *The Permanent Diaconate: Its History and Place in the Sacrament of Orders* (New York/Mahwah, NJ: Paulist Press, 2006), 152.

Consecrated Beauty and the Witness of the Priest

WILLIAM DESMOND

Not unexpectedly, we think of the priest as witnessing to truth and goodness. 'I am the way, the truth and the life,' Jesus said. Jesus, the living incarnation of truth, is agapeic goodness itself, and it is for us to be true to this goodness. Jesus, it seems, says nothing explicitly about beauty. He does not say, 'I am the beautiful, or beauty.' Of truth, goodness and beauty, beauty is perhaps the orphan of the three. This does not make sense, of course, given the glory of the Lord (as von Balthasar reminds us impressively). Beauty might be said to be saturated with significance in a religion in which the incarnational reality of the divine is central, God in the flesh, calling to us.

If we reflect on the priest as witness to beauty, we must always remember that being, truth and good ('transcendental' ideas in traditional metaphysics) are intimately convertible with beauty. My reflections will be about *consecrated beauty*. And this is in line with the fact that the priest is consecrated by God to God, in witness to Jesus Christ and in imitation of the power of his life. There is the sacredness of a chosen life, called to a singular integrity and splendour in which beauty, truth and goodness intertwine.

A priest lives a consecrated life, not because it is first his choice, but because he first is chosen. He is called and he responds. Something is offered, and the promise of the offer is then chosen and lived in a life that witnesses to what it might mean to redeem something of the promise. Redeeming the promise is offering 'something beautiful for God', as Mother Teresa put it. It has been pointed out that *kalon*, the Greek word for beautiful, is related to our word 'call'.

Of course, this matter is not just one of the singular life but of the people of God, the community. It is not that the priest is an artist, an analogy with the Romantic genius. Someone like Gerard Manley Hopkins, priest and poet, raised poetry to the level of prayer, some of it dark in the 'terrible' sonnets. The priest is between God and the people, receiving from the first and communicating to the second. Being in receipt of gifts that are more than himself means he is always embedded in a community of worship, and in that regard, liturgy is the place where the beauty of God is most to be communicated. The liturgy is the sacred art of the religious community, but it is not endowed as sacred by the community but by God as the original source of all good gifts offered to us. Offering and sacrifice are intimately related, though it is not we, or the priest, who makes sacred. We are made sacred (*sacer facere*) through the intermedium of his consecration, which is not his own self-consecration but offered in and through the divine communication.

This 'being called' character of consecrated life puts one in mind of the fact that beauty reveals something of a gift-like event. Thus there is something striking about beauty. A beautiful face, say, stops us, arrests us, and opens up a porosity on our part. This porosity is less a languid passivity as a being taken out of ourselves in relation to the face itself as beautiful. It calls us out of ourselves, calls us beyond ourselves. In beholding something beautiful, something is communicated to us. There is also a resting in something worthy to be affirmed, indeed something worthy of a kind of festive consent and celebration. The offering of beauty is not simply a result of our activity – it comes to us. If we insist simply on our own power over this event, the event does not happen, and we produce a kind of eclipse of beauty. One might draw attention to a more primal receptivity marking the priest as witness to beauty.

I connect this receptivity to the gift of beauty with what I call the *passio essendi*. There is a passion or patience of being, a being given to be, before there is an endeavour to be (*conatus essendi*). This patience brings us back to a more original ontological porosity, where beauty most deeply strikes home. The strike of beauty arouses the passion of being, and in that passion we may construct new images of beauty. But the *passio* of being is not just in what we construct in response to being struck. The living of a life, as witness to divine beauty, originates out of the more primal porosity. Music, one might say, is perhaps the most powerful art to return us to the porosity, while at the same time moving a *passio essendi*, prior to any rationalisation of the movement of desire, and exceeding complete self-determination of it. We do not first move, we are moved. There is music that passes into prayer.

Beautiful things too come to shine, there is a shine on things. It is not *our* shine on things; it is the shine *of* things, but more truly, it a shine *on* things, for the source of the light is not just ours, nor confined to the things of beauty. We behold the lilies of the field, but the shine on things tells of a light that endows their being and others. Beauty itself is inseparable from some sense of formed wholeness. Praise of beauty as consecrated can be awakened in the soul.

I said the priest is not the artist as genius, though there are some family likenesses. James Joyce thought of his artistry as sacerdotal, transforming the everyday into something rich and strange, preparing the occasions of 'epiphany'. His art was a kind of consecrating creativity. But consider this: the Dublin-born artist Michael Craig-Martin, very influential in the field of conceptual art, had a youthful fascination with the power of the priest to consecrate, and as artist he denominated a half-full glass of water as an oak tree. He sold the work to the National Gallery of Australia and then tried to export it there as vegetation. The labelling was rejected by customs, the work was returned, and he had to re-label it as a glass. Is the artist here claiming a certain power of original Baptism? Or does it all amount to the counterfeiting of consecration? One would have to answer yes, if the latter requires the companioning power of God. The autonomous fiat of the creative individual amounts in the end to just 'say so'. It is at most self-ordained. This is not to be ordained. The customs officers who refused the artist's say so at once showed ordinary common sense and (not knowing it) sound theology.

Consecration is not a matter of the creativity of the artist. The family resemblance perhaps lies in that the latter too is an *endowed* creativity, and the companioning power of the divine is *incognito* in all true creation. Consecration is not only endowed, it is singularly dedicated. Just as we cannot endow ourselves, we cannot consecrate ourselves; for consecration might be seen as endowment to the second power to which we cannot be dedicated through ourselves alone.

All of this might sound very noble, and in a way it is, and indeed traditionally the major stress was on the ennobling power of beauty. One might speak of consecration but what are we to make of the fact that desecration, not only of the beautiful, but of all things, is sometimes treated with more interest. There is a certain fascination with the ugly. A revealing instance: a book on beauty edited by Umberto Eco, respectfully noted by critics, was not a big publishing success; by contrast, its companion volume on the ugly was hugely lauded and brazenly outsold its more demure sister.[1] We seem to find an elective affinity for the ugly, the monstrous, the execrable; order seems defeated by disorder, form by formlessness, purity by blemish, serenity by horror.

Can we make proper sense of the ugly without its secretly being parasitical on some sense of the beautiful? The case is analogous to evil and the good. There is also a trend whereby we reveal ourselves to be engaged with radical evil, while all the while we remain mum about the astounding question of radical good. It makes no sense to speak of evil without the incognito companion power of the good. If we have a diminished feel for given beauty, it is not surprising that we have an enfeebled sense of the goodness of creation as given.

In popular culture and the entertainment industry, physical beauty is massively sought after, but in cultural circles of a more avant-garde character beauty is treated with diffidence, if not disdain. It revels in the dubious consolation that serves to tranquilise the false consciousness of the bourgeoisie – so it might go. Admittedly, the case is more complicated in that beauty is, in fact, often instrumentalised by capitalist culture to sell commodities. Beauty addresses us, and gets our attention, and hence is an easy servant to shanghai or press gang the consumer into collusion with the capitalist need to sell. Beauty is groomed as the consort goddess who serves the last god of the religion of shopping.

The whole thing pays a secret tribute to the power of beauty, even as it uses it for purposes that are not always very beautiful. Beauty moves us. There is something elemental, and deep and not understood about our being so moved. It is this moving or being moved that is deflected in the direction of the shopping mall and the cash register. It is quite understandable why lovers of true beauty would hate this. What they love is being prostituted. But, of course, it is part of the power of beauty to beautify. Remember how pervasive beauty is in human life: one half of the human population spends a lot of time looking at the other half. Without beauty would we look at each other at all?

Of course, in relation to religion we can find an anti-aesthetic view that favours dis-incarnation rather than incarnation, and the outcome is iconoclasm. Jean Luc Marion has important reflections on the difference of the idol and icon. The idol is the mirror that only returns to us our own gaze, the icon opens us to the gaze of another, and we are transported beyond the circuit of our own self-absorption. One could see the icon as a paradigmatic instance of consecrated beauty. The priest is not only witness but servant of that beauty – servant not only by presiding at the sacrament(s), but also as guardian of the sacramental sense of creation. The sacramental sense is assaulted both by the religious iconoclasts and the scientific secularisers alike, who share a domineering urge to reduce the surplus mystery of the icon, as image of the divine, to imageless univocity. God may be beyond all aesthetic images, but extreme iconoclasm can produce an emptied space that can as easily become the focus of nothing as the focus of the God beyond all images. In the emptiness other images can come to be generated that blank out divine transcendence. The soul still hungers, and distending into the emptiness it tends to fill it with itself or even with the monsters of its own darkness. Out of the deconsecration of the image comes the desanctification, and then even the desecration of all that is glorious in the aesthetics of the given creation. In desecrated creation the shine on things that might aesthetically tell of the divine is not only dulled but execrated.

What then of the witness of the priest? If we live in such a world, it may not be enough to witness against the loss of the sacred. A consecrated life must testify to beauty in the midst of desecration. In the figure of the priest the sacred is intermediated, and this bears on how beauty has been described in terms of the integral splendour of radiant form. Beauty entails a steadfast integrity and a calling beyond the finite form, and we can see the priest as willing to be that integral call, incarnating something of that splendour, an intermedium of divine radiance, porous to, yet redemptive of, the desecrated creation, most consummately in the splendour of liturgy. How crucial then that the Mass is said with devotion to the mystery of divine communication offered in this making sacred, this sacrifice.

Again you might object: noble and idealistic yes, but listen to the baby wailing, the crowd coughing, the sigh of the battered and unlovely who sit or slouch in the seats of prayer. We often have a very airbrushed view of beauty – all the blemishes of finitude are removed and the idealised picture offers its consolation. Those in the business of denigrating the sacred, or in desecration, take glee in reminding us of squalor.

We ought to remember this strange anomaly about Christianity and beauty. Christianity offers us as the image of images what seems quite nonplussing to airbrushed beauty: the cross. The crucified God: this is so unanticipated from the standpoint of the classical repose of the Greek gods, thought by some to be the epitome of beauty. This means that if there is a Christian beauty, it cannot evade the horror of the cross. It is worthy of note, though, that the image of the mother and child, Mary and Jesus, is perhaps the most pervasive image of Christian art. God in infancy: mothered. God in death: crucified.

The challenge then arises as to whether the priest can witness to beauty in horror. Is not the cross the epitome of horror: the holy of all holies is desecrated in the most unholy of deaths? In some ways, there is something strangely contemporary about this, in regard to those aesthetic circles whose feel for the beautiful has sometimes been replaced by the thrill of horror, without beauty. The cross poses the hyperbolic question, that is, the perplexity that exceeds all our finite effort to fully encompass it: is there a consecrated beauty, even in the midst of desecrated life – a supreme consecrated beauty in this most extreme desecration of the divine life itself?

We are called to be as like to God as possible. Would one have to be God to see the beauty in the horror? Would one have to be gifted with grace to truly see the horror as the mutilation of the promise of divine goodness? To see in the face of evil the forgiving eyes of the God who does not hate the hateful? To see the lovely in the ugly with the look of love. Would this not be the love of an agapeic God? A God who looks on the (un)lovely where we only recoil in disgust? An agapeic God who loves even the evil, forgives it because there is more in the evil than evil?

And the priest as consecrated witness to divine beauty? There is the splendor of chaste form, granting even emptiness as a poverty of form, opening to a mystery beyond all our forms. The door that is open seems empty but it is a door of welcome, and when we step into and through it, it is not empty. The entrance is an opening, a porosity, and the beautiful is incarnated in this opening, in which there is something received, and we are patient, something calls to us, and asks our response, and we act towards what calls to us. There is no simple opposition of contemplation and action. The witnessing priest is both, and the intermedium of the two.

Nor is there ultimate opposition between going down into the darkness of things and being called up to what is above us. The witness testifies to truth sometimes in forbidding circumstances, even in situations where one's life might be at stake. How to think of the priest as witness to beauty in such darker circumstances? Think of the contrast between consecrated beauty and desecration in terms of two different directionalities in which our love can move, either up or down. In beauty, love seems to be called up, beyond itself. The Greeks knew this deeply in terms of the erotics of beauty as called to something higher. I would say there is an agapeics of beauty in the case of the priest, the gifted beauty of surplus generosity, in service of God and fellows. What, by contrast, of the going down? This can be the mutation of love that comes with desecration. There are aesthetic movements that would move down into the heart of darkness, to pits where the sun seems not to penetrate. But recall again other senses of 'going down' that are central to the meaning of Christianity: the Word become flesh, moving among sinners, into death and even into hell itself, there to shine the beauty of agapeic goodness, even among the damned.

The divine Word reopens, even in hell, the primal porosity, communicating a power that is more than hell. Going below into chambers of horror does not necessitate being cut off from redemption. I think of the final few lines of the *Inferno* of Dante. Virgil and Dante descend into the hell hole, but at a certain central point their descent turns into its opposite, namely, ascent out of hell. They climb up over the fixed Lucifer. The frozen Lucifer is beyond all porosity, all permeability: fixed eternally in himself as himself – a parody of divine eternity. The centre of hell is the closure of the porosity onto itself, instead of the opening of the soul to what is beyond it. These last lines, ending on the threshold of a fresh beginning, are beautiful and worth recall:

My guide and I entered that hidden road
To make our way back up to the bright world.
We never thought of resting while we climbed.
We climbed, he first and I behind, until,
Through a small round opening ahead of us
I saw the lovely things the heavens hold,
And we came out once more to see the stars.[2]

Beyond the night and the borrowed gleam of the stars, there is a light that shines on things, and a source of light beyond the stars. The priest as witness of consecrated beauty is neither of above or below but someone of truthful goodness in between. This witness is called to be the intermedium of divine communication and to keep open to the holy the porosity of that between. The beauty that comes to earth endows the between as the place of consecration where God gives himself for praise.

Notes

1. Umberto Eco, ed., *History of Beauty* (New York: Rizzoli, 2004) and *On Ugliness* (New York: Rizzoli, 2007).
2. Dante, *Inferno*, Canto XXXIV, 133–39.

Contributors

Fr **Niall Ahern** is a priest of the Elphin diocese. He was director of formation at Maynooth College and administrator of the diocesan cathedral and is currently parish priest at Strandhill, County Sligo.

Br **Martin Browne** is a Benedictine monk of Glenstal Abbey in County Limerick. He is currently headmaster of the Abbey School at Glenstal. He has been a deacon since 2008 and serves on the editorial board of the ecumenical journal *One in Christ.*

Dr **Anne Codd**, a native of Wexford and a Presentation Sister, currently works as resource person for Pastoral Renewal and Adult Faith Development at the Irish Catholic Bishops' Conference.

Msgr **Hugh Connolly** is a priest of the Diocese of Dromore. He is currently president of St Patrick's College, Maynooth. He has authored a book, published in 1995, on the Irish Penitentials, and in 2002 published the volume *Sin* in the New Century Theology series.

Dr **Patrick Connolly** is a priest of the Clogher diocese and is senior lecturer in theology and religious studies and assistant registrar at Mary Immaculate College, University of Limerick. He specialises in canon law and moral theology.

Prof **Eamonn Conway** is a priest of the Tuam diocese. He has been head of theology and religious studies at Mary Immaculate College, University of Limerick, since 1999. His publications include works on Karl Rahner and Hans Urs von Balthasar as well as on faith and culture.

Prof **Jim Corkery** is a Jesuit and teaches systematic theology at the Milltown Institute of Theology and Philosophy in Dublin. His recent writings have dealt with the theology of Pope Benedict

XVI, theological anthropology, and the fiftieth anniversary of the Second Vatican Council.

Dr **Tom Dalzell** is a Marist priest and head of theological studies at All Hallows College, Dublin City University. He has written on the theology of Hans Urs von Balthasar and on what theology can learn from psychoanalysis.

Prof **William Desmond** is professor of philosophy at the Higher Institute of Philosophy at the Katholieke Universiteit Leuven in Flanders, and also at Villanova University in Pennsylvania. His research interests include philosophy of religion, ethics, German idealism and Hegel, metaphysics and aesthetics.

Dr **Eugene Duffy** is a priest of the diocese of Achonry. He joined the department of theology and religious studies at Mary Immaculate College in September 2007. His main research is in the area of ecclesiology, especially the history and development of collegiality in Church structures.

Fr **Pat Farragher** joined the Family Centre staff in 2001. Ordained to the priesthood in 1990, he has served in Cill Chirain and at St Jarlath's College, Tuam. In 2000, he graduated from Boston College Graduate School of Education with a Masters in counselling psychology and a Masters in pastoral ministry. He is an accredited member of the Irish Association of Counselling and Psychotherapy.

Dr **Éamonn Fitzgibbon** is a priest of the Limerick diocese and is an associate faculty member of the Department of Theology and Religious Studies at Mary Immaculate College. His areas of research interest include ministry, pastoral theology, parish development and renewal, and the theology of John Macquarrie.

Fr **La Flynn** was ordained as a priest of Clogher diocese in 1976. He has been part of the team on Lough Derg for many years and is currently parish priest in Ballybay, County Monaghan. His areas of special research interest include liturgy and adult faith development.

Dr **Michael Paul Gallagher** SJ is rector of the Bellarmino College, Rome, where he also teaches at the Gregorian University. He is widely published, especially in the area of faith and contemporary culture. Many of his books have been translated into several languages, including most recently *Faith Maps: Ten Religious Explorers from Newman to Joseph Ratzinger*.

Dr **Brendan Geary** SM is provincial of the West-Central European Province of the Marist Brothers. Previously he served as Director of Human Formation at Ushaw College, then the Catholic seminary for the north of England. He has worked as a teacher, spiritual director and psychotherapist, and has specialised in working with victims and perpetrators of sexual abuse.

Maureen Kelly is a pastoral worker with the Killaloe diocese. She facilitates parish-based groups in west Clare and works with parishes to develop shared initiatives. Her research interests include change and transition in the Church viewed through the lens of systemic and psychodynamic theory, as well as from theological and pastoral perspectives.

Bishop **Brendan Leahy** is Bishop of Limerick. From 2006 until his episcopal appointment in 2013, he served as a professor of systematic theology at St Patrick's College, Maynooth, having previously been registrar at the Mater Dei Institute, Dublin. He has several publications, most recently as co-editor of the two-volume *Treasures of Irish Christianity*.

Dr **Enda Lyons** is a priest of the diocese of Tuam. He was a founder of the Institute of Religious Education, Mount Oliver, Dundalk. In recent years, he has worked at theology with groups mostly in the west of Ireland. He is the author of *Partnership in Parish: A Vision for Parish Life and Ministry* and *Jesus: Self-Portrait by God.*

Dr **Patrick Fintan Lyons**, a Benedictine monk at Glenstal Abbey, is a part-time member of the Department of Theology and Religious Studies at Mary Immaculate College. He has held posts including professor at Ateneo Sant'Anselmo, Rome, 1993–99, and visiting lecturer, Beeson Divinity School, and Samford University, Birmingham, Alabama, USA.

Fr **Feidhlimidh T. Magennis** is a priest of the Diocese of Dromore. He is currently a principal lecturer in religious studies at St Mary's University College, Belfast. Recent publications include *First and Second Samuel* for the New Collegeville Bible Commentary.

Dermot McCarthy is former Secretary-General to the Irish government and former Secretary-General to the Department of the Taoiseach. He has contributed to several diocesan in-service programmes, reflecting on the renewal of the Church in contemporary society.

Fr **Pádraig McCarthy** is a native of Dublin. He was ordained a priest in 1967, and has served in a variety of parishes in the diocese of Dublin. He is author of *A Wedding of Your Own* and of *My Name is Patrick*, a translation of the *Confessio* of St Patrick.

Dr **Aoife McGrath** lectures part-time in pastoral theology at the Pontifical University of Maynooth and has worked in the lay pastoral area in the diocese of Waterford and Lismore. She has served in a variety of parish ministries and currently conducts research in Catholic Higher Education for the Irish Bishops' Conference.

Bishop **Donal Murray** is retired Bishop of Limerick. He previously lectured in moral theology at the Mater Dei Institute and in Holy Cross College, Dublin, and is widely published, including most recently, *Let Love Speak: Reflections on Renewal in the Irish Church* and *Keeping Open the Door of Faith: The Legacy of Vatican II.*

Fr **Caoimhín Ó Laoide** OFM, a native of Tralee, now serves at Ennis Friary as Novice Master for the Franciscan Provinces of Ireland and of Great Britain. Until 2011, he served as Minister Provincial of the Franciscans in Ireland. Having been ordained priest in 1989, he has worked in parish ministry, service church ministry and retreat ministry in Killarney, Clonmel and Dublin.

Baroness **Nuala O'Loan** was the first Police Ombudsman in Northern Ireland, serving in this capacity between 1999 and 2007. In 2010 she was appointed to the House of Lords. She is a regular columnist with *The Irish Catholic.*

Dr **Kieran J. O'Mahony** is an Augustinian priest and a scripture scholar. At present he works for the Archdiocese of Dublin as academic co-ordinator of biblical studies, having previously lectured for many years in the Milltown Institute, Dublin. Among his books is *Do We Still Need St Paul?*

Fr **Brendan S. O'Rourke**, a Wexford native, joined the Redemptorists in 1967. He has been involved in retreats to priests and religious, counselling, spiritual direction, teaching and parish missions and novenas for several years. He is currently rector of the Redemptorist Community, Esker.

Dr **Seán Ruth** is an organisational psychologist, former senior lecturer in psychology and head of the department of organisational and social studies at the National College of Industrial Relations, Dublin. Since 1992 he has run his own training and consultancy business and specialises in leadership development, conflict resolution, facilitation and team building, strategic planning and managing change.

Bishop **John Sherrington** is an auxiliary in the diocese of Westminster, England. Ordained in 1987, he has a background as a parish priest and as a lecturer in moral theology at All Hallows College, Dublin, and St John's Seminary, Wonersh, Surrey. He has contributed widely to the ongoing formation of priests.

Fr **Gerry Tanham** is currently parish priest of the parish of Michael the Archangel in Athy, County Kildare. He has ministered in several Dublin parishes and has also held office as chairperson of the Dublin Diocesan Council of Priests and of several school boards of management.

Msgr **Paul Tighe** was ordained a priest of the Dublin diocese in 1983. Previously, he lectured in moral theology in the Mater Dei Institute of Education, Dublin, being appointed head of the theology department in 2000. He was appointed as secretary of the Pontifical Council for Social Communications at the Holy See in 2007.

Dr **Rik Van Nieuwenhove** lectures in theology at Mary Immaculate College. His main research is medieval theology (Thomas Aquinas) and spirituality, theology of the Trinity, and soteriology. His latest book is *An Introduction to Medieval Theology*.

Bishop **Willie Walsh** is retired Bishop of Killaloe, which he served as ordinary from 1995 until his retirement in 2010. He has been pastorally involved with ACCORD (formerly the Catholic Marriage Advisory Council) since its foundation in the Killaloe diocese. He has also worked with marriage tribunals at diocesan, regional and national levels.

Prof **Tom Whelan** is dean of the faculty of theology and spirituality at the Milltown Institute, Dublin. His research interests include liturgical and sacramental theology, liturgical methodology, worship and mission, Christian ritual music and musicology, early Roman prayer texts, the Stowe Missal, ministry (including ordained priesthood) and the Eucharist.